PENGUIN BOOKS

CONSERVATISM

Ted Honderich is Grote Professor of the Philosophy of Mind and Logic at University College London. He has been a visiting Professor at Yale and the City University of New York. He is the author of *Violence for Equality: Inquiries in Political Philosophy, Punishment: The Supposed Justifications* (Penguin 1971) and, most recently, *A Theory of Determinism: The Mind, Neuroscience, and Life-Hopes*, as well as many articles in philosophical journals. He is the editor of *Essays on Freedom of Action* and *Social Ends and Political Means* and, with Myles Burnyeat, of *Philosophy As It Is* and *Philosophy Through Its Past*. He is also the general editor of three continuing series of books, *The International Library of Philosophy and Scientific Method, The Arguments of the Philosophers* and *The Problems of Philosophy*.

CONSERVATISM

TED HONDERICH

PENGUIN BOOKS

PENGUIN BOOKS

Published by the Penguin Group
Penguin Books Ltd, 27 Wrights Lane, London W8 5TZ, England
Penguin Books USA Inc., 375 Hudson Street, New York, New York 10014, USA
Penguin Books Australia Ltd, Ringwood, Victoria, Australia
Penguin Books Canada Ltd, 10 Alcorn Avenue, Toronto, Ontario, Canada M4V 3B2
Penguin Books (NZ) Ltd, 182–190 Wairau Road, Auckland 10, New Zealand

Penguin Books Ltd, Registered Offices: Harmondsworth, Middlesex, England

First published in Great Britain by Hamish Hamilton 1990
Published in Penguin Books 1991
1 3 5 7 9 10 8 6 4 2

Printed in England by Clays Ltd, St Ives plc

To my darling Jane

Contents

Acknowledgements

I could hardly be more grateful to Jerry Cohen, Jane O'Grady and Timothy Sprigge for reading the whole of the penultimate draft of this book and making a very large number of written objections and suggestions. This formidable trio greatly improved the book. I am also very grateful to Jonathan Riley for doing all that an exacting editor does, and to Andrew Franklin, Jeremy O'Grady and Janet Radcliffe Richards for comments on parts of the penultimate draft. They too made the book better, as did the postgraduates and others who listened and objected to it during a term's seminar at University College London. Helen Betteridge at University College worked indefatigably on the thing, not only secretarially but also editorially, and did a great deal else to forward its progress. Douglas Johnson and Derek Parfit provided useful reassurance. Finally, I was helped out by many early suggestions as to what to read in order to write about the subject. The suggestions came from John Allen, Brian Atkinson, Alan Brown, Marshall Cohen, David Conway, James Der Derian, Elizabeth Divine, Michael Foot, Keith Graham, John Gray, Kiaran Honderich, Nicola Lacey, Shirley Letwin, David Lloyd-Thomas, Steven Lukes, Kenneth Minogue, Kai Nielsen, Richard Norman, Noel O'Sullivan, Amartya Sen, John Spiers, Richard Rawles, David Ruben, Roger Scruton and Hillel Steiner. None of those who have given me greater or lesser aid shares all my views. Some share few.

– 1 –
Change

Our business is interrupted, our repose is troubled, our pleasures are saddened, our very studies are poisoned and perverted, and knowledge is rendered worse than ignorance, by the enormous evils of this dreadful innovation ...

Edmund Burke

Conservatism by its name announces that it conserves, and it has recurrently said of itself, in a tone suitable for an axiom of politics, that it is against change. Others say it believes nothing should be done for the first time. No doubt there is *some* compendious truth about its opposition to change, but what is it? To understand Conservatism, by which I mean a political tradition including a number of parties and many governments, and to make a judgement about it, we need a clearer understanding of what it is against. Conservatism, or self-aware Conservatism as we know it, sometimes defensive and sometimes aggressive, came into existence as a reaction to the French Revolution. It began in disapproval, shock, fear and resistance. Some say, as a result, that Conservatism is better identified by what it opposes than what it supports. Are they right?

It would go against a certain refrain of Conservatives, having to do with familiarity, to take them as against only bare change. That is something that does not include within itself our loss of familiarity with a thing. Bare change causes, but does not include, unfamiliarity and like feelings. Is Conservatism better conceived as resistance to change where change importantly *does* include our no longer being accustomed to things? It is, we have often been told, the disposition and the politics in favour of the familiar, the old and known, whether in the constitutions of nations and the large ways of society, pinstripe suits, places to fish, or as some say, reflectively and perhaps resolutely, wives and mistresses.

Our subject, however, is not conservatism in a wide sense, where it has to do with more or less anything and is more a matter of a personal disposition or indeed personality than politics. Nor is our subject a related conservatism where that is something that can turn up in any political party, and has turned up in socialist and communist parties. We are not concerned with conservative wings of such parties, so long as those wings remain more or less true to the spirits or principles of the parties. Rather, our subject is the particular political tradition of belief, feeling, policy, legislation and action exemplified by the Conservative Party in Britain and a main part of the Republican Party in the United States, a political tradition that has evolved and contains diversity. That is certainly no adequate account or definition of our subject – such an account is not something we can start with, but something we may end up with – but it is enough to enable us to get under way. Is this politics of the Right well conceived as resistance to the kind of change which includes unfamiliarity?

It has among its leading principles, as they are briefly and coolly traced throughout its history by Anthony Quinton,[1] the principle of traditionalism, which has to do with attachment to and reverence for established customs and institutions. English Tories true to their lineage, like their American cousins in the Republican Party and indeed part of the Democratic Party, can rely on Peregrine Worsthorne of the *Sunday Telegraph* to speak their instincts, indeed weekly. He has recurred to the proposition that the purpose of sound men must be *to keep a country recognizably the same*.[2]

Still, if Conservatism were at bottom a defence of *the familiar*, in the plain meaning of the term, we should have a mystery on our hands, the mystery of how an egregious idiocy could have become a large political tradition. If we do speak in an ordinarily clear way, in saying that Conservatism comes down to a defence of all of the familiar, we also say nothing kind of Conservatism. We do not do it justice.

One simple reason is that over quite short periods of time, if Conservatism were the mentioned thing, it would in effect have to be repeatedly inconsistent. It would need to defend tomorrow or the day after – when the thing becomes familiar – what it opposes today. More absurdly, it would fail to make the most elementary distinction in life: between what is familiar and good and what is familiar and bad – and hence the distinction between bad and good change. *Anything*, after all, can become familiar. Confusion, boredom and torture can. So can being without a job. Perhaps there remains a logician of what was called the New Right in some overwarm Institute for the Preservation of Tradition who supposes that for consistency he must agree that there is a good argument for the Anarchists and Communists outside continuing to drive him crazy. He is familiar with that. Let us not make him our exemplar of the Conservative.

Does the summary idea, that Conservatism recommends the familiar, founder not just on the truth that that would make it wholly irrational, but on the large proposition that in fact Conservatism has often or even always advocated change? One might be excused for thinking so.

Conservatism as we are understanding it begins with what all take to be its greatest piece of writing, Edmund Burke's *Reflections on the Revolution in France* of 1790. Consider this tradition up to this day when we are to turn into private property anything upon which the eye of an entrepreneur may fall, or be directed to by an evangelical politician. We are to privatize the prisons, think about doing the same with the police and the army, and pay a little attention to the far-sighted economist who wishes to privatize the whale as a means to its preservation. Pretty well all this Conservatism, from Burke on, has advocated what we can certainly call *alterations*. It has made a lot of them.

If Burke, when he was concerned with England, did not actually want to turn the clock back to an earlier English constitution, the constitution whose 'balance' he so idealized, he certainly did not want just the England he found himself in at the end of the eighteenth century – let alone the way it might naturally develop. To glance at an early American instance of the unbroken line of Conservative doom-singers, Fisher Ames of Massachusetts could hardly have wanted to leave alone the American state of things in 1807. 'Our disease,' he said, and gave good signs of believing it, 'is democracy. It is not the skin that festers – our very bones are carious, and their marrow blackens with gangrene.'[3] Could *anyone* convinced that democracy, or more democracy, is a kind of dismal affliction, which will end by consuming all that is valuable, be inclined to anything less than a little alteration or indeed a little *transformation*?

Coleridge was no doubt sincere in his idea that English society should be civilized. This was to be done – it is here that the novelty comes in – through the ministrations of a new national church of culture, superior to the Anglican, and under the guidance of what he called a clerisy. To pass on to Benjamin Disraeli, his celebration of the gentlemen of England and his resistance to the new industrial money did indeed issue in national alterations. A somewhat less world-historical figure, President Hadley of Yale University, maintained in 1925 that equality was the ideal of backward races, and liberty the ideal of progressive peoples. He was no doubt inclined, as a rational man, to having less of equality in America and more of liberty.

To come on quickly to the New Right, and the sample provided by William Buckley Jr, he would near to transform American society: individualism in place of what he perceives as collectivism, moral absolutism in place of relativism, more presidential power and less Congressional, more liberty and less social security, and so on. The list is no short one. The Harvard philosopher Robert Nozick is opposed to anything more than the minimal state, has discovered that taxation on earnings is nothing less than a form of forced labour, and has elaborated the idea that starving members of a society may have no moral right to food. Much might be conjectured about his benevolence or humanity, of whether it would be prudent to go shooting tigers with him, or, for that matter, picking mushrooms. The present point, however, is that he clearly is no advocate of exactly the status quo.

In Britain, from the year 1979, Thatcher governments set out to undermine or overturn as much as possible of what others regarded as the decent institutions and practices of the society, institutions and practices which others took to have made a little contribution to advancing civilization. In fact Conservative Party politics, *more* than Labour Party politics, was the politics of alteration. In one large part it was reactionary politics, which is to say intent on alteration in the direction of a society long since left behind. The poor were again to become properly independent, and so on. Reagan governments, if somewhat more constrained in domestic politics, shared this zeal.

We have already concluded that Conservatism cannot be taken to advocate an undiscriminating defence of all of the familiar, since that would be absurd, more so than is likely to be true of any sizeable tradition. Given what has been noted of Conservatism – its record of actual alteration and its commitment to it – are we not able to conclude that any attempt to summarize Conservatism as opposition to change would fly in the face of a large fact: that Conservatism *does* produce and advocate change?

If we do conclude that Conservatism advocates and produces change, we go against a dominant idea in its tradition, although an idea not quite so much to the fore in its moments of aggressiveness.

The dominant idea, which certainly does not issue in a general and undiscriminating defence of the familiar, is taken to be consistent with its record, with what in anticipation was neutrally called the *alteration* advocated or made by Conservatism. Yes, it is said by Conservatives, we have favoured *some* alteration, but do not confuse two kinds of alteration. Conservatism has never been in favour of the alteration, involving unfamiliarity, which is *change*. It has been and is for the kind of alteration, no doubt also involving some unfamiliarity, which is *reform*. If there have been careless musings to the contrary, Conservatism has had at its heart, indeed firmly in its head, a claim about a deep difference between change and reform.

Burke set out to make this 'manifest, marked distinction' several times. It was wholly clear, he said, but one 'which ill men with ill designs, or weak men incapable of any design, will constantly be confounding'.

> ... change ... alters the substance of the objects themselves, and gets rid of all their essential good as well as the accidental evil annexed to them. Change is novelty, and whether it is to operate any one of the effects of reformation at all, or whether it may not contradict the very principle upon which reformation is desired, cannot be certainly known beforehand. Reform is not a change in the substance or in the primary modification of the objects, but a direct application of a remedy to the grievance complained of. So far as that is removed, all is sure. It stops there; and if it fails the substance which underwent the operation, at the very worst, is but where it was.
>
> All this, in effect, I think, but am not sure, I have said elsewhere. It cannot at this time be too often repeated, line upon line, precept upon precept, until it comes into the currency of a proverb – *To innovate is not to reform*. The French revolutionists complained of everything; they refused to reform anything; and they left nothing, no nothing at all, *unchanged*. The consequences are *before* us – not in remote history, not in future prognostication: they are about us; they are upon us. They shake the public security; they menace private enjoyment. They dwarf the growth of the young; they break the quiet of the old. If we travel, they stop our way. They infest us in town; they pursue to the country. Our business is interrupted, our repose is troubled, our pleasures are saddened, our very studies are poisoned and perverted, and knowledge is rendered worse than ignorance, by the enormous evils of this dreadful innovation ...[4]

Some have bravely said that Burke stands on a level with Karl Marx and John Stuart Mill. They are equals in the pantheon of politics. He did for Conservatism what Marx did for the socialism that bears his name, and what Mill did for liberalism. If his tolerance of suspect financial dealings was considerable, and if there is the persistent suspicion that his varying opinions had something to do with his patrons and his pension, he did not, like Marx, father a child on his servant, or, like Mill, never quite achieve the manly. Be all that as it may, he was not, as the passage indicates, very good at holding one idea before the mind long enough to explain it. He was not good at doing one thing at a time.

The most promising thought we can take away from his words is that change is what alters the substance, or the essence, or the primary character, of something. Reform touches only what is extrinsic or accidental to it. Do we by this thought come near to understanding what alteration Conservatism opposes and what alteration it supports? Burke was by way of being a philosopher, of more than politics. At any rate he was an aesthetician. But we shall not get far by supposing that what he has in mind can be clarified by reflecting on philosophical distinctions between substance and attribute. We shall not be helped by the distinction between the elusive substratum of something, say of the wine goblet, and that which the substratum supports, which is to say *all* of the properties of the goblet. His drift is clear enough, and is as well put in this way as any other: *change alters what is somehow fundamental, and reform alters what is not fundamental.*

However that difference is enlarged upon, we are left with a large difficulty: we cannot take it to convey Burke's intention, or to clarify Conservatism. Burke is not against *all* change, which is to say all alteration to what is fundamental to a thing. A large part of the *Reflections on the Revolution in France* is given over to damnation of the very nature of a thing, a thing regarded in its most fundamental nature. It is hardly too much to say that Burke mainly owed his fame in his own time, and that in part he owes his place in history, to the force of his demand for *exactly* the changing of this thing, as distinct from any mere reforming of it. The thing in question was the constitution and government of France put in place by the French Revolution.

The point is a general one, and does not depend on that one piece of support for change, telling though it is. His life had in it a good deal of passion or feeling for change – desires that certain things be altered fundamentally. Another example was his championing of the

American Revolution, inconsistent or not with his vilification of the French. He could have little hope of success in arguing, as in ways he did, that the American Revolution was mere reform. It may be, too, if Conor Cruise O'Brien is right about Burke's residual Irishness, that Burke was in a part of himself inclined to some change with respect to another large fact, England's grip on Ireland.[5] It would be sad, looking on the statue of him in front of Trinity College Dublin, to think otherwise.

About some facts and things, there is room for much dispute as to what part of their nature is fundamental, and hence what alteration of them counts as change. However, if we do not succumb to the brazen stubbornness which turns up so often in political dispute, there is not much room for dispute with the French constitution and government, or with the American Revolution. We know that Burke wished to alter the French constitution and government fundamentally, and that what he supported in supporting the American Revolution was also change. We get our conception of fundamental alteration in this neighbourhood *from* such cases, rather than bring it along to judge them.

No doubt someone will make the different objection about the French Revolution that Burke was not supporting change in attacking the new constitution and government of France, but opposing the change which was the establishing of that constitution and government. He was opposing the fundamental alteration which was the Revolution itself. There is more room for disagreement here. One question that arises is that of how long a thing must be in existence before it ceases to *be* a change, and becomes something settled, to which change can be made.

Let us not struggle with this matter of how long a thing has to exist before it ceases to count as a change. Let us simply give up the idea that Burke was supporting change in trying in the years just after the Revolution to get Europe to go to war against France. That will not affect what is also true: that many decades later he would still have been in favour of fundamental alteration to the given constitution and government if it had persisted. He would indubitably have been in favour of altering it fundamentally when it *was* well and truly settled. To think of certain of his successors for a moment, Conservatives opposed to the Communist government of Russia have been very keen indeed on fundamental alteration of a state of affairs seventy-five years old.

In the quoted passage Burke evidently has in mind more than the distinction between alteration to what is fundamental and to what is not fundamental. He spends more words on something else. He purports to shed light for us by conveying that change alters what was good, and reform alters what was bad. As he says, change gets rid of essential good, while reform remedies evil.

It should be unnecessary to say that we learn nothing useful from these magisterial if inflamed sentiments. There is no more here than the triumph of eloquence over argument. Indeed there is not much more than Irish abuse done into a good class of rhetoric. There is more decorum than in the advice given by one Dublin politician to another, that he should go home and shoe asses, but not greatly more reflection. Certainly we come to know that Burke takes what he calls change to be bad and what he calls reform to be good, but that does not tell us in any useful way what either is, and hence what Conservatism is. He curses changers wonderfully throughout his works, and speaks well of reformers. That does not tell us what it is, independently of his passions, that distinguishes changers from reformers. We learn nothing that distinguishes Conservatism from any other party by noting that Conservatism, exactly like the rest of them, takes some otherwise unspecified alterations of society to be right and others wrong.

Of course several notes are sounded by his words – change is what shakes 'security' and troubles 'private enjoyment' and 'business'. But they convey no other *general* propositions save one which is subordinate to or part of the one at which we have just glanced. It is that change is what has bad effects. That gives us no more understanding of Conservatism than the like proposition about socialists, or any other sane persons, that they are against alterations which they take to have bad effects. We need a clear account of what those effects are, putting aside anyone's condemnation of them, or commendation.

I grant that we all have some sense of what Burke is unstrung by. We get it from the words just quoted. We guess that he is against alteration in connection with the holding and inheritance of property. We may say after reading other passages that he is against any alteration owed to mere theorizing or theory, as against alteration owed to *mute wisdom*. However our subject now is neither inheritance nor the wisdom he regularly praises, but some general distinction between change and reform, and we are given no understanding of precisely that distinction.

Will we have a better sense of what change and reform are when we come to see, say, the difference between theory and mute wisdom? Will we have an effective conception of change when we see that it is what is owed to theorizing, and reform is what is owed to wisdom? And that other distinctions to be made – between the preservation of different kinds of rights and so on – will give us a further and eventually a full understanding of change and reform? No doubt all that is possible, but it is not all that is possible. It may be that when we come to the subject of theory and wisdom, we will in effect be informed that theory is to be understood as what gives rise to *change* and wisdom as what gives rise to *reform* – which difference between alterations we do not know. Burke is certainly inclined to play that game with the poor confounded reader. Each of two distinctions is in effect taken as explained by the other. Both of them, alas, are left unmanifest and unmarked, and so neither can explain the other.

Taking one thing at a time, what we now have is no clear and general distinction between change and reform. As a result, we remain with the further conclusion that Conservatism cannot be characterized even in part as opposition to change. We possess no effective characterization of it, and have no grip on what is different, its fundamental principle. We thus have no possibility either of celebrating or condemning Conservatism, no way of coming to a judgement about it.

Shall we get help from the New Right? Here and hereafter in speaking of the New Right, I shall have in mind a Conservatism of the last quarter of the twentieth century, in the main in Britain and America, but not all of the Conservatism of that period. The New Right, if we pass over the details of its factions, and its dispute as to who is really a Conservative and who is not, included doctrine and feeling that preceded and accompanied Thatcher, Reagan and similar governments, to some extent influencing them and being influenced by them. It also included those governments themselves. The distinctiveness of the governments in question, which I shall not try to define generally, was a matter of such policies as the running down of the National Health Service in Britain after plangent assurances to the contrary, and the illegal activities of the Reagan administration in arming mercenaries to try to bring down an elected government in Nicaragua.

The New Right did not include several governments of another Conservative kind, which came earlier in the quarter-century and were, as one might say, less credal. The New Right was also unlike the Old Right – by which I mean everything but the New – in that the Old was perhaps capable of taking a certain summary of itself as a tribute to its plain sense and sound character. I mean John Stuart Mill's summary of it as the Stupid Party. The New Right, by contrast, whether or not in fact less benighted than the Old, had in it self-announced *thinkers*. They paid attention to themselves and, as remarked, had some paid to them by cabinets and Oval Offices.

Shall we get help in connection with the subject of Conservatism and change, more precisely, from the doughty and yet inspirational Michael Oakeshott, who did much to save the London School of Economics from the Fabian Socialism on which it was founded, and to whom a good part of the New Right deferred? His views on our subject are to the effect that Conservatism is against change, somehow conceived. Not a great deal is said of any kind of alteration it tolerates.

Conservatism esteems the present, he begins, 'not on account of its connections with a remote antiquity, nor because it is recognized to be more admirable than any possible alternative, but on account of its familiarity'. The Conservative, he continues, does not say, with Goethe, *Stay with me, you are so beautiful,* but *Stay with me because I am attached to you.*

Changes are without effect only upon those who notice nothing, who are ignorant of what they possess and apathetic to their circumstances; and they can be welcomed indiscriminately only by those who esteem nothing, whose attachments are fleeting and who are strangers to love and affection. The conservative disposition provokes neither of these conditions: the inclination to enjoy what is present and available is the opposite of ignorance and apathy and it breeds attachment and affection. Consequently it is averse from change, which appears always, in the first place, as deprivation. A storm which sweeps away a copse and transforms a favourite view, the death of friends, the sleep of friendship, the desuetude of customs of behaviour, the retirement of a favourite clown, involuntary exile, reversals of fortune, the loss of abilities enjoyed and their replacement by others – these are changes, none perhaps without its compensations, which the man of conservative temperament unavoidably regrets. But he has difficulty in reconciling himself to them, not because what he has lost in them was intrinsically better than any alternative might have been or was incapable of improvement, nor because what takes its place is inherently incapable of being enjoyed, but because what he has lost was something he actually enjoyed and had learned how to enjoy and what takes its place is something to which he has acquired no attachment.[6]

I shall not in general quote so extensively – as earlier with Burke and now with Oakeshott. It has perhaps been a good idea to give both passages fully, and so quickly to introduce readers with little acquaintance of Conservative writing to the nature or rather the natures of it. Very much of it, including very much of the most celebrated, consists not so much in reflective and explicit argument in good order, but rather in the rhetoric that might be called Ongoing Parliamentary, or Risen Sophomore – that is Burke, at least too often – or else in the delivery of propositions a touch oracular, showing a certain weakness for the numinous. We get the latter from Oakeshott. This fact of style is of some importance in itself, and we shall eventually return to it. Quoting the above reflections fully also serves the end of saving sceptical readers from the thought that it is selective reporting on my part that gives rise to what they may feel about it, which is bafflement.

Oakeshott is a man with an admirable awareness of life, and kinds of estimable feeling about it, but given or driven to something like self-contradiction, which runs through what he says. We are indeed told at the beginning and the end of it that change – resistance to which thing identifies the Conservative – is what ends the familiar, where the familiar may *not* be better than what succeeds it. The familiar, which the Conservative esteems and defends, may not be more beautiful or admirable than what comes after. In fact the familiar, as seems to be allowed elsewhere in the piece of writing in question, may actually be less good than what comes after it – the familiar may be the merely convenient as against the perfect. *On the other hand*, we are as firmly given to understand that change is something quite different: an ending of deep attachments, of love and affection, of enjoyment. It is the ending of the pleasure of a view or of a friendship, or of the satisfaction of being at home. Change for whatever reason *does* take us from good to bad, and indeed is what is welcomed only by the ignorant, the apathetic and the strangers to love and affection.

The running-together of change as unfamiliarity and change as something near to deprivation or injury may distract one from what is plainly true: that neither idea of change is of use in the enterprise of coming to understand Conservatism. That is, one may be led into supposing that there is no objection to be raised to the conception of

Conservatism as an undiscriminating defence of the familiar because that is not really the conception being proposed. Or, one may be led into supposing that there is no question to be asked about the conception of Conservatism as the defence of the enjoyable, because that is not really the conception proposed.

The fact of the matter is that we cannot take Conservatism to be both of these inconsistent things, and that each conception on its own, as we already know, is hopeless. The first reduces a sizeable tradition of political parties and loyalties, a tradition of some considerable rationality, to no more than an absurd defence of all that is familiar. The second is the conception of Conservatism as resistance to that change which consists in a loss or destruction of the enjoyable. This cannot distinguish Conservatives from socialists, or the National Union of Mine Workers, or for that matter the Society for the Propagation of the Gospel in Foreign Parts or the Pennsylvania Amish, all of whom can say that they are opposed to the loss of the truly enjoyable.

Are we to understand something more useful from Oakeshott to the effect that Conservatism is resistance to the loss of a special category of enjoyments, or enjoyments associated with a definable kind of life, or indeed enjoyments of a certain social or economic class of persons? It is notable that no such thought is clarified. If it were, of course, Conservatism would cease to be presented as what it is implied to be, something whose description can be given by way of decorous or uncontentious generalities got from a true view of our common human condition and not much sullied by politics.

We have not come to the end of weak Conservative ideas about the change it opposes. It is the change that is quick and easy as against slow and difficult. It is the change that is unnatural. It is the change that threatens or destroys our personal identities and hence our senses of ourselves – our identities and our senses of ourselves somehow depend on our being in and seeing ourselves in a continuing setting. It is the change which consists in defaulting in a great contract between generations. It is the change that threatens activities which are ends-in-themselves, as distinct from means to other ends. It is the change that is total, which preserves nothing of the past in it. Or, if this is different, it is the change that is not part of growth.

What can be said of all of these ideas, on the assumption that they can be made clear, is that they do not give us distinctive features of Conservatism, sometimes because they do not call for serious attention by doing justice to it. Further and more important, they do not reveal its fundamental nature. Let us look at two.

Consider the light idea that Conservatism is marked off by its opposition to alterations which endanger our personal identities. These latter things, our identities, are never given much definition by the proponents of the idea. Do we here have a *substantial* consideration? I fancy, to glance back, that Oakeshott, if he found himself without some of his friends, the copse, customs of behaviour, homeland, good luck, some past abilities, and also the clown, would still be Oakeshott. He himself would also have a pretty good idea of who he was. No doubt he would be a gloomier man, but our subject is not his morale, but his identity.

Still, let us allow that alterations of the kind in question may somehow affect who we think we are, or better, *how we think of ourselves*. Does opposition to such alterations, with no more said, distinguish Conservatism from other things? I fear that it does not. To take one example, it is a plain fact that a good deal of ideology of the Left, including a Marxist tubful having to do with what is called alienation, opposes change which is said to endanger identities.

It needs adding that if Conservatism were characterized as general opposition to alteration of identity, it could not have much to say for itself. It must indeed be no more than *alteration* of identity that is in question, rather than *loss* of identity or *endangering* of identity. The latter two descriptions import the idea not merely of identities, but of good or valuable identities – including senses of oneself that ought to be preserved. But the intrusion of some idea of good and bad identities makes for difficulties of which we know. That is, we need but certainly are not given an idea of what sense of self and the like *is* valuable. We are left with no real distinction.

To consider Conservatism as opposition just to alteration of identity or self-conception, then, the question must arise of why identities in this sense should not alter or be altered. Suppose the life of a woman or the existence of a class of people is one of constraint, being bullied, defeat or suffering. Suppose too, as we are invited to, that some alteration in circumstances will produce something called alteration of this identity. What she or they are likely to say, happily, is that they would not mind a new identity. If Conservatism were to be opposition to *any* change of such identity it would be as absurd as if it were to be, as we know, an undiscriminating defence of all of the familiar.

Consider now one other idea in the list, that Conservatism is the politics which opposes the change which is a kind of defaulting on a great contract between generations. Burke requires that we be mindful of what we have received from our ancestors and of what is due to posterity. He famously continues:

> Society is indeed a contract ... It is a partnership in all science; a partnership in all art; a partnership in every virtue, and in all perfection. As the ends of such a partnership cannot be obtained in many generations, it becomes a partnership not only between those who are living, but between those who are living, those who are dead, and those who are to be born. Each contract of each particular state is but a clause in the great primaeval contract of eternal society ...[7]

This, like so much in Burke, is a grand mingling of several themes and intimations. Let us for the moment attend only to a principal one, having to do with change. We, of this generation, have a contract with eternal society. This is a contract in virtue of which we have received from eternal society – or more particularly from its past – a great benefaction, and in virtue of which we must make a return to it – or more particularly to its future. Change consists in our defaulting, our not making good on our part of a rather prolonged deal.

Putting aside everything else that must come to mind, which is a lot, consider what it is we are to inherit and transmit. Evidently we are to transmit the good as somehow conceived rather than the bad. But what does this good consist in? Certainly we get no help from the utterance that the good in question is what is transmitted by reform rather than change. We need not an allusion or two, but a decent inventory of this good to be transmitted, or better, a general description. We have not got it.

Does it include those particular goods-for-some, say great profits, which are also evils-for-others? Does it include taxing the poor to encourage the rich? Does it include education for those best able to pay for it rather than best able to use it? Does it include, while we are near the subject, the dragging down of the universities? Does it include that particular tradition of sensibility, as it might with charity be named, that reaches its apogee in the Creative Departments of advertising agencies? Does it include a wretched puppet press, full either of nipples or pompous servility? Does it include government by toadying place-seekers? Does it include a government led by a prime minister whose intellectual horizons and hence her policies are such that not even the university most heavy with tradition could bring itself to follow the precedent of giving her an honorary degree? Such questions abound, and, as you see, they can raise up a feeling or two.

In the absence of a general description of what we are to inherit and pass on, we have no conception of the defaulting which is the change condemned by Conservatism. For all we know, it is a defaulting such that we ought in fact to do some of it, perhaps a lot. For all we know, to turn for a moment to the New Right, we should do some defaulting even when we enter into the further vision of Roger Scruton in one of his Hegelian moments. He is not abashed by the idea that Burke's eternal society is no speechless organism, but has a personality, and a will too.[8] Eternal society, so far as I can tell, is not speaking very clearly, not through Burke and not through our professor of aesthetics either. Still, we will return to it.

What we have so far in sum is that Conservatism cannot be identified as opposition to change where change is (1) just the ending of the familiar, or (2) the alteration of the fundamental, or (3) destruction of the good, or (4) what affects our identities or self-conceptions, or (5) defaulting on a long contract.

A larger proposition – that we get no adequate conception of Conservatism by way of *any* general notion of change on offer – is in a way agreed by some who are of Conservative inclination themselves. In beginning his admirable tour of the Conservative horizon, Noel O'Sullivan allows of what he takes to be most promising, Burke's 'manifest, marked distinction' between change and reform, which we considered earlier, that it is not contentful. In practice, he tells us, what constitutes reform will be different in different situations. He is not the first of his persuasion to say so. Conservatism, we are often told, means different things in different societies and at different times. O'Sullivan remarks that sometimes reform will involve defensive actions, and sometimes it will involve taking the initiative in changing the status quo, as when Disraeli extended the suffrage and so dished the Whigs. The fact of the matter is that 'the meaning of reform cannot be specified in advance of events'.[9]

We can, on the contrary, hope to find the kind of change to which Conservatism is opposed, and, quite as important, the kind of continuity it opposes. It cannot be that there is *no* such thing, *no* summary description that can be put on it. It cannot be that a fundamental refrain in a large political tradition is without a general content. It cannot be that Conservatism, in so far as it has recurrently objected to change, and allowed the need for reform, has not conveyed anything clear to itself and to others. It may be that its thinkers have not really disclosed their thoughts about change, let alone what guides those thoughts and others, but that is another matter.

We shall come to an answer by degrees, in the course of our inquiry. The answer is to be had by reflection on what else may be thought to identify Conservatism. It was remarked above that there is the possibility that getting a grip on the distinction between theory and mute wisdom will give us a satisfactory characterization of change and reform – that change is what comes from theory and reform is what comes from the wisdom. As also remarked above, there are indeed weak games that can be played in such an enterprise (pp. 8–9). We can none the less be optimistic that by care, and by looking at more things than theory and wisdom, we can come to an answer to the question as to the kind of change which Conservatism opposes.

To do this will be to find a distinction of Conservatism. It is one of our aims to find all of its distinctions. A second aim is to appraise many particular doctrines and arguments of Conservatism. A third is to come to a decision as to the nature of its fundamental and general commitment. The fourth is to come to a judgement on Conservatism.

– 2 –
Theory, Etc.

Because half a dozen grasshoppers under a fern make the field
ring with their importunate chink, whilst thousands of great
cattle, reposed beneath the shadow of the British oak, chew the
cud and are silent, pray do not imagine, that those who make
the noise are the only inhabitants of the field …

Edmund Burke

To turn to larger subjects, Conservatives have long said they are
distinguished by being against theorizing about society, and of course
putting theory into practice. They say theory is one of a bundle of
things they eschew, and a failing of their opponents. It is something,
they say, which is incapable of dealing with the complexity of society.
It is not clear what they take theory to be, or that they take it to be a
single thing. In this connection, however, book-writing Conservatives
are inclined to recall someone not actually in their tradition, Alexis
de Tocqueville, best known for his mixture of sympathy and pessimism with respect to the new democracy in America. In particular
they recall his unkindness to some of his own countrymen, the French
Revolutionaries. He said they had a 'fondness for broad generalizations … and a pedantic symmetry', a 'taste for reshaping institutions on novel, ingenious, original lines', a 'desire to reconstruct
entire constitutions according to the rules of logic'. They were closer
to writers than statesmen. 'All they needed, in fact, to become literary
men in a small way was a better knowledge of spelling.'[1] All of that,
perhaps including the poor spelling, was in de Tocqueville's view
catastrophic for France.

To pass from theory to ideology, whatever it is and however it is
related to theory, few things have been taken to be more pernicious
by Conservatives. They have traditionally said they eschew it. John
Adams, who did much to set American Conservatism on its early
course, recorded in the margin of one of his books his view of the
nature of ideology.

The political and literary world are much indebted for the
invention of the new word IDEOLOGY.

Our English words, Idiocy or Idiotism, express not the force
or meaning of it. It is presumed its proper definition is the science
of Idiocy. And a very profound, abstruse and mysterious science
it is. You must descend deeper than the divers in the Dunciad
to make any discoveries, and after all you will find no bottom.
It is the bathos, the theory, the art, the skill of diving and sinking
in government.[2]

Russell Kirk, who did a good deal to get the New Right in America
under way by, at a recent count, his twenty-two books, is of much
the same mind about this science of government and society. He says
in the introduction to his ever useful *Portable Conservative Reader* that
Conservatism is not a political system and certainly not an ideology.
It is no less than 'the negation of ideology'.[3] Elsewhere he is sharper,
although idiosyncratic in his conception of the unbearable as against
the loathsome. 'When a man is both a professor and an intellectual,
he is loathsome; when he is professor and intellectual and ideologist
rolled into one, he is unbearable.'[4]

What are called abstractions, third, however they are related to
theory and ideology, are as little to the taste of Conservatives. John
Randolph of Virginia, one defender of the peculiar institution of the
American South, slavery, did not put abstract ideas wholly out of
question, perhaps not even the idea of universal humanity. But he
supposed that his adversaries, or some of them, did not take account of
something else, *circumstances*, and quoted Burke at them. 'Circumstances are infinite, are infinitely combined, are variable and transi-
ent: he who does not take them into consideration is not erroneous,
but stark mad, ... metaphysically mad.'[5] That theme of 1829
carries on to 1982. Russell Kirk is not much less firm in his hostility
to abstractions, which he specifies as '*a priori* notions divorced from
a nation's history and necessities'.[6]

If Conservatives say they have nothing to do with theory, ideology
and abstractions, they also take themselves to be distinguished by
resistance to traditions and habits of thought which issue in these
things. The traditions and habits include what are called rationalism,
reliance on intellect or reason, and utopianism.

As for rationalism, in one way understood, Oakeshott is in part
against it. What he has in mind is a kind of reasoning about means
and ends exemplified in engineering and a good deal else. Such

reasoning involves the specification of an end and the devising of a specific means to achieve it. Such rationalism is tolerable in some endeavours, but reliance on it, or exclusive reliance on it, is not tolerable in politics. Engineering is all right, but not social engineering. To refuse to bring this sort of thinking to bear on society, or just this sort of thinking, is the mark of a Conservative.[7]

Fifth, to come to morality, we have it that Conservatives are distinguished by not propounding systems of morality, moral principles of great generality and doctrines about moral rights. Conservatives recoil from Utilitarianism and its Greatest Happiness Principle, that we are to pursue the greatest happiness of the greatest number. The principle, if there is not agreement among Conservatives about what is wrong about it, or even what it is, is agreed to be hopeless. Some take it to be clear but a mistaken principle. Others also take it to be clear and true, but uselessly truistic. Others take it to be equivocal and near to meaningless.

Disraeli sometimes takes the last option. He began a tradition which still has a trickle of undergraduate essays in it. The bad thing about the Utilitarian advice to pursue the greatest happiness of the greatest number, he said, is that it does not say who is to decide on the greatest happiness of the greatest number. If it is the greatest number themselves, the majority of a population will have been persuaded by their particular education, history and no doubt their government that their government is pursuing the greatest happiness of the greatest number. But of course, since countries differ, no two peoples agree – thus we get no single piece of moral advice in the Utilitarian principle. Further, 'if to avoid this conclusion we maintain that the greatest number are not the proper judges of the greatest happiness, we are only referred to the isolated opinions of solitary philosophers, or at best to the conceited conviction of some sectarian minority'.[8]

Also with respect to morality, Conservatives recoil from what is taken to be the fancifulness, or worse, of much talk of rights – Natural Rights, abstract rights, rights in theory, human rights. They do so except on the occasions when such talk serves their interests, say when their foreign policy can be advanced by declarations as to such rights of persons in societies other than their own, perhaps the Russian or Polish. For the most part they do not take seriously, for their own societies, anything other than established legal rights. To choose for illustration a doyen of the New Right, there is the economist Friedrich Hayek, one of the several Dismal Scientists who have influenced

Thatcher governments. He is opposed above all to 'social justice', or the 'mirage' of social justice. This conception encumbers no true Conservatism, and is 'empty and meaningless'. It is useless since its essential idea is that individuals are to be rewarded in accordance with their moral merit, but the moral merit of each individual is hidden, and can be known by no one. God, if he knows, does not pass on his rankings to us.[9]

Sixth and finally I bring no news – remember Russell Kirk on the not merely loathsome professor – by remarking that Conservatives take themselves to be distinctive in what might be called the persistent effectiveness of their reflections. They take themselves to be distinguished from the aforementioned elaborators of theories, ideology and abstractions, usually the same unfortunates subject to traditions of rationalism and the like, and also the purveyors of moral systems and the discoverers of elusive rights. Conservatives are no scribblers or word-spinners, no intellectuals, no moral philosophers. They are not inconsequential, and they are not so noisy. Burke again, as if to a French correspondent:

> The vanity, restlessness, petulance, and spirit of intrigue of several petty cabals, who attempt to hide their total want of consequence in bustle and noise, and puffing, and mutual quotation of each other, makes you imagine that our contemptuous neglect of their abilities is a mark of general acquiescence in their opinions. No such thing, I assure you. Because half a dozen grasshoppers under a fern make the field ring with their importunate chink, whilst thousands of great cattle, reposed beneath the shadow of the British oak, chew the cud and are silent, pray do not imagine, that those who make the noise are the only inhabitants of the field; or that, after all, they are other than the little shrivelled, meagre, hopping, though loud and troublesome insects of the hour.[10]

Let us chink a little. Let us see if we can move towards making all of this clearer. Can we clarify this bundle of oppositions taken as identifying Conservatism by seeing something of the *alternatives* said to be preferred by them? As might be expected, we here encounter another bundle.

One thing Conservatives put against theory is what is named common sense. The novelist George Gissing took this course at the turn of the century, and was also typical of many Conservatives in

claiming that the Englishman is by nature Conservative. He noted
that political theorists, in connection with monarchy and the like,
scoff at privilege which will not bear examination, forms which have
survived their meaning, and compromises which sound ludicrous.
Instead they propose consistent, rational and ideal schemes, having
to do with ideals and the Rights of Man. But Englishmen will have
nothing to do with all this.

> If you talk to them (long enough) about the rights of the
> shopman, or the ploughman, or the cat's-meat-man, they will
> lend ear, and, when the facts of any such case have been
> examined, they will find a way of dealing with them. This
> characteristic of theirs they call Common Sense.[11]

Gissing cannot have in mind, if he is to be paid attention, what
commonly is intended when we speak carelessly of proceeding by
common sense. We mean little more than being governed by what
we take to be true or right. Proceeding by common sense, so understood, does not distinguish common men, or Englishmen, from theorists, since all of them claim to be governed by what is true or right,
whether on the subject of gravity, constitutions or the cat's-meat-
man. Further, Gissing must have some other thought, since in resting
conclusions on common sense, he wishes to give an independent
reason for their being true or right, which independent reason cannot
be just that they are true or right. Gissing's other thought is kept
from us.

One clear thing implied in the report of his opinion is that common
sense, whatever it is, can naturally be introduced as something
superior to more of the disdained things than theory. It is superior
to talk of natural and like rights – Gissing has rights in mind as much
as theory – and also ideology, abstract principles and social justice.
That is an indication that any intended idea of common sense,
whatever it is, is a pretty general one. However, Gissing does not
share with us whatever idea he has.

Others who speak of common sense in contexts different from
politics also keep to themselves whatever relevant thought they have
in venerating common sense. Nor can they or we get a lot of help
from those philosophers, including some resolute Scots, who spent
much ink on it. It is worth remembering, too, that Bishop Berkeley,
after having resolved 'to be eternally banishing metaphysics, etc, and
recalling men to Common Sense', took himself to be going about the

task in arguing for the uncommon conclusion that the material world is just in the mind, God's mind when no one else is on hand.

Much else that is said by Conservatives of their alternatives to theory, ideology and so on is also of uncertain meaning. Burke opposed the subversives of his time who claimed rights to frame a government for themselves, choose their governors and cashier them for misconduct. Against these claims as to rights of men, as distinct from constitutional or other legal rights, he asserted a certain conclusion, that all Englishmen ought to accept with joy the fact of a hereditary monarchy and peerage. This conclusion was taken by him to derive from something quite different from prattle of rights. It derived from 'following nature, which is a wisdom without reflection, and above it'.[12]

Let us not linger over this well-turned piece of mystery-mongering. It remains just that, partly because Burke does not linger over it either to any effect. Let us instead pass on from wisdom to instinct. It too is prized by Conservatives as a kind of badge. Some assign it to ordinary folk generally, who are taken to be natural Conservatives sometimes led astray.

> There is a natural instinct in the unthinking man – who, tolerant
> of the burdens that life lays on him, and unwilling to lodge
> blame where he sees no remedy, seeks fulfilment in the world
> that is – to accept and endorse through his actions the institutions
> and practices into which he is born. This instinct, which I
> have attempted to translate into the self-conscious language of
> political dogma, is rooted in human nature ...

Thus Roger Scruton, in his role as the unthinking man's thinking man.[13]

There is the irrelevant suggestion there, perhaps, that instinct is to be characterized in terms of its particular contents or deliverances – as might also have been said with common sense and wisdom-above-reflection. That is, we are able to distinguish instinct from, say, rationalism or the impulse to theorize, not by attending directly to these sources of propositions, but by attending to two classes of propositions, two political dogmas. The idea is that we are to characterize instinct as that which issues in the proposition that only legal rights matter, that everybody should have the dignity that comes from paying for their own medicines, and so on, and characterize theory and the like as that which issues in empty talk of human rights, keeping a National Health Service going, and so on. Of course, if we are really to achieve success, we shall need to find a *rationale* or *unifying principle* or at least a *good summation* of the Conservative bundle of propositions.

We shall be much concerned with various Conservative propositions and the matter of a general rationale, but our present enterprise is to find out whether Conservatism is distinguished by, so to speak, a distinctive mental means to the end of conclusions about society. That is supposed to be true. In thinking of instinct itself, are we to have in mind whatever gives also rise to the activities of, say, such social insects as ants and bees? Are we, that is, to have in mind whatever it is that issues in rigid and stereotyped forms of behaviour neither learned nor modified by experience? I think Scruton's high regard for unthinking man precludes our using that reasonably clear conception. Nor, to cast around, will we get help by pondering the utterances, indeed what is called the theory, of Freud. He also has a conception or two of instinct, not so clear. Libido does not seem quite the right thing. The fact of the matter is that Scruton does not pause to guide us, and says nothing clear himself.

Nor do we get help from other members of the New Right. Kenneth Minogue of the new-style London School of Economics merely reminds us, taking time to try to distance Conservatism from something disagreeable, that Conservatives have identified themselves with instinctual man – as against reason-intoxicated man, 'who has produced those grandiose social blue prints (such as the collectivization of agriculture or the "thousand-year Reich")'.[14] With respect to the distancing of Conservatism from Fascism, did not the thousand-year Reich have something to do with what was called exactly instinct? But I digress.

We might spend some time on other Conservative ideas of the sources of Conservative politics. 'Intimations' come to mind, since they are part of what Michael Oakeshott favours in place of specific means-end reasoning, and also the ideas of the 'pre-rational', imagination, affection and habit, as well as something very different, the market. The latter, as we shall see later, is in a way Friedrich Hayek's answer to where Conservatives do or should discover the distribution of things that is superior to any distribution owed to social justice.

Let us pass by intimations, the pre-rational and so on, and turn instead to what are the two most promising ideas or groups of ideas. The lesser of these is to the effect that what Conservatism puts in place of theory and a good deal else is a kind of *empiricism*. This is a

reliance on experience in a certain sense, on looking at the facts as
they are. I have in mind reliance on experience where the experience
is akin to observation or what philosophers call sense-experience,
as distinct from experience in the sense of experience-over-time or
accumulated experience. In the history of philosophy, such an empiricism has been opposed to rationalism, although not the rationalism
of means-end reasoning. This empiricism on which Conservatism
relies is conveyed in what was noticed earlier, Randolph's commitment to taking account of 'circumstances' as against abstractions
(p. 18). It may also be part of what is had in mind by those, like
Gissing, who talk of common sense.

Burke, as we know, also puts circumstances to the fore. He declares, certainly to some effect:

> I must see with my own eyes, I must, in a manner, touch
> with my own hands, not only the fixed but the momentary
> circumstances, before I could venture to suggest any political
> project whatsoever. I must know the power and disposition to
> accept, to execute, to persevere. I must see the means of cor-
> recting the plan, where correctives would be wanted. I must see
> the things; I must see the men.[15]

A related or contained idea is that Conservatives owe their politics
to their own or to their mentors' specifically political involvement,
involvement in governing or administering, no doubt down to parish
and ward. They are really in touch. This involvement brings with it
a kind of power of discernment. As Kenneth Minogue has it:

> Political judgement ... cannot be based on the deductive appli-
> cation of metaphysical principles to problems arising in the
> sphere of government. Conservatives regard ruling as a special
> kind of skill, possibly arcane and certainly not universally dis-
> tributed among members of the human race. It is learned by
> practice and example and therefore is likely to be most highly
> developed among members of a long established ruling class.[16]

As the passage indicates, there is a connection between empiricism
as a source of Conservative politics and the yet more acclaimed source
to which we now come. This is *the test of time*. One succinct statement
of this source is owed to Lord Quinton, about whom it might be said
incidentally that my brisk distinction between New Right and Old
(p. 9) is not so well drawn as to locate him in either – despite his

owing his rank to Margaret Thatcher and his decent willingness, to no avail, to elevate her to the rank of honorary doctor of the University of Oxford. We have it from *The Politics of Imperfection* that Conservatism is owed to a fundamental conviction, 'a conviction of the radical intellectual imperfection of the human individual, as contrasted with the historically accumulated political wisdom of the community, as embodied in its customs and institutions'.[17] It is not that we are imperfect morally – which true thought is not peculiar to Conservatism – but imperfect intellectually. The consequence of this is that we should not attempt to guide ourselves by the large and abstract projects of individuals, but rather guide ourselves by 'the accumulated political wisdom of the community'.

This conviction as to our imperfection, of which more will be said in the next chapter, issues in three principles, one noted already (p. 2). The one relevant now is that of political scepticism. It is

> the belief that political wisdom, the kind of knowledge that is needed for the successful management of human affairs, is not to be found in the theoretical speculations of isolated thinkers but in the historically accumulated social experience of the community as a whole. It is embodied, above all, in the deposit of traditional customs and institutions that have survived and become established and also in those people who, in one way or another, have acquired extensive practical experience of politics.[18]

This principle evidently is in pretty intimate connection with the given conviction of intellectual imperfection, as distinct from being any distant deduction from it.

Other descriptions have been given of these sources of Conservative politics. 'We are afraid,' writes Burke, 'to put men to live and trade each on his own private stock of reason; because we suspect that the stock in each man is small, and that the individuals would do better to avail themselves of the general bank and capital of nations and of ages.'[19] He celebrates 'prejudices' in this connection, perhaps meaning the beliefs, customs and institutions that have been established over time, most importantly prescriptive rights or 'prescription', and legal rights to private property above all.

There are many other words spoken of what we can call the source of accumulated wisdom. We cannot avoid hearing that Conservatism directs itself by the old and tried, the tried and tested. 'The Conservative places his faith in arrangements that are known and tried, and wishes to imbue them with all the authority necessary to constitute an accepted and objective public realm.' Thus Roger Scruton.[20] The American sociologist Robert Nisbet would have us all eschew the present plague of 'futurists' and 'futurologists' and look to the past. We will not thereby become tiresome nostalgics. 'Properly worked, the past is, as all comparative historians from Herodotus on have said, a vast and wonderful laboratory for the study of success and failures in the long history of man.'[21]

So much for a sketch of what Conservatives say they are for, with respect to the sources of politics, and what they say they are against. To try to judge the worth of what they say as a characterization of Conservatism, an encapsulation will be useful. Conservatism, we are told, is distinguished by the fact that *it consists in political, social and economic beliefs that have passed the test of time, and are of an empirical kind, and hence are not theoretical, ideological, abstract, greatly general or greatly systematic.* Second, *Conservatives favour political, economic and social beliefs and the like of the given character rather than others.*

The second claim, if it goes naturally together with the first, does not follow from it as a matter of logical necessity. Nor does the second claim, that Conservatives favour such beliefs, entail the first, that they actually have only such beliefs. It *might* be the case that they favour them, but have not yet achieved beliefs and the like of the preferred character, and are still restricted to ideology and so on.

With respect to the supposed character of Conservative beliefs, the encapsulation does leave out occult suppositions that common sense, wisdom-above-reflection and instinct are defining features of Conservatism. We forget about these partly on the assumption that any useful content they have is already captured by referring to the test of time and so on.

The encapsulation also leaves out the common refrain anticipated earlier when we were considering change (p. 9), that Conservatives have and favour beliefs (items of wisdom) that issue in reform, and lack and do not favour beliefs (theoretical beliefs) that issue in change. The distinction between the two kinds of beliefs depends on a suitable distinction between reform and change, which distinction we never got.

The two claims assigned to Conservatives in the encapsulation sum up certain *beliefs about beliefs and the like.* That is, the two claims sum up a set of Conservative beliefs about the nature and grounds – a non-theoretical nature and so on – of a large and diverse body of other Conservative beliefs, doctrines and attitudes, these being about change, incentives, government, property, freedom and so on. The latter large and diverse body of items, if we are to make any progress at all in considering the many claims and beliefs about it, needs to be divided into two large categories. The first we may label factual or either true or false, and the second evaluative. It is important to distinguish the two categories for the reason that what is arguable or whatever about one category – say that its contents are empirical – may not be so of the other.

The division is between what is true or false in an ordinary sense and what is acceptable or unacceptable, where being acceptable is not being ordinarily true, and being unacceptable is not being ordinarily false. Evaluative and in particular moral truths, so called, are not truths in the ordinary sense – ordinary truths, despite philosophical controversy, may still be taken as propositions which have the distinction that they correspond to facts. Despite recurrent and indeed contemporary attempts to assimilate acceptable moral judgements to ordinary true propositions, there is evidently a fundamental difference.

There is a fundamental difference between, say, 'Selling cemeteries to property developers helps keep down local taxes' and 'Selling cemeteries to property developers is right and proper,' or between 'Wall St brokers have incomes, on average, of $300,000 per annum' and 'Wall St brokers should or ought to have incomes, on average, of $300,000 per annum.' It is impossible to *look up*, or *calculate* in the literal sense, a moral fact. In the sense of the word 'fact' in which ordinarily true statements correspond to facts, there are no moral facts. There is perhaps more agreement on this among philosophers and others than on anything else in this neighbourhood.

To begin with the factual side, which will mainly concern us, what we have is that Conservatives do not make and do not approve of factual claims which have not been subjected to the test of time, are unempirical, and hence are theoretical, ideological, abstract, greatly general or greatly systematic.

What seems fundamental is the test of time, and propositions not having been subjected to it. This subject is not easy to get into view, and harder to keep there, partly because it does merge into another more familiar one. We are not now concerned with the fact that Conservatives take some, most or all of the propositions of their opponents to be *false*. Something of this sort must be the case, but it in no way distinguishes Conservatives. It is as true of Social Demo-

crats, old Liberals, Socialists, and the Manhattan Circle of Trotskyists
that they take some, most or all of the propositions of their opponents
to be false. Our subject, rather, is the idea that Conservatives dis-
approve of another thing about certain factual claims, *their not having
been tested over time*, whatever that comes to, and on this account do
not themselves make such claims.

Similarly, our present concern is not that Conservatives take their
own factual propositions to be *true*, although something of that sort
might be the case, but that they take them to have a further satisfactory character or characters. They stand in a certain relation to
actual history or have a certain provenance: they *have* been tested
over time.

It is apparent, incidentally, that many Conservatives who are less
careful than Quinton (p. 25) speak of institutions, arrangements,
customs, laws and established rights as having the given good character, as distinct from what can be said to be embodied in them, a
proposition of some sort. They speak of an existing institution, say
the distribution of income and wealth as it exists in Britain and
America in 1990, or perhaps that type of distribution. This, as it
seems, they contrast with other possible distributions involving
greatly less inequality in income and wealth. The egalitarian distributions, they would say, have not been subjected to the test of
time.

What *can* be meant by saying that an income and wealth distribution, *as distinct from* a proposition about its necessity or worth, has
been tested over time? As it may seem, just that the distribution has
lasted. But that is clearly not the conclusion to which Conservatives
are attracted, but the premise for such a conclusion. Clearly, what
Conservatives must be taken to have in mind when they say an
income and wealth distribution or British democracy or whatever
has been subjected to the test of time is that it has lasted *and* that
something follows from that fact, a proposition of some sort, or rather,
that a proposition has a certain satisfactory character or provenance.

So – we are considering the central idea that Conservatives are
identified by their adherence to factual propositions which have been
tested over time. Very many Conservative propositions of the factual
kind are to the effect that one thing of which we know, say one
economic fact, *is necessary to* another fact. It is not too much to say
that Conservatism, in so far as its factual beliefs are concerned, mainly
consists in such beliefs – whatever Conservatism may come to in sum,
whatever its rationale or informing principle may be. One such belief,

already anticipated, is that an unequal distribution of income and wealth, providing incentive, is necessary to a certain level of economic well-being, perhaps defined in terms of Gross National Product or in some related way. There are many similar beliefs.

Authority is necessary to social order; more pay for policemen, and more liking for them, is the only way of dealing with the incidence of mugging; what is called economic freedom is necessary to what is called political freedom; limited government, a government's holding the ring rather than getting into it, is essential if tyranny is to be avoided; a limited money supply is the only way of defeating inflation; great wealth is necessary, by way of private patronage, to cultural progress; complete secrecy about our secret police, whatever they get up to, including the subversion of democracy, is necessary to national security; good breeding is required for knowing where to put the spoons on the dinner table.

Indeed, a glance back at our survey so far of Conservative opinions gives a good indication of the role of necessity-beliefs. Fisher Ames took less democracy to be necessary to social health, Disraeli took the sustenance by legislation of the gentlemen of England to be necessary to something or other, and the New Right took the ending of the Welfare State to be necessary to an improvement in national character.

Let us proceed in terms of one example of large importance, the first mentioned above. Let us consider the true or false claim that a certain unequal distribution of income and wealth is necessary to provide incentive, which itself is necessary if we are to have a certain level of economic well-being. Certainly something like this is a Conservative belief, although it might be stated more fully and carefully. For a start, it might be turned into this: *a certain unequal distribution of income and wealth is necessary, in our societies where people are not forced to work or enslaved, if we are to achieve a certain economic level.* We can call this, although it is unclear and in a way ambiguous, the Conservative Incentive Proposition. By contrast, there is what we can call the Socialist Incentive Proposition. It is that *the mentioned unequal income and wealth distribution is not necessary in our societies, more or less as they are, still without coercion or enslavement, if we are to have the mentioned economic level.* The thinking behind this is that something else, perhaps another incentive not including the unequal distribution, would work as well. It could partly be the incentive of being a contributor to a fair society.

Our question is this: What is to be said of the idea that the Conservative Incentive Proposition has been subjected to the test of time – time-tested – and thus is in a sense not theoretical, while the Socialist Incentive Proposition has not been time-tested and thus *is* in the given sense theoretical?

To judge the idea, we need first to make *it* clear. We need to do what is not done or not done well by the proponents of the idea. Life for you and me would be easier if Burke and his successors were inclined more to definition and less to declamation, but that is not the case. I do not mean to suggest that their opponents, the Left, are *wholly* different in this respect, that they are angels of clarity. Some are Marxists who owe much to Hegel. However, there *is* a difference, underdescribed as a difference of style, to which we shall return.

There are various understandings of the idea that only the Conservative Incentive Proposition has been time-tested, and we shall look at four.

(1) The first, in part, is that one can look to an actual history which has Conservative inequality and economic well-being in it, but not the other incentive and the same economic well-being. A society, that is, has consistently been more or less Conservative for a long time. More fully, what we have is that *the truth of the Conservative Incentive Proposition can be tested simply by looking at what has happened, just the historical record, and this is not the case with the Socialist proposition.* The society has at no point been Socialist. To proceed in this way is evidently to take the Conservative Incentive Proposition in a certain way, as having to do with a distribution of income and wealth generally or widely conceived, one that has long persisted, throughout past centuries of the history of the society. It is also to speak of an economic level generally or widely conceived, one which has persisted as long. Both conceptions cover variations.

Do we do a favour to Conservatism if we take it to maintain that the Conservative Incentive Proposition, so understood, can be tested just by the historical record of the society, and the Socialist Proposition cannot be tested in this way? We most certainly do not. We here give one relatively clear sense to talk of *theory* – it is what has not been time-tested in this first sense – but it would be unkind to Conservatives to assign to them an opposition to such theory. It has to be allowed that the spokesmen of Conservatism, if they are no plain speakers, *do* suggest this, but we do an injustice to the broad tradition of Conservatism if we take the spokesmen to be right. It would be a silly tradition if it condemned something upon which, as it turns out, it must rely itself. That it does rely on theory in the given sense is easily seen.

To accept the Conservative Incentive Proposition is to accept that if we did not have the given distribution of income and wealth, and did not have some form of coercion, we would not have the given level of economic well-being. But *that* could not conceivably be established just by the truth that we have long had such a distribution and such an economic level. It would be as absurd as to suppose that Cedric's having for twenty-five years been a cat's-meat-man and a Conservative proves that if he were not a cat's-meat-man he would not be a Conservative. He might well be. His Conservatism might be in the blood, or owed to pure reason, or imperfect reason, or the result of an unhappy childhood.

The *only* way of establishing either the Socialist or the Conservative proposition about incentive, as understood, is by theorizing: that is, by going beyond the facts as they have been and considering whether it *would* be the case, in circumstances where the distribution of income and wealth was different, that there would none the less be the given level of economic well-being. The Conservative and the non-Conservative despite their different answers are in exactly the same boat in so far as going beyond the facts is concerned. Therefore, if Conservatism *were* a politics which took the Conservative Incentive Proposition as we have understood it to be different in kind from the other proposition, from the point of view of theory as we have understood it, Conservatism would not get an *A* or a *B* in rudimentary logic but a very low mark indeed, such as to call out for a period of re-education.

Do we now hear sounds of protest, perhaps rural rumbling of the kind that led Mill to his description of Conservatism as the Stupid Party? Do we hear that all this is logic-chopping or whatever? Chinking? No matter. Nothing will unseat the truth that the mere fact that *X* has always gone with *Y* is nowhere near a proof either for those who say *X* is necessary to *Y* or those who deny that *X* is necessary to *Y*. Cedric may indeed have been cat's-meat-man and Conservative for forty years, without thereby establishing that his choice of profession was or was not necessary to his politics.

(2) Enough of that. Let us think about another understanding of the idea (p. 29) that the Conservative Incentive Proposition has been time-tested and thus is not theoretical, while the Socialist Incentive Proposition has not been time-tested and thus *is* theoretical. Here what we have is the thought that we can look at past history and find in it (i) times when there was a certain unequal or Conservative distribution of income and wealth, providing a certain incentive, and

a certain level of economic well-being, and (ii) other times when there was a more equal or Socialist distribution of income and wealth, providing less incentive, and a lower level of economic well-being. A Conservative who takes this to be true, evidently, is taking the Conservative Incentive Proposition in a different way, as the claim that a fairly specific extent of inequality is necessary, if there is no coercion, for a fairly specific level of economic well-being.

Can our Conservative take this to be time-tested? The short story is that he can, essentially for the reason that it has actually been tested in the past: there have been times when the inequality has been missing, and, he maintains, so has the well-being. He *also* maintains, however, that the Socialist Incentive Proposition, understood similarly, is not time-tested. That proposition is that Conservative inequality is not necessary to a specific level of economic well-being. Is he right in saying this has not been time-tested? The short answer is that he is as wrong as he could be. The Socialist proposition, which he takes to be false, has in the relevant way exactly the same history as his own. It too, on his view, has actually been tested in the past, in exactly the same way. That is, when there has not been Conservative inequality, there has not been the specific level of well-being.

Certainly, *if* things are as he supposes, the Conservative can be happy. His proposition is true, and the Socialist proposition is false. But that more substantial issue, to which we shall certainly come, is not our subject now. Our subject now is whether the Conservative Incentive Proposition, as understood, has a certain satisfactory provenance, unique to itself. It does not. Our subject now is whether what a Conservative says about the histories of his own and somebody else's beliefs is true. It is not.

(3) We have been considering necessity-claims. Conservatism can be taken to include factual claims of another kind. They too are characterized by the spokesmen of the tradition as untheoretical in the given sense. In slightly technical language, these are claims to the effect not that one thing is necessary for another, but that one thing is just sufficient for another. That is, they do not say that if X is missing so is Y, but typically say that if all of X is present so is Y. Nothing but X is needed. To persist with the same example, we may be told that just an income and wealth distribution of which we know, putting aside what might be the case if it were missing, *does* secure us a certain general economic level. This we are supposed to know from our history. By contrast, it may be said, we do not have a proof that what some call the incentive of a fairer and hence more

co-operative society would keep GNP as it is. All we know is that it is our existing wealth distribution as it is, and the particular incentive that it involves, does keep GNP as it is.

One thing to be said of this sort of thing is that it is less important. Sufficiency-claims must be very much less important to Conservatism than necessity-claims. In general, to recommend X by saying that it is sufficient for Y is not much to recommend it. I do not, in a certain common situation, give much of an argument for a given means to an end by pointing out that it is such a means. I do not give much of an argument if the situation is one where *other* means are available, and these would be less costly, more humanitarian, or have some other recommendation. I do not much recommend your getting very drunk by saying what is true, that it will make you forget your troubles, if ringing up your mother would have the same effect and not involve the hangover.

The main thing to be said of Conservative sufficiency-claims of the given kind is that like necessity-claims they may be perfectly theoretical. The persistence of one distribution of income and wealth, and one level of economic well-being, does not by itself establish that nothing less than the first is sufficient for the second. To speak differently, Conservatives may defend a certain general extent of inequality in income and wealth, and no less than that extent, as what gives rise to a level of economic well-being. Consistently with the history to which they point, however, it may be the case that a *lesser* extent of inequality would have done as well. Suppose that I was struck at an impressionable moment long ago, not by a vision of the dauphiness of France at Versailles before she came to the throne and before the Revolution, as in the case of Burke, who never thereafter forgot the joy of it, but by the more mundane sight of Lord Hailsham with his lower garment very well supported. I cannot safely conclude that because I have worn both a belt and also braces since then, for forty years, and my trousers have stayed up, that nothing less is sufficient to secure that end.

Here again, then, with sufficiency-claims, Conservatives are necessarily involved in theoretical reasoning of the given kind. They must maintain what is *not* a simple matter of there having persisted, for a long time, one unequal distribution of income and wealth, and one level of economic well-being. They must maintain that if the inequality had been less, there would not have been the given well-being. There remains a second understanding of Conservative sufficiency-claims, like the second understanding of Conservative necessity-claims. This faces the same fatal objection as its predecessor. Let us not rehearse it.

So much for some related understandings of the idea that Conservative beliefs as to necessity and sufficiency have been tested over time or consist in accumulated wisdom. These understandings have the great recommendation that they are actually about the beliefs, about them and their support or evidence or logic, rather than about something else: who believes them. There is a different sort of understanding of talk of the test of time and accumulated wisdom.

(4) Such an understanding is not about the beliefs themselves, but *is* about who believes or has them. It is in a way simpler, and more to the fore in what Conservatives say, and open to a simple reply. We may hear of 'the laboratory of the past' here, but the thought in question is not that of Nisbet, the sociologist not fond of futurologists (p. 26). He supposes that Conservatives now among us or anyway their comparative historians learn by studying successes and failures in the past. That claim, to whatever extent it is true, could be thought only in a moment of delirium to distinguish Conservatives. Others also learn a thing or two from the past.

The calmer Conservative thought about Conservative thought, in one form is that if an institution or practice has lasted, although with intermissions, there is the argument for it that it has had the good opinion or favourable judgement of many people, some succession of generations. No matter the theoretical nature of Conservative propositions in the senses so far considered, they none the less have been judged to be true or defensible in a kind of long investigation. No matter that Conservative propositions cannot be read off the facts of the past in some unique way, they have been believed by many people. Conservative propositions *are* untheoretical in the sense of being a summation of many judgements. Burke may be taken to have this in mind in speaking of the smallness of one man's stock of reason as against 'the general bank of capital of nations and of ages' (p. 25). Anthony Quinton, alas, depends on it. It is contained in or indeed *is* his principle of political scepticism (p. 25).

This idea, at best, can only be as strong as any idea to the effect that what is true is a matter of how many people believe it. It is, at best, only as strong as any idea to the effect that truth is decided not merely by authority, but by the authority of numbers, if that can be called authority at all. We are recommended certain beliefs, not for reasons having to do with them and their logic, or indeed the facts, but on the ground of a kind of democracy in which each of a number of generations counts as a voter on truth. The democratic analogy, of course, given the scepticism of Conservatives about democracy, to which we shall come, is not likely to be brought into play by them.

The kind of argument in question is rightly embarrassing and rightly disdained when it turns up elsewhere, say in science and philosophy, or anyway philosophy other than political philosophy, or in ordinary life of a moderately enlightened kind. Why should it have a hearing here? What, if anything, stops us from supposing that we are contemplating the flat-earthers of politics? How are these thinkers different from those fundamentalists in religion who have lately seen through Darwin's plot and substituted, for evolutionary theory, the Clap of Creation and God's subsequent industry in calling up the various species?

That is not all. The particular argument we are considering, about beliefs of a political kind, depends absolutely on whether political history can be regarded as having been an *inquiry* or *investigation*. Was the succession of generations a sequence of unfettered reflection, free gathering of evidence, informed testing of hypotheses? Has the past been near to being the kind of laboratory where all political experiments are possible, and unconstrained verdicts given?

To suppose so is nonsense. There is no need to approach that rough answer by degrees, or to spend time in qualifying it. History, if it is to be summed up quickly, and if we are to get a laboratory into the story, has been a laboratory where people have always been preventing political experiments, knocking over the apparatus when they were started, concealing results, and, when necessary, setting fire to the benches. History has been a struggle, not an inquiry, and what has lasted in it, in terms of actual politics and economics, has been owed to human desires other than the desires for truth, validity, consistency and the like. This is no doctrinaire proposition of a Marxist kind which reduces all of history to what is called 'class struggle', but a denial of a yet more contentious account of it, an account so idealized as to be dreamlike, an account worthy of Burke lately back from Versailles. If Conservatism did necessarily embrace the view that the past has been a respectable laboratory, it could not claim much attention.

We have made four attempts and found no creditable characterization of Conservatism in terms of factual beliefs owed to the test of time or accumulated wisdom. Let us now proceed more quickly, first with the claim that Conservative beliefs of the factual rather than evaluative kind are distinctively *empirical* in some general sense. Again it is no easy thing to get clear what, at bottom, is being maintained. I fancy that readers of these lines, however mindful of what was reported earlier (p. 23), will discover that they have no clear idea. What *is* meant by saying of such Conservative beliefs as those to the effect that one thing is necessary for another or sufficient for another, that they are empirical?

We cannot see with our eyes that authority is necessary to social order, or even that more pay for policemen is the only way of dealing with mugging. We are not helped to *see* such things, further, by being involved in governing or administering. Members of cabinets and government departments, whatever else they may acquire, do not acquire the gift of making *visible* to themselves what others cannot see.

Of course we shall now be told that what Conservatives have in mind is not that their beliefs are *literally* empirical, really a matter of sense-experience. That concession, however, gives us only obscurity. It is all very well for Burke to announce that he wants 'in a manner' to touch with his own hands not only the fixed but the momentary circumstances (p. 24), but what manner is that? A manner, presumably, such that he could, if he were still with us, in that manner touch with his hands the circumstance that what is called economic freedom is necessary to what is called political freedom. I should like to see him do it. Or, if that is the wrong kind of wish, itself too empirical, I should like to be told a bit more about this second sight, or, rather, second touch.

In the end, as always in such contexts, what starts as an obscure and provocative thought may be reduced to what is clear and arguable but in another way unsatisfactory. The claim that Conservatism is empirical, having run into a question or two, may be reduced to the unstunning idea that Conservatism *pays attention to the facts*, anyway some facts. Let us suppose something of the sort is true. It would be one more unkindness to Conservatism to suppose that it takes itself to be uniquely distinguished by paying attention to the facts, takes itself to be wholly or significantly different from other political traditions in this respect. That could be no more than a kind of pomposity, benighted if actually serious. All right for the House of Lords, or the annual barbecue of the Conservatives of Dallas, but not so good in the outside world. Conservatives in fact are often enough heard dismissing exactly the fact-grubbing tendencies of their opponents: those statistics about poverty, health, race, schools and so on. Furthermore we have hardly any distinction between empiricism, taken as just paying attention to the facts, and rationalism, or between the empirical in this weak sense and the theoretical.

Here is a slightly better suggestion as to empiricism, and one which makes for a fairly clear opposition between the empirical and the theoretical, in one more sense of the latter term. Theories as commonly understood and as understood in science are not empirical reports. They are not reports of observations or readings-off of facts. They are not data, not the products of the empirical method taken by itself. Rather, theories are accounts of the visible facts, explanations of them, often explanations in terms of something unobservable. The facts are that apples fall from trees, and the theory of gravity offers an explanation of the facts. If there are difficulties in finally clarifying the distinction between data and theory, there evidently exists a distinction to clarify.

Certainly there are theories, in this fundamental sense, to which Conservatives are opposed. One for which they can have no love is Marx's theory of history. It concerns the facts that there are in societies what may be called productive forces, which include labour and technology, that societies have such class structures as the one associated with capitalism, and that they have superstructures, which include a system of laws, a customary morality and perhaps a religion. With respect to this triad of facts, what explains what?

It is Marx's theory that the first two items, productive forces and class structure, explain the third. It is not that what is ordinarily taken to be morally right, just or godly explains other facts of society, but rather that other facts explain what is taken to be right, just or godly. Eternal verities dear to most Conservative hearts, and enshrined in law, customary morality and religion, are not very eternal. They simply are products of capitalism or whatever. The theory, which Jerry Cohen has made the best and certainly a valiant attempt to purify and save,[22] verges on or involves a conspiracy theory: that those in control of the productive forces, and well located in the class structure, contrive to get themselves and others to accept a morality and other institutions which will help to keep things as they are.

But not liking the theories of their opponents is plainly no distinguishing feature of Conservatives. Further, not all of their opponents like all theories of those opponents. Truth to tell, I have no enthusiasm for Marx's machinery myself, despite the feeling that it contains a large truth.

Can we, as we must if we are to have a chance of finding anything that might individuate Conservatism, take it to be opposition to such theories *in general*? Can we take it to limit itself absolutely to the related empiricism? If we do so, we again malign it. To take Conservatism to be opposition to such theories in general is tantamount to taking it to be opposition to *explanation*. Could it be that a large political tradition is to be distinguished by not wanting answers, or attempted answers, to the question of why things happen, why things are as they are? We must be loath to think so. Conservatism is not notably intellectual, or keen on education for all, and the thinkers of the New Right may not strike one as masters of argument, or mistresses, but Conservatism is not a wholly general campaign against inquiry, against what might be called the effective part of intelligence.

We must be as loath to take seriously that Conservatism is against much else of the factual kind which is in one way or another unempirical and which its exponents so carelessly disdain: all generalizations, all systematic thought, logic, consistency, all political thought of a literary character, all of what comes from those meagre, hopping and troublesome creatures less in possession of Burke's pasture than the ruminant silent majority. Also all abstraction, to which subject we will return (p. 61).

Not much more needs to be said of the commodious proposition that Conservatives only have and only favour factual beliefs which have passed the test of time, are empirical and so on, and hence are untheoretical in various senses. The proposition needs to be delivered, if necessary by private contractors, to the rubbish heap of history. Putting aside all that has been said so far, it is just a fact that there *are* Conservative theories in any sense one chooses. Above all, there are theories in the standard sense lately noted, which is to say supposed accounts or explanations of observable facts. Some, as we know, have to do with incentive. Some have to do with private property. Some have to do with what is called Freedom. One more is what was called monetarism, and for a time after 1979 was taken to be the final solution to all economic problems. Yet another is the conspiracy theory that gripped the very souls of many Conservatives, and seemed to be in the very ink of the London *Times* or at any rate written into the contracts of employees. It was not to the effect that the Communists were engaged in an imperialist plot, which no doubt they were, but that they were engaged in a plot of which there was no conceivable counterpart elsewhere in the universe.

If there are Conservative theories, there is also Conservative ideology, in any sense of the word which is at all relevant. It must come

as no surprise, although John Adams takes ideology to be worse
than idiotism (p. 18), and Russell Kirk of the New Right echoes his
opinion, that other Conservatives have quite abandoned that sunken
ship. Robert Nisbet in one of his better moments gives a clear and
arguable definition of 'ideology'.

> Leaving aside the historical meanings it has had, such as its
> pejorative reference to a certain class of ideas in Napoleonic
> times and its use by Marx for the collective consciousness of a
> social class, the sense of 'ideology' in our age is quite clear, and
> altogether useful. Stated briefly, an ideology is any reasonably
> coherent body of moral, economic, social and cultural ideas that
> has a solid and well-known reference to politics and political
> power ...[23]

He states, with every reason, that Conservatism is such an ideology.
It is for him one of the three major ideologies of the past several
centuries in the West, the others being Liberalism and Socialism.
Noel O'Sullivan is as sensible, although he takes up a somewhat
grander conception of ideology. For him, an ideology is or involves
'a self-conscious attempt to provide an explicit and coherent theory
of man, society, and the world'. Conservatism is allowed to be such
a thing, and not a mere collection of emotional and pragmatic
responses to change.[24]

As for the nearby proposition that Conservatism is itself a single
large theory, Anthony Quinton somewhat reluctantly climbs aboard
it, protesting that it is not an 'abstract theory'.[25] He later adds a
traditional comment.

> Conservatives generally insist that different social arrangements
> are appropriate to different times and places. They do not, like
> classical liberals, or later doctrinaires like the Fabian socialists,
> endorse a timeless ideal of civilized order which should be
> imposed, if necessary by force, on those communities whose
> historical experience has not led them to it.[26]

Is he right to see Conservatives as not supposing themselves to have
a politics of universal application, as not inclined to impose it on
diverse communities? His words were written before President
Reagan made it clear he knew what was best for the Nicaraguans,
and would try to see that they got it, by paying for a war. They were

not written before the British intervention in the Russian Revolution.

Let us now remember the large distinction made earlier (p. 27) and spend a little time on Conservative claims about evaluative as against factual Conservative beliefs. Is there more promise here? What we are told is that these are not Utilitarian, not greatly general, not greatly systematic, and not taken up with 'social justice' or with imagined rights, these being any rights other than legal ones. Conservatives do not have moral commitments of these kinds. It is also said that the different evaluative beliefs of Conservatives are owed to the test of time, are somehow empirical, and are not theoretical or ideological – but let us excuse ourselves further reflection on these claims, which face yet greater difficulties with evaluative as against factual beliefs.

Disraeli's argument against Utilitarianism (p. 19), which amounts to asking the question who is to decide what makes for the greatest happiness of the greatest number, is the kind of bluff into which politicians fall when, rightly enough, they are made insecure by moral philosophers. *Any* moral principle of interest raises the question, as much or as little as Utilitarianism, of who is to decide what will be in accordance with the principle in question. Utilitarianism is more capable than many of giving an answer. But we need not become involved in all that. What needs to be noted is only that opposition to Utilitarianism is no defining feature of Conservatism. Whether or not he made sense in doing so, Marx too gave over some lines to trying to refute it. This book, as you will have gathered before now, is no Conservative work, but neither is it any defence of Utilitarianism.

Friedrich Hayek instructs us (p. 20) that ideas of 'social justice', by which he means moral principles for the distribution of goods in societies, are absurd because they set out to distribute the goods in accordance with the moral merit of individuals, but the moral merit of each individual is undiscoverable. I do not know where our instructor has spent the present century. He must have found some safe house into which few persons from the outside world intruded. There have been *no* notable principles of distributive justice, at any rate of the kind to which he is opposed, which have been based on moral merit. Most of them have been based on a consideration of individual need, which precisely does not have to do with individuals having different degrees of moral merit. If we assign to Conservatism our instructor's *aperçu* we assign to it a nonsense.

But that is not the largest point. Can it be, as seems to be suggested, that Conservatism is distinguished by having or being informed by *no* general answer of whatever character to the question of how goods in a society are to be distributed among its members? Can it be that it does not have and is not informed by *any* such general principle or commitment? Can it be, to persist with Hayek, that Conservatism makes *no* response to the distribution question but this curiously indeterminate one: goods are to be distributed in whatever way they are distributed by the mechanism of a market? That must be doubtful, as a moment's reflection indicates.

Suppose that the market persists, but begins to function oddly. Suppose, to make the point clear quickly, that it begins to function *very* oddly. There is the result that inheritors, capitalists, entrepreneurs, risk-takers and other persons valued by Conservatives really do consistently lose money. The Athenaeum and other gentlemen's clubs must be mortgaged, Chambers of Commerce decline sadly, and hitherto rising families can no longer send their children to the better schools. However, unenterprising and unfamilied persons less prized by Conservative governments, including members of those remaining communes and encampments of hippies, do very well indeed, by expending no more effort than now. They do not try hard, but they do bid successfully for the newly privatized National Parks, and of course Stonehenge, from which they then seek to make no profit. Are we to think – can we think for a moment – that Conservatives will happily accept, having got over the shock, that things are still in good order, since goods are still being distributed by the mechanism of a market?

But let me not obscure a fact by agreeable fantasy. It is near to certain that Conservatism has some general answer or makes some general response to the question of distributive justice. It is imaginable that a large political tradition lacks such a thing, but wholly unlikely. The very existence of such a tradition, whatever the facts of its historical development and the inevitable diversity within it, might be supposed to depend on such an answer or response. It is near to certain that if a market does in fact distribute goods in a way supported and defended by a political tradition, then that is the way called for by some general principle of distribution favoured by the tradition. This principle will specify a recognizable *end*, not a *means*.

It is an assumption of this book that Conservatism, whatever else may distinguish it, does indeed rest on and is informed by a general principle, whether or not a recognizably moral one. It is one fundamental aim of our inquiry to find that principle, whether or not moral, and thus to come to a conclusion about the worth or decency of Conservatism. The assumption, if not taken to be necessarily true, is as reasonable as similar assumptions about other traditions, institutions, organizations and the like. We rightly accept that a nation as a whole, in its dealings with other nations, pursues an overall end. So with a church, a bank and an army. In each case, the end explains different features or properties of the thing in question. It makes sense of what otherwise would be a kind of mystery, an accidental or coincidental bundle of features or properties. It is worth adding that the assumption that Conservatism rests on a general principle is surely something like a necessary condition of what is true: that Conservatives are recognizable by themselves and by others. They and others recognize their policies. Still, the final proof of the existence of a Conservative rationale must be the finding of it. Until then what we have is an assumption, however reasonable the assumption.

Reflection on Conservative disparagement of talk of non-legal rights leads in the direction of these same conclusions. Conservatives often say, as we know, that they will have nothing to do with such talk, that such rights are no part of their ideology. It is possible to have some sympathy with *one* cause of their disparagement. Jurisprudential and like persons, partly inspired by the enthusiasm of Ronald Dworkin,[27] do in fact take rights too seriously. I mean that they seem to conceal from themselves, and succeed in concealing from others, that to say someone has some sort of non-legal right to something is just to say, with some relatively unimportant preamble, addition or implication, that *he ought to have the thing if he so chooses*. It is typically to make a moral judgement, and has as little or much foundation as moral judgements generally. It is exactly as much in need of argument. To have this clear in one's mind is also to see, importantly, that there is no substantial argument from the premise that someone has a right to a thing to a conclusion to the effect that he ought to have it. We make no significant progress in moving from judgements about non-legal rights to judgements as to what ought to be the case (cf pp. 107 f).

Still, if we do use this language of rights, is it the case that Conservatism must contain an answer to the question of what non-legal rights are possessed by individuals? If it is the case that Conservatism in a particular society is a defence of just the legal rights existing in that society, however unenlightening that truth may be, is it also the case that it is an argued defence of moral rights? Is it the doctrine that on account of a general moral principle individuals ought to have those things to which they have legal rights – that for a general moral reason they have moral rights to those things to which they have legal rights? It would be premature to say so, partly because not all organizing principles are moral principles. It is not mistaken to expect that Conservatism does rest on some organizing principle or other.

That expectation is not to be confused with something else: the proposition that *Conservatism makes explicit any general principle or rationale*. We shall have to discover in the course of our inquiry whether that is so. Is Conservatism distinguished by its not bringing its principle or rationale into clear view?

There is more to be said about the market and the rationale of Conservatism (p. 94), but let us end here by glancing at the most celebrated piece of political philosophy of the New Right. It is Robert Nozick's *Anarchy, State and Utopia*, mentioned earlier (p. 4). What we are offered is a conception of the just society. That society, we have it, is one where the distribution of goods has a certain history, or one of two histories. (1) All goods in the society fall into two categories. They are possessed by persons who have mixed their labour with them, or with the raw materials, and have also satisfied some other requirements. Or they are possessed by persons to whom they have come by way of voluntary transactions, certain sales or gifts, which transactions began with the possession of the goods in question by someone who mixed his or her labour and satisfied the further requirements. (2) Alternatively, if goods got into the wrong hands, in terms of these principles, things have since then been rectified.

Robert Nozick gives a reluctant summary of this political philosophy, a reduction of it to a maxim, a maxim on the model of such familiar ones as 'From each according to his ability, to each according to his need'. His maxim is:

> From each according to what he chooses to do, to each according to what he makes for himself (perhaps with the contracted aid of others) and what others choose to do for him and choose to give him of what they've been given previously (under this maxim) and haven't yet expended or transferred.

He boils this down into:

> From each as they choose, to each as they are chosen.[28]

Nozick is to be commended for assuming, as evidently he does, that Conservatism does have at its base a general principle or rationale. It is a pity that he is so rare among Conservatives in this respect. However, does what he says *make explicit* such a principle or rationale? Does what he says in fact go some way towards supporting the idea that Conservatism keeps its ruling idea to itself? Whatever else is thought of them, his words are not so explicit as might be supposed at first reading. We shall return to the matter (p. 212).

- 3 -
Human Nature

... frailty and depravity ...

John Adams

Shall we find the true nature of Conservatism, in particular a rationale, in what it believes about human nature and in conclusions it draws? Conservatives say so. They say so much to that effect that we are spoiled for choice. One of their various themes has to do with our low characters. Many have directed us to the doctrine of Original Sin, of Adam's Fall. We are to see what all our natures still are, a good while later, from the tale of the Garden of Eden, and from St Paul's doctrine about it, upon whose gloomy mystery so much theological labour has been expended to so little effect. 'By one man,' he said, 'sin entered into the world, and death by sin; and so death passed upon all men, for that all have sinned.' Somehow, we all share Adam's personal shortcoming, whatever that was, not to mention responsibility for his own awful act, whatever it was.

Other Conservatives direct us to the seventeenth century and Thomas Hobbes. Of his philosophy they remember that he took human nature to be such that if certain political arrangements are not made, life will be 'solitary, poor, nasty, brutish, and short'. (Not exactly, as a candidate wrote in the fateful year 1979, in an examination answer, 'solitary, poor, nasty, British, and short'. Still, he should have had a mark or two for foresight.) John Adams spoke for early American Conservatives when he remarked on 'the general frailty and depravity' of human nature. To leap forward to the present, we may hear from a resolute Tory realist, as indeed I have, that human nature is such that Bob Geldof, the organizer of pop music concerts for famine relief, was necessarily in it for the money, his own personal percentage. To turn finally to some New Right thinkers impressed by sociobiology, we have it that as we all go about our late twentieth-century business, it is our genes that are in control of us all, and we are essentially identical with hunter-gatherers going about their Ice Age business. Hence, perhaps, the need for more privatization.

What *is* this human nature of which we hear so much? Although biological science is sometimes in the wings or even on stage when it is spoken of, it does not include all of what is needed to make standard members of the human species. Toes do not get into it, or lungs, or indeed minds, or that we are of a certain average height, or have forty-six chromosomes, or are featherless bipeds. It is clear that when human nature is talked of by Conservatives, and their opponents, what is in question is almost always *one or another or several of our attributes taken to be of relevance to human affairs, notably political, economic and social affairs*. We are such and such, and hence there follows some conclusion as to what ought to, needs to, or can be the case, or is to be excused or readily understood. To revert for an example to previous reflections, we are such that certain incentives are required if we are to get down to work, and hence there ought to be such incentives.

To say this – that claims as to human nature are premises for certain moral or political conclusions – is not to follow one recent student of human nature, Christopher Berry, indeed follow him in the direction of overboard.[1] It is not to come near to saying that claims as to human nature have their value in being themselves dualistic: they are both factual and also somehow evaluative, normative or prescriptive. Or, to be more precise, it is not to suppose that claims as to human nature, *as they function* in political and like argument, are more than true or false claims, and in fact are hybrids. I may certainly say that children have the possibility of learning, and then draw an evaluative conclusion from that, that they ought to be given education. But to say that *they can learn* is not in itself to say *they ought to be educated*. No amount of theory will make it so.

A bit more will be said of the matter (p. 49), but we shall indeed take it that claims as to human nature, in their function as premises, are claims whose use depends only on whether they are true or false in the ordinary sense. There is good reason for this. The whole point of arguments from human nature, as with many other sorts, is to have arguments that are satisfactorily rooted in *facts*. This remains the case when the premises do also have something which does not play a role in argument, an evaluative content. That is common enough. It is indeed the case that to speak of ourselves as selfish, perfectible, rational, only weakly rational, free, a little lower than the angels, and so on, is to speak not only in a factual but also an evaluative way. But to use such claims as premises for evaluative conclusions is at least typically to use them on the assumption that they are true rather than anything else. I do not have to do more than prove we *are* selfish or only weakly rational, as distinct from justify my implied evaluative feeling, in order to get my argument going.

Must we have in mind, in thinking of human nature, only those of our attributes relevant to human affairs which are *universal*, possessed by all members of the species without exception? That is sometimes said, and some arguments having to do with human nature are strengthened by being based on what is supposed to be a universal fact. However, we do no service to Conservatism if we insist on this. If there were a widely shared but not universal relevant attribute, that would be sufficient as a basis for certain common arguments. (By way of analogy, if it is needed, not every last tiger has to be fierce for it to be a good idea to keep out of their cages.) Indeed some Conservative arguments pertain to attributes of half of the human race, either the men or the women, or to persons of lesser races or darker colours, or to the strong or able as against the weak or less able. It was Burke who distinguished a better class of persons from 'a swinish multitude'.[2] It was Thomas Carlyle, in the nineteenth century, who discerned the existence of 'heroes', whom he summoned to take command of English society and rescue it from anarchy, by drilling.[3]

Must the relevant attributes be *unchangeable* ones, items that not only have persisted among us all since the Ice Age, or the Garden of Eden, but could not have been otherwise? David Hume, no doubt the greatest of British philosophers, and a bit too confidently claimed by Conservatives to be of their number, was keen on an unchanging human nature, a subject-matter for the science of man he attempted to establish. Virginia Woolf, a novelist to the taste of some, and of the Bloomsbury Party in politics, was not merely of the different opinion that human nature was changeable, but also that it did change, in or around December 1910.

However we might decide between them, or about whether they are talking about the same thing and hence do really disagree, and whatever exactly we take 'unchangeable' to mean, we do no service to Conservatism to insist that it concern itself with unchangeable attributes. While some Conservative arguments are helped by an assumption as to an unchangeable human nature, others have to do with attributes that are owed to particular societies, and would have been otherwise if the societies had been different. Michael Oakeshott has it that our 'current human nature', owed to bad influences, includes a lust for change.[4]

Finally, by way of preliminaries, are we to think only of those of our politically relevant attributes that are *genetic or biological* as distinct from being owed to environment? It needs to be allowed that much Conservative argument having to do with human nature does take it to be something that *is* a matter of our common heredity, not something owed to society and hence something which could be altered by changes in society. It is commonly remarked that the Left in politics takes human nature to be something formed to some significant or great extent by social history, while the Right takes it to be something settled by natural inheritance. Jerry Cohen, who is of a Marxist persuasion, is true to his inspiration when he tells us that society continually alters human nature. In a society, as he says, committed to certain norms of smell, it may become part of a man's human nature to want a deodorant.[5]

Whether or not we agree with that revolutionary thought, it would not be a good idea to suppose that the human nature of which Conservatives speak is necessarily wholly genetic or biological. Indeed we already have that indicated by Oakeshott's mention of our lust for change, owed precisely to bad influences. There are other Conservative arguments that presuppose a human nature at least partly owed to environment, as we shall see, and, further, there is also a quite general reason for not restricting Conservatives to genetic conceptions of human nature.

The general reason is that it is as good as impossible to find human attributes relevant to politics – at least if we leave aside our being a little lower than the angels – of which we can confidently say that they are owed wholly to heredity. It is as hard to find relevant attributes which can confidently be assigned wholly to environment. Further, it is about as difficult to say of a particular relevant attribute what part is owed to biology and what to environment. Consider kinds of selfishness and rationality. In short, if we supposed Conservatism to be concerned only with genetic attributes or attributes owed mainly to genetic influences, we would run the risk of limiting it to non-existent or disputable attributes.

We shall take it, then, that our present subject is (i) Conservative propositions, true or false, about human attributes relevant to human affairs and particularly politics and economics, the attributes not necessarily being universal, unchangeable or wholly genetic, and (ii)

Conservative arguments based on these factual propositions. Do we here find the rationale of Conservatism?

A first thing that needs noticing is that we do not have a proposition of the given sort, such a premise for a conclusion, in the idea that we have *the attribute that we have rights*, that idea as naturally understood.[6]

It may well be, as the Declaration of Independence has it, that it is self-evident that all men have certain inalienable rights, including rights to life, liberty and the pursuit of happiness. It is arguable, no doubt, that each of us has a right to some amount of private property, or to a fair return for our labours, and perhaps that each of us has more specific rights dear to some Conservative hearts, say the right to a three-car garage, a heliport, or better medical treatment, if we can pay more for it than others. It may even be that some useful sense can be attached to a sadly worn label which may be put on these various items – it may be that they can usefully be called Natural Rights.[7] They could be so labelled because they are rights defended on the basis of widely shared human attributes. (I do not mean to imply that Conservatives have ever been keen on Natural Rights as traditionally understood – quite the contrary, as we have seen.)

None of that is going to transform these claims as to rights into *factual* claims. To say that we have the attribute that we have the right to bequeath our property to our children, in the non-legal sense that necessarily is intended, or, what comes to the same thing, just that we have the non-legal right to bequeath our property to our children, is *not* to say something that is true or false in the ordinary or standard sense. That we may say that it is 'self-evident' or in some other sense 'true' that we have the right makes no difference whatever to the point. Saying that someone has a non-legal right, as already remarked, is at bottom to say no more than that he ought to have the thing. It is to make a moral or evaluative judgement or claim. Certainly claims as to rights may be *based on* human nature, *based on* attributes we have, but that is nothing to the present point. Claims as to rights are not to be confused with those attributes, or with propositions asserting their existence. We shall consider Conservative claims as to rights in later chapters.

We need not be detained long, second, by certain admittedly factual and half-arguable propositions as to our human nature, and conclusions drawn from them, which are less fundamental to Conservatism – certainly less fundamental than the refrain about our low characters. One, which comes into view occasionally, is that our human nature is extremely complex, somehow a mystery beyond our discerning. It is therefore such that political recommendations of the opponents of Conservatism are too simple, bound to be futile since they do not take into account the complexity of our attributes. Burke made his contribution to this line of thought when he said, not taking long enough to dwell on it, that 'the nature of man is intricate'.[8] Clinton Rossiter, who gave us *Conservatism in America*, dwells a little longer. He writes: 'the confession of an eminent psychologist, Gardner Murphy, "Not much, I believe, is known about man," is applauded by the Conservative, who then adds, "Not much, I believe, will ever be known about him."'[9]

It must come to mind that if we take this seriously, and suppose our natures *are* hidden from us, more follows than that the simple opponents of Conservatism are in trouble. *Everybody*, in so far as arguments from human nature are in question, is in trouble. Conservatives are in trouble. A complex response to a real mystery is no better than a simple one.

The given line of thought, moreover, does not accord well with more fundamental Conservative propositions about human nature. It more or less contradicts them. *These* propositions are to the effect that human nature *is* in several ways simple, open to relatively simple description, of which some idea was given earlier by way of the refrain having to do with Adam, Hobbes, *et al*. Further, a fundamental Conservative strategy with respect to the given proposals of their opponents is precisely to assert not that human nature is hidden from us, but that if we are not naive we *can* see very clearly that we have certain attributes, exactly not the attributes presupposed by dreaming Utopians and the like.

There are, third, a number of human-nature propositions of a light-headed kind advanced by Conservatives. Propositions of this general kind, pertaining to more than human nature, have about them a sort of fey audacity. It may be that their principal importance is not so much what they say, but rather what they indicate of the nature of Conservatism, or reflective Conservatism. It may be that they tell in the same direction as certain facts of Conservative *style* mentioned earlier, such styles as Ongoing Parliamentary and Numinous (p. 11). That is something to which we shall return.

One such proposition is suggested after its author lets us know, in talking of the meaning and purpose of life, that he is not merely listing his own tastes and prejudices. 'I am attempting to categorize the most important kinds of human pleasures and satisfactions, those which give the fullest meaning to life.'[10] The proposition is that man's nature is such, his spiritual needs are such, that the game of cricket is a profound and absorbing activity, and ought to be made compulsory. To make it compulsory would be in accordance with the ultimate purpose of the state, which requires it to play its part in the formation of desire. This perception of ourselves and the ensuing recommendation are not to be found, as might be expected by the innocent reader, in the playing-field memoirs of an Edwardian gent, but rather in the political thought of a lecturer in politics, in this case Lincoln Allison of the University of Warwick. The perception and the recommendation are conveyed to us in his *Right Principles: A Conservative Philosophy of Politics*.

Needless to say, the proposition about our natures, and the recommendation as to cricket, are pretty quickly reduced by qualification. Still, something of them remains, at least enough, as Allison says, that liberals ought to be shocked by them. To pay the proposition and the recommendation a bit of attention, it is pretty unclear what attribute of some of us, no doubt some potentiality, will be served by making cricket compulsory. Perhaps a potential for giving life a meaning, or for comprehending moral significance, or for winning, or for noticing that it is going to rain. Our author touches lightly on all of these.

We can carry away the thought that arguments based on human nature must begin by giving us a decent idea of which of our attributes is in question. Allison is clearer elsewhere in his book, where, being concerned with other attributes of ours, he reports approvingly that 'what modern science says about man's nature is that he is tough, nasty and highly-sexed'.[11] Perhaps we shall get to the heart of Conservatism by contemplating such perceptions, and what is taken to follow from them. We do not get to it by inquiring into what it is about ourselves that might justify compulsory cricket.

A fourth human-nature proposition offered by Conservatives is that man is by nature religious. 'We know, and it is our pride to know, that man is by his constitution a religious animal; that atheism is against, not only our reason but our instincts; and that it cannot prevail long.' Burke draws from this, as many Conservatives have after him, that the principal institution of religion in a society, 'a religion connected with the state', must be protected. We must have an established church, and also – I take it that not even Burke could so quickly drift off the subject, but rather supposes these following things to be connected with an established church – 'an established monarchy, an established aristocracy, and an established democracy, each in the degree it exists, and in no greater'.[12]

If our being religious by constitution is perhaps not a Conservative proposition of the light-headed kind, it nevertheless cannot detain us long. Just what supposed human attribute is in question is obscure. It can hardly be what is suggested by some, which is an awe of nature or the universe, its mystery and immensity, and also the endless past of time and its endless future. *That* feeling, hardly properly described as religious, seems not to stand in very close connection with, say, the Archbishop of Canterbury, or just the institutions of society to which he gives his official blessing.

Something the same can be said of a second candidate for the attribute in question, which is a desire for consolation in the face of death, or a third, which is a desire that life should have a meaning, or a suspicion that despite appearances to the contrary it does have. So too with an inclination to real religious belief – say belief in what was defined, in times now forgotten, as a Being omniscient, omnipotent and wholly benevolent. As we may be rightly reminded by Methodist lay preachers and Marxist priests, none of this necessarily issues in support for an established church and the like.

The best candidate for the human attribute in question, and the one Burke has in mind for the most part, is itself an instinctual belief, whatever that may be, to the effect that religion gives to us and preserves morality in a society. It is the belief that religion is 'the source of all good and all comfort', where the morality in question is of some conventional or orthodox kind, and the conception of what is good and comfortable is likewise. It is a part of that supposed instinctual belief, or a conclusion to be drawn from it, that we are to have an established church and so on.

Objections abound but two will suffice. If we have agreed that conceptions of human nature do not have to be of *universal* human attributes, they nevertheless will be of little use in argument if they are of minority inclinations. At best, that is what we have here. Secondly, even if we were to allow that the given instinctual belief about the usefulness of religion were widespread, that would not take us far. If we are engaged in anything like serious reflection, the real question about the belief, whether it is owed to evolution, society, history, prelates or Burke, must be whether it is clear and true, or clear and otherwise acceptable.

The point is of more general application. It is unlikely that *any* human-nature argument which begins by assigning us a *belief* can be of much force. What we are in fact offered is a curious kind of appeal to authority. It is one thing to say that human nature is such-and-such, perhaps greedy, and hence that certain beliefs pertaining to us are true: for example, that we need to have certain incentives. It is another and greatly weaker thing to say that human nature is the source of some belief or other, say about religion and social order, or, as in the present case, that our attributes actually include among them such a belief, and hence that the belief is true.

To revert to Burke, it cannot really be supposed that we here get to the foundation of Conservatism. It may well be that established or official religion plays some part in the politics into which we are inquiring, but we do not see that part clearly by beginning with the given notion of human nature. In taking leave of it, it is also worth remarking that Anthony Quinton and others are persuasive in arguing that there are two traditions of Conservative thought, one of a religious character but the other secular. David Hume in his role as sceptic or atheist may come to mind, as may a distinctly less philosophical strain of members of the New Right. There is also Anthony Flew, to whom we shall come, who alternates between denying the existence of God and the existence of equality.

Let us leave religion, and also pass by another Conservative proposal as to our human attributes, essentially that we have a desire or need for private property, which latter institution will get attention later. As for another idea, that we are by nature opposed to change, that in some sense we are conservers of the past, there may indeed be *some* interesting truth in this neighbourhood, but it can hardly be of the greatest importance in considering the political tradition of Conservatism, for the reason that this tradition cannot usefully be regarded as opposition to change. The proposition that it cannot, arrived at earlier in this inquiry, will certainly not be put in doubt by the truth that many of us are in ways inclined to continuities of certain kinds.

What of the related idea that Conservatism is founded on a conviction as to our intellectual as distinct from our moral shortcomings, our meagre or moderate intellectual powers? As noticed in another connection (p. 25), such an idea is Anthony Quinton's principal contribution to the understanding of Conservatism. In his view, all of three principles of Conservatism derive importantly or fundamentally from 'a conviction of the radical intellectual imperfection of the human individual'.[13] It is this conviction, we are told, which issues in the Conservative opposition to theory and to alteration based on it.

One difficulty about this is that, as we have already seen, the fundamental nature of Conservatism does *not* consist in or include oposition to theory and what comes from it, and indeed Conservatism *does* embrace theory and what comes from it. Furthermore, it is impossible to persuade oneself, at least in an uncommitted moment, that reflective Conservatives have a much different opinion than the rest of us of our common intellectual powers. What some of them may attempt to be convinced of is the dimness of their opponents, but that, assuredly, does not distinguish them from their opponents.

There is another point of importance, which pertains to more arguments mentioning human nature than the one in hand. Suppose it were absolutely true that Conservatives both had a uniquely lower opinion of our intellectual capacities, and that they opposed theory and change, and that we had clear ideas of those things. Would it then follow that they opposed the theory and change for only the reason of our dimness? Would it follow that they had the kind of somehow secure argument which talk of human nature promises, one which starts out just from a satisfactory basis of *fact*? That is not conceivable. Their opposition would necessarily have *another* ground, which very likely would have more claim to being the rationale of Conservatism, and which would certainly invite examination.

Any sane person, in a situation of extremity, will make use of the help of a half-wit. If I have blundered into a cage of apes, or into a train filled with English football fans, or for that matter into a part of the New York subway system, and have no idea about how to get out, I will indeed attend to the advice of a half-wit, or at any rate a plausible three-quarter-wit with some local experience. Similarly, if I find myself in a circumstance, say a society, which is to me intolerable, I will not disdain advice owed only to an imperfect grasp of things if no better advice is available.

It becomes clear by way of such reflections that the best that could be said about Conservatism, along the given lines, is that it is the politics which has a lower opinion of our intellectual capacities, *and also* a view of certain societies as tolerable, and hence opposes theory and change of a certain kind. For a start the societies are taken not to be awful societies, calling out for change. But then an understanding of Conservatism, and support of it or opposition to it, will have essentially and importantly to do with the mentioned view. It is that which may be *more* distinctive of Conservatism, that which needs more consideration either in supporting or opposing the politics in question. We are led away from Conservatism as a politics founded on an idea of human nature to Conservatism as a politics founded on something else which is left inexplicit. That is not good news for those who supposed they had the security of a *factual* basis for their prescriptions.

To come to the three most considerable human-nature arguments by Conservatives, the first may be unexpected despite some items noticed earlier. Its premise is that somehow we are creatures of society. If much Conservative thinking is on the theme that our nature is fixed by our common heredity, by biology or genetics, or at any rate on the theme that there is something like a universal human nature, there is also what may seem to be the opposite theme, that we have differing natures, owed to our different social and cultural environments. This contradiction or seeming contradiction in Conservative ideology, indeed double contradiction, is no great reassurance. It is the sort of thing that will nag at a suspicious mind. Still, we can rise above that. The idea now before us is that attributes of ours – attributes relevant to political and economic proposals and so on – are owed to our particular language, the family as it exists in our particular society, perhaps images of manhood, and in general the culture, institutions, practices and habits of our particular society.

Burke was committed to such an idea, and often set out to express it. Shall we, since sociology has happened in the meantime, and may be thought to have some use, get something more orderly and better defined in a recent expression of the idea?

The human infant, in order to achieve its humanity, in order to have an identity ... requires acculturation ... those who speak the same language share the same experience, and what makes *this* people what they *are* serves to distinguish them radically from other people ... that human nature is disposed to maintain conduct through habit ... is part of its constitutive complexity ... humans are, in a mutually reciprocal fashion, inescapably naturally dependent and cultural beings. Individuals are a product of their times.[14]

... human nature is unintelligible outside its specific cultural context. ... Man's nature is constituted by the specific cultural context within which it is ineluctably to be found. ... In short,

becoming human is becoming individual and we become individual under the guidance of cultural patterns ...[15]

Thus Christopher Berry, or rather, a fair selection of the propositions in which he may be more concerned to expound sym-
pathetically than to assert a Conservative view of our nature. The
exposition leaves something to be desired. That, no doubt, has something to do with the unruly subject-matter being expounded.

Just what attributes are supposed to be given to us by society is
not made wonderfully clear. Can it be that we are offered the idea,
to which we have been near before now (p. 13), that it is actually
our personal identities? Certainly the very last sentence quoted, and
perhaps the first, can be taken to suggest this. But surely it *cannot* be
that what makes me one person, numerically the same person as the
one who started this book some time ago, and numerically different
from you in the same society, is something or other owed only to the
common culture we share. It is not easy getting clear what our
criterion of personal identity actually is, or its genesis, and good and
great philosophers have struggled to find out. Some say a person's
identity is a matter of a single human body or brain, others that it
has to do with a stream of memories or what is called psychological
continuity.[16] I doubt that anything arguable could make my identity
dependent on my society.

It would be yet wilder to suppose, as the first sentence quoted
might be misunderstood to mean, that I am a member of *the human
species* in virtue of being a member of the particular society in which
I find myself. (It was once supposed, perhaps, with the aid of Kipling,
that being British was a necessary condition of being human, but
that supposition has on the whole been abandoned.) It does not
much matter, but it is of course true that one's being human, in this
literal sense, consists in more than one's human nature as generally
conceived (p. 46).

We do better for Conservatism by assigning to it the thought that
a people or nationality owes to its society – to its language, institutions
and so on – what is peculiar to and common to the people or
nationality, and that the common part of each member's being is, to
say the least, most important to it. That is not yet satisfactorily clear.
What is this 'most important' part of an individual's make-up? One
answer, perhaps the answer which accords best with Conservative
utterances, is that it is the part of an individual's being which most
enters into the individual's sense or conception of himself or herself

(cf p. 13). This might not be what fixes personal identity in the sense noticed above.

What we have, then, is that I owe to my society those of my attributes shared only with other members of my society, perhaps my habitual attitudes above all, which mainly give me my own self-image. In my own view of myself, I may be first of all an American, which fact is owed to American society: its peculiar language, its matrimonial customs, baseball, apple pie and its other great customs and institutions.

To turn to the conclusion into which this enters, it is that we ought not to change the society in which we find ourselves. We ought to apprehend and resist recommendations of social, economic and political alteration. The whole argument, in sum, is taken to be this: my society gives me my self-conception; hence large changes in my society, a large break in its continuity, would lose me my self-conception; therefore large changes must be resisted. 'A radical break will have to de-nature individuals, that is, will have to strip "them" of the sources of their identity.' [17]

In all of this we are dealing with propositions of a certain vagueness. None the less it may well be that we could get a clear and true one near to the premise of the argument. It would be along the lines that a man owes to his society those of his attributes which he mainly has in mind in thinking or conceiving of himself. We could get to such a proposition, I trust, without recourse to certain supposed facts of language which are so reverberating for certain thinkers on the subject. I have in mind the fact that the language which does so much to form the Argentinian gaucho has in it 240 expressions for the colour of horses' hides, and the fact, as Christopher Berry also reports, that there is in Shambala no linguistic distinction between yesterday and tomorrow, which must make life's little arrangements difficult, and the fact that the Japanese, perhaps less surprisingly, lack a single word for the first-person pronoun.

That we very likely could get a clear and true proposition about the social ground of our self-conception, however, does not take us far ahead. That is, it does not by itself come close to giving us the conclusion that we should resist social change. Admittedly it is then true that large change, over time, will alter significantly the self-conceptions of individuals. But, as was asked earlier, what is wrong with that? What is obvious is that the argument as stated above is in fact an enthymeme: it is not complete but leaves out one of its essential premises. Actually stated fully, the argument is this: my society gives me my self-conception; hence large change in my society would lose me my self-conception; *that self-conception is of great value*; therefore large change must be resisted.

But, to repeat, what is so valuable about my conceiving myself in a certain way? Is it not possible that an alternative conception would be somehow superior? Is it not possible that social change giving rise to this alternative would be desirable? Would it not be agreeable, say, to come to think of myself as being able to say the difference between yesterday and tomorrow? I could then think of myself as able to remind people about my birthday on time, and so on (cf p. 17). It is very notable that Marx too, although he does not depend on Shambala, suggests the idea that our self-conceptions depend greatly on facts about society, and he is all for changing both.

In dealing with the questions, or rather in not dealing with them, Conservatives too often depend on the seeming confusion noted in the quoted passages, between my conception of myself and my personal identity in the more fundamental sense. *Certainly* I would have a breathtaking argument against social change if it were going to *end* the person I am, as distinct from the kind of person I now am or perceive myself to be – social change which would bring it about that there is *no one* identical with the person I was before the revolution. That would really get through to me. It would not be far from the persuasive argument against change that supporting the revolution would be attempted suicide. But all that nonsense is not to be confused with what we actually are considering, which is all that we can sensibly be considering: that my self-conception or self-image, how I think of myself, would change as a result of social change.

We do not here get to a rationale of Conservatism, for at least the reason that we do not have specified the *recommendation* of a certain sort of self-conception, and hence the value of a certain sort of society. It is very clear indeed, despite an occasional Conservative willingness to bite the bullet and approve of *any* strong society (p. 68), that Conservatives do not value any sort of self-conception and hence any sort of society. They have, since the French Revolution, been actively involved in attempting to subvert or quarantine certain self-conceptions and societies. They have no love for Socialist Man and what engenders him, and perhaps still less for Socialist Woman. The proposition that Socialist Man and Woman, in so far as they exist in South America, should not get a step nearer Texas, has been a self-evident truth in the White House for some time now. There is a related and simpler argument, by the way, not quite so much to the fore in Conservative utterance, which is open to the same sort of objection. It is not that exactly our self-images are owed to our society's language, institutions and so on, but that others of our attributes are so owed – perhaps the collection that makes up our common national character – and that this must be protected by resisting social change. What one needs to ask about this, of course, is what is so good about this or that national character or whatever. Without an answer, there is no line of thought worth considering.

There is yet another and quite different argument beginning from the proposition that some set of our attributes relevant to politics, economics and so on is owed to our particular society. Again it is perhaps easiest to think of those attributes which constitute what can be supposed to exist, our national characters, or, more particularly, that part of each individual's make-up which is his or her Englishness, Americanness, or the like. The argument concludes with the proposition that we should have nothing to do with political or economic proposals and the like which pertain to people of all societies, universal proposals. Above all, we must have nothing to do with proposals or claims as to natural rights or human rights, or, to be more careful, *certain* such rights.

Why not? No doubt one implied answer is one we know, that this would very likely involve change in our society and hence change in our valuable self-conceptions. There is another and more passionate line of thought. It depends in part on what can be taken as a truth, that any universal proposal about human life in all societies must have to do with *some* conception of universal human nature. It must somehow derive from a view of attributes shared by all or nearly all of us, in whatever societies. Anything that did not derive from such a thing would, to say the least, be out of touch with its subject-matter. The given Conservative line of thought also depends fundamentally on something else: that there exists no such conception, that there exists no effective and relevant conception of human nature other than the assortment of social or national ones. If that is true, arguably enough, there can be no persuasive or even rational political and economic proposals having to do with people generally.

Christopher Berry has been quoted already to the effect that the Conservative supposes there is no general conception of human nature that is 'intelligible' (p. 55). For the Conservative, further, 'any idea of human nature understood as pertaining to any individual anywhere is necessarily an uninformative empty abstraction ...'[18] A trawl through *The Portable Conservative Reader* will produce many more declarations to roughly the same effect, some of them noted earlier in connection with the supposed disinclination to theory and in particular abstraction.

It is true, I think, that *homo conservans*, as Roger Scruton is inclined to call him, is no great reader. It is none the less remarkable that he, and more particularly certain of those who purport to do his reading for him, have not happened on certain general conceptions of human nature that are intelligible, informative, contentful rather than empty, and in general conceptually adequate. The history of human reflection, from Plato to Malinowski, has been replete with conceptions of attributes taken as common to all people and relevant to the ordering of human affairs. A good many of them, as this chapter has already indicated, have been precisely Conservative conceptions.

No doubt many of them could do with a bit of attention, being unenlightening or in one way or another obscure. It would be a standing miracle, however, such as to put Our Lady of Fatima in the shade, if anything like all of them could be put aside as unintelligible or the like. Something close to the supposed miracle was contemplated earlier (p. 50) in another connection. To suppose that it has occurred, that *nothing* conceptually satisfactory has ever been said of human nature generally, is to be a little out of touch.

Here is a conception of universal human nature, not greatly different from many others, which will be of use to us later (p. 232) and for which I am willing to say a word or two. *All of us share in certain fundamental desires: for the material means to a decent length of life for ourselves and those close to us; for further material goods, say those supplied by dentists rather than interior decorators, which make life easier; for kinds of freedom and control of our lives in our societies and in smaller contexts, such as work; for the respect of others and also self-respect; for kinds of intimate and other relations with others; for various goods of culture, including knowledge and skill.*[19]

That conception, which is logically consistent with what can be said of national characters, raises questions of various kinds. One, which will come naturally to mind, and can be despatched quickly, is the question of to what extent the six desires can be explained biologically, and to what extent environmentally, including socially. Let us say no good answer is possible. Nothing follows as to the intelligibility or the like of the conception, or of course the extent to which it is true of all of us.

To remember a persistent Conservative complaint, is the conception 'abstract'? Well, a description of a set of things which is abstract in the fundamental sense is one which concentrates on or abstracts certain features of the things and leaves out others. Hence this description of members of the human species, concentrating on their fundamental desires, is abstract. For a start it does leave out national differences. However, *any* useful general description of anything is abstract in this sense. Very certainly a description of members of one nation by way of attributes which make up their national character is abstract in this sense. Conservatism is like any other body of doctrine in being *replete* with abstract descriptions in this fundamental sense.

Is the given conception, still using the word in the fundamental sense, 'too abstract'? The only proper meaning that can be attached to a description's being 'too abstract' is that it leaves out what is somehow essential to the inquiry or argument in question, perhaps by failing to make some distinction. It is too abstract to talk of 'women' or 'freedom' where different kinds of them are important to the endeavour in hand. We shall not at the moment pursue an inquiry or argument based on the given general conception of human nature, but we have no reason to suppose in advance that the conception has this weakness. Particular objections, as distinct from any sort of general declaration of opposition, would be needed in order to establish such a conclusion.

Is a conception of members of a nation in terms of their national characters, if not 'too abstract', at least 'less abstract' than the given conception of all persons? Hard to say, and, truth to tell, not worth puzzling about. What is more worth noticing here is that when one political party charges another with dealing in abstraction, or too much of it or more of it, what they are annoyed about is very likely no fault in sense, or failure in communication, but rather the attention being paid to what is common to a class of things or can be claimed about all of them – as distinct from what separates them into sub-classes, or the different claims or rights the sub-classes may be supposed to have. No doubt it is annoying to have one's opponents take up the general point of view, since it may raise up the spectre of one's bank balance being redistributed, but that point of view need involve no conceptual shortcoming whatever.

To turn for a moment to what may be regarded as a separate sense of the word, is the conception of human nature in terms of fundamental desires abstract in the sense of not being 'concrete', whatever that comes to? Well, it seems *more* concrete, or no less

concrete, than any summation likely to be supplied of the attributes
that enter into the national character of a people. Is the given
conception abstract in the sense of not being furnished with examples?
It is, and since this seems to trouble some Conservatives, they may
take a little time out from argument and simply contemplate themselves and others.

There are further questions that may be raised about the given
general conception of human nature. Given the resistance of Conservatives to such a thing, and the use we will be making of it, it will
be as well to notice them. Further and better particulars may be
asked with respect to each part of it. It may be asked what the desire
for freedom and control comes to in detail. If I am unable to make
an answer to please all comers, including those who go on thinking
up more questions on the basis of what they have been told already,
that will not render the conception unintelligible. It may be asked,
differently, if the satisfaction of the various desires is not inter-
dependent. Indeed it is. No one possesses respect in the entire absence
of freedom. But it would be absurd to suppose that complexity of this
kind and others produces unintelligibility or the like. It needs to be
allowed, too, that the given conception is disputable. That is, there
is the possibility of an argument to the effect that it is incomplete,
somehow one-sided, or has been assembled with an eye to political
conclusions that can be drawn from it. None of that, if true, would
make it a nonsense or close to it. Finally, it can be granted that
political conclusions drawn from the conception may be ill-judged,
unrealistic, or worse. That is as irrelevant to the point in hand, the
charge being considered.

Finally, does this reply to the charge against general conceptions
of human nature concentrate too much on the intelligibility and the
like of the given conception – that is, on those of its properties other
than its truth or falsehood? Is it falsehood that Conservatives mean
to ascribe to any such general conception? No doubt some have this
intention. None, to my knowledge, gets down to the business of giving
reasons, of entering into argument. Nothing else need detain us.

To glance back for a moment, we have noticed or considered
Conservative thoughts about our human nature as consisting in
attributes which are (i) our possessing certain rights, (ii) something
mysteriously complex and beyond our discerning, (iii) spiritual needs
satisfied by cricket, (iv) religious instincts, (v) desires or needs for
private property, (vi) desires for continuity rather than change,
(vii) our imperfect intellectual powers, and (viii) attributes taken as

somehow owed to particular societies. In no case have we succeeded in finding anything – it may turn out to be relevant to our disappointment that we postponed consideration of private property – that could naturally be described as the rationale of Conservatism (pp. 41 f).

Whether or not we shall find such a thing, we shall come closer to it in the last two kinds of reflection about human nature to be considered, at some length. The first is the one anticipated at the beginning, the refrain about our low characters. It issues in two families of arguments, one about order in society, one about incentive.

The refrain itself has in it the episode in the Garden of Eden, Hobbes's pessimism, what is thought to be plain commonsensical realism about all our motives, sociobiology and a good deal else. It can be expressed in the proposition that *we are first self-concerned rather than moral, first concerned with the interests of ourselves and those close to us rather than altruistic or governed by any general moral principle, and that we act accordingly*. It is important to see that the refrain is reasonably summed up in just that proposition rather than something wilder. Certainly Conservatives have sometimes seemed to work themselves up into a frenzy in revealing to us our fallen natures: we are, they say, monsters compounded of blindness to the interests of others, greed, lust, malice, treachery, disloyalty, envy and deception, untouched by morality and always but one step away from lives of careless sloth or mindless anarchy.[20] If Conservatism involved such a view, which is no more than caricature, it would involve nothing of sense or balance, no arguable judgement of ourselves.

Nor is there good reason to drag into Conservatism at this point, as some do, a certain philosophical tradition which propounds a kind of hedonism, often called psychological hedonism. Jeremy Bentham gives some expression to this in the opening declaration of his best-known exposition of Utilitarianism. 'Nature,' he says, 'has placed mankind under the governance of two sovereign masters, pain and pleasure ... They govern us in all we do, in all we say, in all we think: every effort we can make to throw off our subjection, will serve but to demonstrate and confirm it.'[21] There is much to be said for the doughty Bentham. If Burke is to be elevated to the pantheon of political philosophy, Bentham must be there already. Still, his dictum might be thought to be imperfect, since it has allowed a reader or two to come away with an idea that is, to say the least, unpersuasive.

It is unpersuasive to suppose, although this can be taken as suggested by his words, that each of us is at every moment pursuing something like a sensation of pleasure or avoiding a sensation of pain. We do not always, indeed hardly ever, pursue or avoid *feelings*. Our lives are not aimed at them, however much they involve them. How then is Bentham to be understood? He is in fact to be taken quite differently, as making something close to this point: at every moment of action we are in some sense doing what we want, however reluctant our wants may sometimes be.[22] That is close to a logically necessary truth about action: that it somehow derives from desire or volition.

Taken this way, however, Bentham cannot be understood as excluding the propositions that sometimes, often or even always we go *against* self-concern, that the desires or volitions which move us to action are in part or in whole for the satisfaction or the good of others, others unrelated to us. In short, the more arguable understanding of psychological hedonism does *not* give us a doctrine of self-concern, the Conservative doctrine or any other. That Bentham *must* be understood in the given way is clear since he himself, also in his opening passage, declares that *Utilitarianism* is consistent with our subjection to pain and pleasure, indeed founded on that fact. Utilitarianism is certainly not self-interested in the relevant sense. It is precisely not the doctrine that what is right is what makes the agent happy, or serves his interest above all.

If we are to assign to Conservatism something reasonable and relevant, it must therefore be something along the lines suggested: that we are *first* self-concerned, and *first* act on this self-concern. It is only this, incidentally, leaving room for some unselfish motivation, which is in accord with certain other items of Conservatism. One is a certain recommendation as to engaging in charity, however limited by good sense. Another is a defence of kinds of private property, notably stately homes and works of art, in terms of stewardship, of their owners being custodians for generations to come.

However, if we do assign to Conservatives a defensible view of ourselves, neither just a little below the angels nor incarnations of evil, it becomes uncertain that we have anything that much distinguishes it from the other principal political traditions, say socialism. These too need to be looked at with a reasonably discerning eye. Admittedly Jean-Jacques Rousseau did purport to believe, having averted his eye from his own example, and in particular from his relations with the more saintly Hume,[23] that we are all naturally good. Admittedly William Godwin, who instructed us of our moral obligation to save the life of an eminent and useful personage rather than that of our humble mother or brother, if the awful choice has to be made, did write that 'man is perfectible or in other words susceptible of perpetual improvement'.[24] Marx too has some pretty heart-warming things to say about natures. Really we are all creative producers. Still, it would do no justice to socialism to suppose that in general it takes quite so agreeable a view of us, or depends on any such things. It is in the interest of Conservatives to assign to their opponents a fantasy, but they need not expect to be taken too seriously.

No doubt it is wise to admit the possibility that a careful inquiry into attitudes and judgements generally, of all comers, would issue in the conclusion that Conservatives have a healthier scepticism than others about us all. Conceivably there is a somewhat *a priori* reason for the conclusion, which is that those who are more in possession of the world's goods are more likely to take a jaundiced view of their fellows, notably the burglars, and hence of mankind generally. Or, they may get their scepticism from a view of themselves, their acquisitive selves. On the other hand, there must be the thought, tending in the other direction, that those who are *less* in possession of the world's goods, being deprived and envious, are likely to have the darker view.

If we were in the end to assign to Conservatives no more than we reasonably could, which is a *somewhat* greater scepticism about us all, that would still not provide much by way of a fundamental characterization of their politics. That conclusion, by the way, is not alien to the thought of many Conservatives. Anthony Quinton is firm about his party's not being unique in its view of our moral imperfection, which firmness, as noticed earlier, leads him to try to find its uniqueness in its view of our intellectual imperfection.[25]

No doubt it would also be wise to allow that there is a *somewhat* greater tendency on the part of Conservatives to explain the low character they assign to us by reference to genetics or biology as against social environment, history and the like. Again this difference of degree – Conservatism would be made silly by taking it to explain the low character overwhelmingly by genetics – could hardly give us a fundamental characterization of Conservatism.

Do we get further ahead by considering the two propositions or families of propositions which Conservatives base wholly or partly on their view of our self-concerned natures? In fact we cannot fully consider these now, since each of them leads into a large subject which requires separate attention on its own. We can make a start, and arrive at preliminary judgements.

The first family of propositions has to do with the character of a satisfactory society and government. It is forever said by Conservatives that a satisfactory state of affairs, given our low natures, must be one of *order*. Kirk speaks out eloquently for his fellows, although the structure of his argument is not crystal-clear, and he gets rather more into his conclusion than the need for the particular kind of order which is a matter of society and government.

> In every culture, what does the imaginative conservative aspire to conserve? Why, to conserve order: both order in the soul and order in the state. With Luke, the man of conservative impulses says to himself, 'No man having drunk old wine straightaway desireth new; for he saith, The old is better.' Out of the deep well of the past comes order; and as Simone Weil reminds us, 'Order is the first need of all.'
>
> From revelation, from right reason, from poetic vision, from much study, from the experience of the species – so the conservative argues – we human beings have learned certain ways and principles of order. Were we lacking these, we would lie at the mercy of will and appetite – in private life, in public concerns. It is this order, this old safeguard against private and public anarchy, which the conservative refuses to surrender to the evangels of Progress.[26]

Let us stick to society and state, which is enough to be going on with, and leave aside the soul, for which Kirk has a somewhat unusual and not standard Conservative predilection.

It is clear that just a recommendation of order, in the ordinary sense, is not what he and other Conservatives intend in their declarations. They are not thinking of order where that is just the fact that people accept certain principles or procedures and act in accordance with them, without confusion, riot, violence and the like. Conservatives do not have in mind, say, a conceivable society of order in which self-organising groups go about their business in an effective and co-operative way, none having an ascendancy over another. Nor do they have in mind a conceivable society of order in which one group has an ascendancy, but an ascendancy owed only to their powers of argument or persuasion.

Conservatives have in mind a society of order in the sense of a *hierarchical* society, as we may name it, with classes or grades of people ranked one above another, and those above having what is called *authority* over those below, government having supreme authority. Conservatives, in Peregrine Worsthorne's perspicuous rendering, see that if socialism has made an advance, then 'the urgent need ... is for the State to regain control over the people, to re-exert its authority ...'[27] Does this particular desire for order distinguish them?

The authority, in brief, consists in power or force that is legitimate or accepted. It thus involves some allegiance, deference or sense of political obligation in those over whom it is exercised. Much can be said of the nature of allegiance and the like, and, by God, much has. But to forget or diminish the fact that authority also involves force and the threat of force, most notably in the ongoing institution of punishment, is to misconceive it entirely.

Authority is very likely to be power according to, and limited by, a constitution, law and other tradition. Its legitimacy or acceptance is then bound up with these latter facts. Further, the authority is likely to be possessed by a class or grade of persons who are taken by themselves and others to constitute an élite, to have personal properties which may enter into the justification of their powers. They have strengths and virtues which suit them to their role as a ruling class (cf. p. 24). Also, the hierarchical society or the society which is subject to authority is one which is always in sight of being, or at any rate has the possibility of becoming, authoritarian or repressive – a society where those in power exceed or anyway press the powers accorded to them, perhaps by paying insufficient attention to constitutional or traditional rights of those below. Authoritarianism, not our subject now, will be at a later stage (p. 141).

There can be no doubt that Conservatives have long advanced or anyway intended the argument that our primarily self-interested natures call for and justify a hierarchical society in the given sense or something close to it. The argument has a certain charm for them. It has the charm that its conclusion, taken as a proposition more or less independent of the premise, has about it a kind of impressive realism, a realism which must discomfit their opponents. It may seem barely possible that a large and modern society could be otherwise than hierarchical, and, say, merely be persuasive.

However, to repeat, do we here have an argument which individuates Conservatism? Do we here have a reality of Conservatism displayed? The answer is that we do not. We do not for a simple reason which carries all political philosophy before it, as well as the ruminations of Conservative politicians over generations, and also the artless cultisms about 'law and order' of British governments of the New Right. The simple reason, in part, is that others than Conservatives firmly support hierarchical societies. In the other part, the reason is that Conservatives have never in the past, do not now, and never will support all societies which are hierarchical in the given sense.

The society and government of the Soviet Union are hierarchical in the given sense, as are the societies and governments of the Eastern Bloc generally. As we are reminded when something else is the subject, there is no great shortage of policemen in those places. There is much the same fact of hierarchy about China and Cuba. Political traditions which are certainly not Conservative support these governments and societies, and the Conservative tradition does not support them. Whatever else is true, and whatever can be claimed about the existence of conservative wings of political traditions generally, and of communist or socialist ones in particular, Conservatism is fundamentally opposed to certain forms of society and government despite their being, to any reasonable judgement, hierarchical.

The fact of the matter is evidently that Conservatism is for one particular species of hierarchy and against another. The worn conceptions of order, authority, allegiance, constitution, law and so on, used by themselves, do not come within a country mile of individuating this commitment. No one of sound mind and actually engaged in reflection can suppose so. Roger Scruton, whose devotion to authority raises in one a hope of finding in it the true being of *homo conservans*, is indeed led by his preoccupation with authority to something other than the usual denunciations of Communist states. But he too recovers his balance quite regularly and distinguishes himself from simple piety about all authority, of whatever kind, in accordance with whatever political principles.

Conservatism is therefore not at all clarified by describing it in terms of a low view of our natures and a resulting commitment to hierarchy. Also, to know what we all do know, that it is friend to *certain* hierarchical governments and societies and no friend to others, is still not to lay hold on its rationale. Its nature cannot simply be *read off* its support for some and not other governments and societies. If any persuasion of this is needed, it can be had from the fact that many have looked at the two sorts of societies – their constitutions, governments, political arrangements, national histories – and purported to see that what distinguishes Conservatism is something of which we know, opposition to change and theory. These things, we know, do not distinguish it. Nor do we get a rationale of Conservatism, if it is merely insisted that the sketch given above (p. 67) of the society of hierarchical order was too general, that Conservatism is for a kind of hierarchical society, which kind is evident to more perspicuous persons. *Obviously* it is for one kind, but the kind needs to be made explicit, which in this context it never is.

Evidently there is more to be said about Conservatism and government, and more that is not too far from the matter of order, but let us now leave this neighbourhood for a time. As remarked above, a second proposition or family of propositions is said to be based on the view of our natures as primarily self-concerned. What we get here is an argument which moves from our self-concern, and some other items, to a conclusion about the need for incentives and what they issue in, kinds of inequality. To be clear about the argument as it is usually talked of or gestured at, it will be useful to set it out fully.

(1) Sustained or increased economic well-being in a society is desirable or imperative.

(2) We ought to be free, which is to say not compelled to contribute to sustaining or increasing this well-being.

(3) If we are not compelled, we will contribute only out of either self-concern or kinds of altruism.

(4) We are primarily self-concerned rather than altruistic or the like.

(5) Given this fact of our self-concern, incentives are necessary to induce us to make greater contributions to well-being, perhaps including incentives provided through the privatization of what have for some time been governmental or public activities or enterprises.

(6) Therefore the incentives ought to be provided, and we should accept the inevitable inequality which results.

It was remarked earlier that Conservatism and socialism, if reasonably conceived, are not worlds apart in their conceptions of human nature, and more particularly in their views of ourselves as self-concerned. There is also some similarity between them, if a lesser one, in something that follows from the first similarity. It is that both give some place to incentives somehow conceived. Given this, we may wonder if their respective rationales are more likely to be better discerned *elsewhere* in their respective arguments or lines of thought having to do with incentive. One place where the Conservative rationale is likely to be found, it may be supposed, is precisely in its presumption as to the fundamental economic or social goal in question. Let us in any case begin at the beginning of the argument, which procedure is good sense if not a habit of Conservatives.

What is the 'economic well-being' whose desirability is fundamental to the argument? (If we had spoken instead of 'prosperity' or 'a higher standard of living' or even 'better lives for all', what would those things have come to?) The question was not considered earlier when we encountered the matter of incentives in connection with the subject of theory (pp. 29–34).

Shall we take economic well-being to have to do with no more than *economic totals*, say Gross National Product? That would be to proceed in a common but unhelpful way, one that would not serve our purpose, which is to try to find the fundamental principle of Conservatism in order to make a judgement on it. In fact the Conservative goal of well-being is not near to being well described simply in terms of economic totals, which is to say in a way which leave entirely inexplicit what *distribution* of well-being is in question. The above argument about incentives, if it is to be regarded as the Conservative argument, has to do with economic well-being where that does not turn out to be a total of well-being so distributed, say, as to benefit recent immigrants into a society above all, or one-parent families, those in greatest need, or vegetarians. The money is not mainly to end up in their pockets. Nor, certainly, is the distribution the one which will serve the end specified by Utilitarianism, the *greatest* total of happiness no matter how distributed.

To make much the same point differently, we do not get an answer to our question by listening to low electioneering and thus supposing that Conservatism aims only at making *everybody better off*. That, as recent experience of New Right governments in Britain and America so awfully demonstrated, is false. I cannot myself resist the speculation that the electioneering of the parties in question, which to some considerable extent distinguished it from much previous Conservative electioneering, was in fact carried forward by species of gross self-deceivers (cf pp. 184, 199 f).

Even if we could rightly believe that Conservatism aimed at a distribution which involved a universal improvement in living standards, as may somewhere in the past have been the case, that would not help at all. It is clear that of the *large number* of conceivable or possible distributions of that general character, it is *one* which

Conservatives favour, indeed one to which they are committed. Consider the two possible distributions, each involving a universal improvement, but such that one benefits one-parent families more than other members of the society, and the other benefits those in need more than other members of the society. Neither of these would be embraced by Conservatives. They have, still supposing that they seek to make everybody better off, something else in mind (cf pp. 41 f).

Clearly the distribution they have in mind is some more or less traditional or conventional one. But what, in summary, *is* that distribution and the recommendation, principle or implicit idea of it? Certainly the recommendation is not just that it *is* traditional or conventional. It is far from being true, as we know, that Conservatives would be on the side of *any* distribution that had become traditional or conventional (pp. 2, 11). To know the nature of what distribution they favour would be to come close to knowing the very nature of their politics. If Conservatives, perhaps those industrious theorizers of the New Right, were to have given us a plain and effective answer, would we have much need of their reflections on human nature and incentives? In general, if two lines of planning or activity involve somewhat similar or at least related means, but divergent ends, it is evidently by way of their ends that they can be distinguished.

Since Conservatives do not make clear what 'economic well-being' or the like comes to, can we distinguish their tradition and discern their fundamental principle by looking directly at the rest of the argument set out above? We can in fact go some good way towards doing the first thing, distinguishing them from their opponents.

The second part of the argument, which is essential to its final conclusion, excludes what is called social compulsion from consideration. We are not to secure contributions to economic well-being in this way. We here encounter, at long last, what can confidently be judged to be a first true mark of Conservatism. It is the political tradition which is partly identified by its opposition to what it calls social compulsion. Whatever may have been true of ancient conservatism, say feudal conservatism, we here have a mark of the tradition of Conservatism with which we are concerned. We here have something more useful than anything discovered in our inquiry into the subjects of change and theory. It is a distinction related to others that can be brought into view by considering the incentive argument.

This significant exclusion, however, is no matter of *necessity*, connected with human nature or anything else, but a matter of decision. That decision is to the effect that we ought not to engage in 'compelling' members of a society to contribute to it. We can ask for the ground or basis of this decision, as we ask for the ground or basis of any decision which accords or denies a freedom to persons, say the decision to compel obedience to the criminal law. The freedom in question is certainly not what is called the Freedom of the Will, or Free Will, which, whatever else is to be said of it, is not the sort of thing which we can in the ordinary sense give or deny to anyone. Something will be said of Free Will shortly, in connection with a final Conservative idea of human nature.

To put the question differently, and properly, why should members of a society not be compelled, constrained, led, called upon, encouraged, argued into, convinced, educated, re-educated or inspired to contribute to its economic well-being somehow conceived? Certainly many of the possibilities in this spectrum – possibilities of *social persuasion* as they can best be called – are utterly underdescribed by the term 'compulsion' and by rhetoric about a slave state, captivity, oppression and so on. Why should some means of compulsion, education, or whatever not be used with respect to what is, *ex hypothesi*, a good end? Why should we proceed differently here than with the good end of securing obedience to the criminal law? Certainly social persuasion, if the point matters, is in no way alien to our societies. We go in for other kinds of it a good deal.

There is a logical possibility of saying that the absence of the given sort of social persuasion, our not being persuaded to contribute, is just obviously right, or, more precisely, a good-in-itself. There is the same possibility of regarding the opposite thing, the establishing or maintaining of such social persuasion, as a good-in-itself. Neither of these responses is convincing, not more convincing than any *ad hoc* announcement that something is a good-in-itself. It is more convincing to attempt to justify a decision for or against the practice by reference to an antecedently argued general principle. Those in favour of the practice in question may refer to a principle of equality. As for those against such social persuasion, or what they call compulsion, to what do they turn? The fact of the matter is that they do not tell us. We could have learned their rationale from a clear answer, as in the case of the question about the nature of the goal of economic well-being.

Consider the fourth premise of the argument. It reflects the fact that Conservatism as against other political traditions assigns a lesser place in our make-ups to social altruism as against self-concern. We concluded at the beginning of this inquiry into human-nature arguments that they start from true or false propositions about human attributes which are not necessarily universal, unchangeable or wholly genetic (p. 48). In fact to assign to Conservatism the view that we are *incapable* of social altruism, which incapability is universal, unchangeable and wholly genetic, would be to assign to it something close to an absurdity. Indeed, when discussing other subjects than incentive, notably societies on which they are not keen, Conservatives are quite prepared to allow the possibility of creating or fostering social altruism, and to condemn governments for doing it. They allow the possibility of what a moment ago was named social persuasion.

What must come to mind, and what is true, is that the Conservative's relation to social altruism is not near to his having the true or false belief that it is impossible, but rather is an opposition to it which is at best a compound of elements, one large element being a decision or preference for something else. The decision or preference for something else is bound up with the opposition of Conservatives to social persuasion. That other thing which they prefer, of course, is an incentive system. But *what* is the ground for the rejection of social altruism and social persuasion, and the recommendation of incentive? Once again we are left in the dark. We do certainly have a further distinction of Conservatism here, but no indication of what can be said in explanation or justification of its commitment.

Turning now to the fifth part of the argument, what is an incentive in the relevant sense? We have not so far inquired. To make a distinction, it is the expectation or offer of some satisfactory return for work, endeavour or the providing of something, which satisfactory return is not, so to speak, a satisfactory part of the work, endeavour or provision itself. The latter satisfactory thing is something about which no question of whether or not to provide it after the work is done can arise. Incentive in the relevant sense, more particularly, is the expectation or offer of (i) the possession, use or consumption of the product or fruit of the labour or the like, or (ii) something else of value, if not necessarily of the value of the product or fruit. It may be a matter of a family's having for itself the food it grows, or someone's financial reward in lieu of a product: the higher salary attached to a higher position in a business, office or factory, the bonus attached to greater productivity within a grade, the profit to be earned by an entrepreneurial initiative. Incentive in the relevant sense, then, is in a certain way *extrinsic*, rather than any incentive

which is intrinsic to or inseparable from the work or whatever itself.
The work or whatever, whatever is to be said of the force of intrinsic
incentive, might have been carried forward in the absence of the
external incentive, perhaps as a result of some other external motivation. One of these possible motivations, already rejected in the
second part of the argument, is some kind or degree of social persuasion.

Intrinsic incentive is also of several kinds. It includes the anticipated satisfaction of achievement or distinction, and of the recognition by others of that achievement or distinction. It includes the
anticipated satisfaction of increased power, independence or scope
for decision-making, again partly a satisfaction owed to the necessary
recognition by others of that power or the like. It also includes what
cannot be so quickly summed up, satisfactions having to do with self-
development and with the very experience or very nature of work
and endeavour, perhaps its complexity.

If it would be mistaken to assign to Conservatism a view of our
self-interestedness very greatly different from that of other political
traditions, and a view of the necessity for incentives – extrinsic incentives – that was wholly different, it is right to say that it asserts a
greater need for such incentives. Here we have a third if related
real distinction of Conservatism. More particularly, it assigns an
overwhelming place to extrinsic as against intrinsic incentive.

But why does Conservatism pay little or no attention to intrinsic
incentive? Consider positions in society which involve notable
achievement or distinction and perhaps power, independence and
the like. We are all subject to a very considerable intrinsic incentive
to get into such positions. They have a great attractiveness which is
independent of the income or profit attached to them. Why do
Conservatives, as they uniquely do, tend to ignore this fact, and to
call for high incomes and sizeable profits? The thought is inescapable
that they suppose that such returns are justified in some way *not*
having to do with incentive, justified by some consideration other
than the consideration that the income and profit are a necessary
means to getting a certain contribution to economic well-being. But
what is that consideration? What is that rationale? The question
remains unanswered.

To come now to the last sort of Conservative reflection about
human nature to be considered, it is briefer, more reluctant and more
inexplicit than other reflections. This is partly owed to a certain
insecurity, an insecurity which may come from an awareness that

the subject-matter in question, Freedom and Determinism, is an ancient and still all too busy preserve of philosophers. None the less, if fewer and weaker paragraphs are written on our free or determined human natures, there is an assumption that lies under and runs through a good deal of Conservative thinking and feeling, to the effect that we possess a certain freedom.

What is clearest is what necessarily goes with this, which is opposition to the doctrine of determinism. The latter has occasionally been conceived in an effective form, as a philosophy of mind and action based partly on neuroscience, which is to say the various sciences of the brain and nervous system. This philosophy of mind and action asserts that each of our mental events, including our decisions and intentions, and also each of our actions, is the final effect of a causal sequence or causal chain of a certain nature. Each such sequence or chain, like any other causal sequence, is such that the final event and every other event in it, given the initial events of the sequence, had to happen. It was the only event that could then have occurred.

A causal sequence issuing in a particular mental event, say an intention to act, will have in it events owed to the heredity of the person and also events owed to his or her environment. These antecedent events will of course include other mental events, which, like all mental events, are somehow intimately bound up with simultaneous neural events. As for a causal sequence which issues in an action, it may be taken to have as one of its earliest members the intention to do the action. In this determinism, then, causal sequences for intentions and causal sequences for actions combine to form single longer sequences.

The details and problems of such a determinism are many and varied, and its clarity, truth and human import have for long been disputed.[28] A part of the human import of determinism is clear enough when stated ordinarily, as it was a moment ago. It is that given the initial events of certain causal sequences, each mental event and action occurs necessarily or inevitably – there was no possibility that anything else could have occurred in its place.

Conservatives, as I say, although no doubt there are exceptions to the rule, are opposed to neuroscientific determinism, or rather, are opposed to it and to all determinisms of the same character, and this general opposition lies under and runs through much else of what they think and feel. Their response is in fact clearest in these consequences. The first point, that they will declare themselves to be opposed to neuroscientific and like determinisms, is of less significance, and does not effectively distinguish them. The degree to which their opposition informs their ideology does more to distinguish them. Again, as in the case of incentive, we have something of definitional importance.

Other determinisms of the same character, of which Conservative writers are more aware, are historical antecedents of neuroscientific determinism. They include the seventeenth- and eighteenth-century doctrines of Hobbes and Hume. To Hume it was evident, although he was not so well supplied with evidence as his successors, that every event without exception 'is so precisely determined by the energy of its cause that no other effect, in such particular circumstances, could possibly have resulted from it'.[29] That neither Hobbes nor Hume can be uncontentiously claimed as Conservatives has much to do with the fact that both were determinists of what might be called the clear-minded sort.

There is also the determinism of Marx, which is more or less identical with his theory of history. Whatever its historical or moral importance, which is great, it is no masterpiece of order and clarity. What it comes to, in the view of an amateur, and stated differently than when we noticed it in connection with Conservatism and theory (p. 37), is that all of our thoughts and actions are somehow determined, those of one great category determined by productive forces, and those of the other category determined, to speak of their nearer rather than remote causes, by what is called class structure or economic relations.

The first category of determined thoughts and actions have to do with, or are within, that class structure or set of economic relations. The second category has to do with, or are within, the superstructure of a society, including law and customary morality. Exactly what does the determining in each case, despite much divining of Marx's intentions, remains obscure, as does the mode of the determining – it seems not safe to suppose that the latter is a matter of standard causation.[30] None of this uncertainty has made less vigorous the opposition of Conservatives to Marx as determinist.

To turn from what Conservatives deny to what they assert, a part of it is a kind of freedom of individuals which everyone allows to exist. It was encountered in connection with incentive (p. 72). It is that freedom of individuals which is their voluntariness in deciding and acting. This voluntariness in deciding and acting, to speak generally, consists in not being subject to certain constraints, compulsions or the like, which is to say *not being made in certain ways to decide or act against one's desire, want, volition, will, disposition, personality or the like*. It is being able in certain respects to decide or act, rather, *according to* one's own desire, want or the like. This voluntariness consists in the absence not of all constraints, or the possession of all powers or abilities, which condition would be godlike, but in the absence and possession of some (p. 83 f).

Different individuals, and different groups and classes of individuals, are subject to different constraints, have different powers. The constraints to which I am subject, as noticed in connection with incentive, are to a significant extent a matter of the decisions and actions of others, above all those who are in power in a society. The extent of my voluntariness is importantly fixed, evidently, by the enacted laws and institutions of my society. It may be increased by education or by a reduction in my taxes, safeguarded by such defenders of my interests as my lawyer, dramatically reduced by my being sent to gaol.

The freedom which consists in kinds of voluntariness, more of which kinds will be our subject in the next stage of this inquiry, is perfectly consistent with determinism. That is, determinism does not at all exclude states of affairs in which we decide and act *as we want*, are not subject to certain constraints. It is not and does not entail the view that we are always or indeed ever subject to compulsion. Determinism can be true without at all reducing this freedom which is voluntariness. The point is depended on by a tradition of philosophers who have the name of Compatibilists, not because they deny the existence of any freedom other than this one which is logically compatible with determinism, although many of them do deny this, but because they suppose that this freedom is all that the rest of us ever have in mind in this neighbourhood. It is, they say, all of the ordinary or standard understanding of freedom.

Voluntariness is not the different kind of freedom, which, if it exists, is more properly regarded as a fundamental fact, even *the* fundamental fact, of our human natures. Conservatives are inclined to assert and to rest a part of their ideology on this different freedom, which evidently is inconsistent with determinism. If determinism is true, there is none of it.

The final analysis or even description of this supposed freedom has always been supremely difficult. Philosophers have spent much time, to little effect, with such obscure notions as that of the Creative Self or the Self-Conscious Mind, taken as a kind of inner engine of this freedom. They have been involved with such absurdities as the idea of a Self-Causing Cause within us. Robert Nozick, no doubt aware of what his politics requires, has recently set out to enlighten us about this freedom, but succeeded in immediately wandering off the subject.[31] Despite this difficulty or impossibility of giving an analysis of it, the central idea of this freedom can be gestured at easily.

I am free in this sense, first, if at the moment when I came to a particular decision, or formed a particular intention, or set about acting, there was the possibility of some other decision, intention or setting-about, and, second, that alternative was a matter of my origination. The first fact about such a supposed decision or the like makes it other than an effect, other than the upshot of a causal sequence. The first fact, perhaps, is no more than the negative fact that the decision or whatever is not an effect. The second fact, entirely more obscure, makes such a decision or whatever other than arbitrary or a matter of chance. This freedom of origination, what has traditionally been called Free Will, is in virtue of its first feature logically inconsistent with determinism.

All of us, prisoners of a common culture, are inclined to take Free Will as a fact, perhaps our own Free Will above all. We are inclined to take it to be necessary to what we are inclined to think is another fact, which is our responsibility for our actions, responsibility of a certain fundamental kind. It remains true that the Conservatives among us distinguish themselves by the use they make of their inclination. It informs much of their ideology, but has perhaps been clearest in connection with the institution of punishment by the state, or rather, with a supposed justification of this punishment.

It is far from true that Conservatives have been or are alone in depending on the supposed justification of punishment, but it is safe to say that among political traditions theirs has been to the fore in embracing it. They say, in many different ways, that a part if not the whole of the justification of punishment by the state is that it is *deserved*. It is retribution, what is fitting, a return for harm done, a debt to be paid. They are to the fore, that is, in embracing what in the past has been called the Retribution Theory of Punishment. What is essential to the theory is that it somehow seeks to justify punishment by pointing to some relation between it, or something bound up with it, and the offender's past act, and more particularly a relation between punishment and the past act taken, in part, as having flowed from the Free Will or origination of the offender.

This supposed justification in itself, whatever may be added to it about punishment's also having the recommendation of preventing or reducing future offences, has nothing to do with affecting future behaviour. Nor is it in itself a matter, whatever may be added about prevention, of taking the past act as *evidence* of the likelihood of future offences, or in some other way relevant to future behaviour. The retribution idea about punishment, as the philosopher Immanuel Kant was pleased to point out, has the consequence that if we were apprised in advance of the end of the world, one of our last bits of tidying-up ought to be the execution of the last murderer.[32] Whether or not he was right in inserting capital punishment into the idea of retribution, he was certainly right in taking the idea to have nothing to do with deterrence, reform or any such agreeable effect.

Conservatism, to repeat, cannot be taken as distinguished by its view of persons as being not only voluntary in many decisions, intentions and actions, but also originators of them. We do come to a further distinction of Conservatism in the use, often enough the resolute or fervent use, to which it puts this conception of human nature. If it is put to use in connection with punishment, it is also used as significantly elsewhere in the ideology of Conservatism, as we shall come to see.

We wondered earlier if Conservatism is to be distinguished as that political tradition which is inexplicit about its rationale (p. 43). That remains somewhat unsettled. We subsequently concluded, when considering the matter of our low natures, that Conservatism *is* distinguished by its resistance to three things: what was called social persuasion, its related attitude to social altruism, and its ignoring of intrinsic incentive. We concluded, as well, that it does not make clear the rationale or principle which issues in these conclusions. We now have it that Conservatism is also distinguished, fourthly, by its greater inclination to support, in particular, the Retribution Theory of Punishment.

Do we now also have its rationale or principle? Well, we might speculate that Conservatism rests on something that might be called a principle of desert. We might have speculated similarly about its utterances on incentive, the several parts of the incentive argument we considered. But what is that principle? You can spend much time with the *Portable Conservative Reader*, indeed read every word of it, and not be informed. You will find much that may seem to imply the thing, or even mentions it, but no clarification. The same is true, to my knowledge, of all other Conservative writing.

To return to punishment, it is very clear indeed that to say the

justification of punishing a man is that *he deserves it* is to say something
that calls out for explanation. Perhaps the most natural understanding of the claim that a man deserves something is that it is right
that he get it or have it. But that turns the argument that something
is right for the reason that it is deserved into the beauty that it is
right for the reason that it is right. It offers *no* reason for the supposed
rightness of whatever it is. There is exactly the same absurdity
concealed at the base of a number of contemporary versions of the
Retribution Theory, and there are embarrassments nearly as great
in various other understandings of the claim that someone deserves
something.[33] For all of that, there must surely be *some* sense to be
attached to saying a man deserves a particular penalty, which sense
saves this argument about desert from being nonsense. We shall
return to the matter, and, if briefly, to the question of the truth of
the competing doctrines of determinism and Free Will. Conservatism,
as is plain, somehow depends to some extent on what is not easy, to
say the least, which is showing the doctrine of Free Will to be true
and that of determinism to be false.

So much for philosophical reflection on Conservatism and human
nature, or philosophical reflection in a narrow sense. One thing
remains to be said, and can be said as well in a personal way as any
other. It has to do with what previously concerned us, our low
natures.

When I came to England in 1959, I came from a decent place to
join a nation of decency. It was to join a nation which to my mind
had been and was still raised up in a certain way by a war. That was
a war which touched on it uniquely and which had been made
necessary by, among other things, a generosity of feeling, which
feeling was a part of its struggle against Germany and contributed
to victory, and was in the end stronger than before. Whatever the
worth of that explanation, it is true that the decency of England,
that part of the character of its people, was in 1959 still in a kind
of ascendancy. I mean by decency or generosity, of course, some
uncondemning comprehension of the lives of those who are without
the luck of family endowment or an edge of competitiveness to their
personalities or simply health, and some real willingness to enter into
arrangements for their help.

As all have come to see, that general decency or generosity, by
which I do mean something more general than the particular com-
passion which informs a good deal of socialism, has been confused
and weakened. It has been confused and weakened by British govern-

ments since 1979. It has been confused and weakened by governments, appropriately led, which manifestly lack this decency, and put in its place the patent hypocrisy which is always the resort of those who lack it.

Conservatism in England since 1979, Conservatism in power, in many ways like the Conservatism of the New Right elsewhere, has not merely depended in many of its arguments and policies on a view of human nature – a view of it as first of all self-interested. It has, necessarily by way of subterfuge, set out to degrade that human nature. It has set out to make more true what at first could not be more than pretended. In this it has to some small but awful extent succeeded. Some members of these governments, blinded by political struggle, are incapable of seeing what they have done. I should not myself choose to be a child or grandchild of a member of a government which set out to drag down, in so far as it could, the character of a people.

– 4 –
Freedom

To the civilized man *the rights of property are more important than the right to life.*

Paul Elmer More

Every major political tradition without exception lays claim to being the tradition of freedom, or anyway the freedom that matters. The truth of that generalization can be obscured – freedom can be made to seem the concern of just one political tradition or indeed one party for a moment or two, or even a decade or a lifetime. This is accomplished with the aid of responsible organs of opinion, as some used to say, or balanced newscasting, or television programmes under no constraint but getting their facts right, or of course a free press. But the generalization remains stubbornly true.

Marxist advocates of revolution may still be heard to announce in our societies, in so far as they can be heard to announce anything, that freedom is exactly what they will secure for our toiling masses, and our toiling middle classes as well. Liberals of several remaining sorts, undismayed by the sad outcome of John Stuart Mill's struggle to say what it is, take *liberty* to be their very own property.[1] Roy Hattersley, on behalf of Britain's Labour Party, does not delay longer than the opening sentence of his book to declare that 'the true object of socialism is the creation of a genuinely free society in which the protection and extension of individual liberty is the primary duty of the state', which proposition seems to him self-evidently true.[2] So with Conservatives. Burke, as he said, flattered himself that he loved a manly, moral, regulated liberty as well as any gentleman of the Constitutional Society, which English club approved the somewhat different liberty sought and secured in the French Revolution.[3] One section of the New Right, sometimes called the Neo-Liberal section,[4] has been pretty well unable to write a sentence of self-description that does not remind us of its mission of liberation. It has been sent by Friedrich Hayek and other Austrians to save us.

Furthermore, and more important, every major political tradition does not only announce that it is for freedom, but in fact *is* for it – some freedom or other. Parties of these traditions, when they are in power, do indeed secure or increase certain freedoms. They would be hard-pressed not to do so, since it is close to a logically necessary truth that any act of legislation or government will have effects that can properly be described as securings or increasings of freedoms. All that is required, in brief, is that somebody be enabled by the act of legislation to do or to have something. Even the racial purifying of a people, to take that terrible and not wholly irrelevant example, may indeed be said to have secured a freedom for some of them.

There is therefore no possibility at all of distinguishing Conservatism as just the political tradition that values or protects freedom. It is absurd to suppose that one can usefully summarize it as 'the politics of liberty'. I fancy no reflective Conservative will try to claim so, at least when not on television or fund-raising in Dallas or writing a leader for *The Times* of London. Is it the case, however, that Conservatism can be distinguished as the tradition that values or protects certain freedoms as against others? Can we here find a rationale of the tradition? Let us see.

The subject of this chapter is freedoms other than those which are part of the choosing and influencing of governments. The latter freedoms, including what are called political liberties and democratic freedoms, enter into the subject of the following chapter, which is government. The freedoms considered in the present chapter, none the less, will have much to do with government, in the first instance for the reason that they are secured or protected by it. They are a matter of the scope or extent of government, or, to speak differently, its bounds or limits. To widen or narrow the scope of government is at once to increase some freedoms and reduce others.

What must come to mind first among types of freedom in connection with Conservatism is *freedom to acquire and hold private property*. It is what we will mainly consider, but let us begin by looking at it just as an example of other types of freedoms we shall notice.

It is like them in not being itself Free Will or a kind of Free Will – say Free Will with respect to property (pp. 74 ff). Such a thing, if it exists, and however the idea of it may invigorate or give teeth to certain political conclusions, is not at all within the gift of political parties or makers of constitutions or legislators. If anyone gave us Free Will with respect to anything I guess it was God.

The freedom to acquire and hold private property, like the other types of freedom we shall consider, may be said to consist in *one* important part in legal facts. In part, this freedom consists in an absence of legal constraint or coercion, in there being no law which prevents or hinders persons or partnerships from possessing things in a certain way, and also, quite as important, in there being a body of law which facilitates their doing so. There exists a body of law which does not frustrate the desire of individuals to possess things in a certain way but rather facilitates their acting in accordance with that desire. To speak differently, the freedom to acquire and hold private property consists in one important part in the possibility or existence of one person's or one partnership's legal rights and of related legal obligations on the part of others. My right to the house or newspaper I own entails an obligation on your part not to intrude on it without my permission.

That is not to say that the type of freedom in question, or any like freedom, is to be regarded as consisting just in the existence of law. The freedom to own property, like all freedoms to be considered, is to be regarded, in sum, as a power or ability. It is, in sum, *being able in certain respects to act on a desire*, or *not being subject to certain constraints* (p. 76). The power I have, the constraints to which I am not subject, are not only a matter of law. If I have this power to come to be an owner of a house, television station, business, bank, patent, vaccine, bottle of pain-killers or square meal, then, if I am an ordinarily efficient person, all that remains in order for me to *be* an owner is that I desire to be so. To have this power, clearly, more must be true than just that there exists a facilitating law about property. It *may* be – as is the case with familiar instances of this type of freedom – that I need to have money, often a good deal of money. I must not be subject to the constraint of poverty, or the constraint of being short of cash at the moment. To have the money, which is itself a kind of property, I may need to have the virtues or vices of character that procure it, or to be the child of well-off and generous parents. There can be and have been societies where the additional thing, over and above law about property, which an individual needs in order to become an owner, is something else easier to come by. In any society, however, to have the freedom in question, an individual will need more than what we can call the *legal opportunity* or *legal help*. He or she will require what we can call *other means* as well. It will have to be that he or she is not constrained by the lack of these other means.

It is true that we have now taken a certain conceptual or terminological decision, and in so doing passed by a prolonged and unedifying wrangle, one in which the Left has been as declamatory as the Right, sometimes even as fervent as the single-minded Friedrich Hayek.[5] We have taken a type of freedom to consist in much more than legal opportunity or help and of course the absence of legal obstacles or hindrance. It is not enough for freedom to acquire and hold property, as we are understanding it, that laws are as they are. There is a different way of thinking and speaking.

Here, freedom to acquire and hold private property *is* effectively taken to be no more than the existence of the legal opportunity or help. All that is required is the absence of legal constraint. A bit more may be added, and different language used, but nothing that affects the present point. There is a certain logical consequence of this way of proceeding, one that is dear to Keith Joseph and similar politicians of intellectual aspiration.[6] It is that those of us in our societies who have not inherited a cent or a penny or got one by other methods, and *cannot* do so, are perfectly and absolutely free to acquire a flat in Mayfair or an apartment on Fifth Avenue or merely, as may be more to the point, sleeping accommodation more permanent than a cardboard box. What we lack is not freedom, which in this way of thinking is more or less identical with legal opportunity or help, but rather what is usually set aside as power. Here the word 'power' is used in a narrower sense than we used it above. It is used here as 'other means' was used above.

The English language does not settle the matter but allows both possibilities – (i) speaking of freedom in the larger sense, where it is a power or ability which includes legal opportunity and help but also other means, power in the narrower sense, and (ii) speaking of freedom in the smaller sense, where it comes down to legal opportunity and help but not other means, power in the narrower sense. There are these two possibilities not only in connection with property but also in connection with other types of freedom, say the freedom to establish or advance a political party.

Whatever the rhetorical satisfactions, and the aids to political smugness or viciousness, no substantial question is affected by speaking carefully in either way. We might have defined the freedom to acquire and hold private property in the second way, just in terms of legal opportunity and help, just the absence of legal constraint, thus taking freedom by itself as not near to sufficient to make it actually possible for someone to get or have property. We would then have to say that power, in a sense, is also necessary. We would, if we had proceeded in this way, be in exactly the same position of inquiry in which we find ourselves at this moment. No substantial question would have been answered, begged or confused. In place of asking, as we shall, whether light can be shed on Conservatism by considering its attitude to a certain type of freedom, or what particular freedom of this type it supports, we would have the question of whether light can be shed on it by considering its attitude to a certain type of *freedom and power*, or what *freedom and power* it supports. Any good answer to one question will be precisely as good an answer to the other.

Further, if Conservatism is in the end to be blamed or praised for its attitude to freedoms in the larger sense, so it is to be blamed or praised for its attitude to freedoms in the smaller sense taken along with powers in the smaller sense. A political party is precisely as much to be blamed because it denies to some people what it chooses to call a power as because it denies to them what others call a part of a freedom. Or, if praise is what is in question, it is precisely as much to be praised because it does not accord what it calls a power as because it does not accord what others call a part of a freedom. One advantage of proceeding as we shall is that all of our subject-matter will automatically be kept in view. *No one* in their senses, of course, could take part of the subject-matter, power in the narrow sense, to be *irrelevant* to the characterization or appraisal of a political tradition. Few Conservatives, whatever their predilection with respect to linguistic matters, are in this respect out of their senses.

There can be no doubt of the prominence in Conservative writing of a particular sort of freedom to acquire and hold private property. One of Burke's most extended damnations of the French Revolution had to do with its confiscation of a kind of private property, such corporate property as that of the church. What he celebrates most in the English ordering of things is the principle of inheritance. He once delivered himself of the opinion about property, indeed, that the state exists only for its conservation.[7] To come forward quickly to 1914, the American literary essayist Paul Elmer More was unhappy that John D. Rockefeller was mealy-mouthed in defending the massacre of some strikers on his property. He let him know that to the civilized man, which perhaps Mr Rockefeller was not, the rights of property are more important than the right to life.[8] Perhaps Burke and Paul Elmer More are a touch stronger in their feelings than other Conservatives. Even Roger Scruton, however, who is of the Neo-Conservative section of the New Right rather than the Neo-

Liberal, which section is more attracted to authority and the pleasures of accepting it than to any freedom, allows that property is what some take to be Conservatism's principal fetish.[9]

That is not to say that many Conservatives, so far as I know, have done much to clarify either the type of freedom which is the freedom to acquire and hold private property, or the particular instance or instances of the type which they defend or propose. Still, philosophers have laboured to good effect in clarifying at least the type of freedom.[10] More needs to be said.

The freedom to acquire and hold private property, speaking of the type, involves

(i) persons who are candidates to own it,
(ii) the things, not necessarily material, which can be privately owned,
(iii) facts of relational kinds about the owners and others and the owned things, these being legal duties on the part of others and legal rights on the part of owners, as well as other facts about would-be owners which are their other means to their acting on their desires.

Instances of this type of freedom, which can be very different in the three respects or elements, involve particular limits as to what persons can possibly be owners, particular limits as to what things can be owned, and particular duties on others as well as particular rights of owners and other necessary facts about owners. Thus a society may exclude convicted criminals, married women or foreigners and the like from the category of possible owners of some things. It may, second, exclude coastal lands or hospitals or railways from what can be privately owned. It may, third, allow or not allow owned things to be destroyed by their owners or wholly bequeathed without taxation, and it may either require or not require that would-be owners of fillings in their teeth, kidney machines or a share in a joint enterprise be able to buy them at a market value.

What particular instance or sort of freedom to acquire and hold private property is defended or advocated by Conservatives? Or rather, since the matter is not simple, what instances or sorts are defended or advocated? Any answer must proceed in terms of the three elements or aspects of private property and of course their effects, sometimes their joint effects. A short answer must be a general and impressionistic one.

In the past history of Conservatism, it has certainly been more given than other political traditions to restricting the category of persons who can put themselves forward as possible owners. Women and certain races and social classes come to mind. With respect to the twentieth century, however, and to pass by the primitive racial restrictions imposed by whites in South Africa, which have had the tacit support of very many British and other Conservatives, it may be best to say that there is no great difference in this first respect between the sort of property-freedom defended by Conservatives and the sorts defended by other political traditions. At any rate this is not the place to look for a fundamental difference.

There is such a difference, to come to the second element or aspect of private property, in what things Conservatives allow or would allow to be owned. They defend or seek to have a wider range of things open to private ownership, which is to say, effectively, not in *public* or *communal* ownership – not owned by central or other governments and administrations or by other specially authorized and socially responsible bodies. Conservatism, for part of its history, stood in opposition to liberalism. This opposition, in good part, had to do with forms of government which have since declined. In its more recent history it has more clearly stood with liberalism in opposition to socialism and to socialist strains in other ideologies. To a great extent this has been an opposition to extensions of public ownership and in particular an opposition to extensions or existing extents of the range of things that are public property.

The New Right in Britain, for much of its life, was near to being mainly identified by its credal commitment to *privatization*. Before 1979 there was a general acceptance that what were then called *public utilities* – water, electricity, gas – are best provided for a society by one kind or another of public ownership. The New Right substituted and acted so far as it could on the ideal of shareholders, entrepreneurs, and in general what is called free enterprise. So with *public services*: housing, education, health, pensions, transport, communication, sanitation, security of several kinds. So with *essential industries*: steel, coal, oil, defence. So too we were to have free enterprise with gaols, juvenile secure facilities, public swimming pools, weather forecasting, the deterring of parking offenders by hoisting away their cars, telephone tapping, and rat catching. We were to have, if the hopeful Murray Rothbard had his way, the blessings of the profit motive with respect to the police and the courts.[11] We were to have, that is, private protective agencies and private arbitration services. We are to have in the future, if the Adam Smith Institute has its way, the 'civilianization' of at least parts of the army.[12] We are not to regard as actually insane the anarcho-capitalist anticipation of the day when nuclear weapons are in the hands of the Coca-Cola Corporation. In sum, what has been recommended and attempted is a contraction of the public sector, and a growth without discernible limit of the private sector. We are to have the large range of ownables that goes not with big government but with, in one sense, small.

One large consequence of having a society run according to Conservative ideas of property-freedom is that a certain class or type of individuals have a yet larger or greater advantage than such individuals have in a society shaped by more restrained ideas of property-freedom. Or rather, the agreeable situation of the given class or type of individuals is the consequence of two things. One is indeed the wider range of things open to private ownership. The other, a matter not of the second but rather the third element of private property, to which we are coming, has to do with possessing the specific other means required in order to come to own the things in question.

More fully, a Conservative society makes the private sector of its resources, endeavours and services larger than the private sector in societies shaped by other ideologies, and its public sector smaller than the public sector in other societies. That is one thing. The second is that the access of individuals to the private part of any society's resources and so on (and thus to profits or returns from them, including greater power) is largely dependent on ability to pay and hence to some considerable extent dependent on abilities and inclinations to make money – entrepreneurial and like abilities. That is, access to the society's private resources is dependent to some considerable extent on being a person of *an entrepreneurial or efficiently acquisitive class or type*. In contrast, access to the public part of a society's resources and so on is greatly more dependent on a fact about individuals other than their ability to pay. That fact, in short, is *need*. It includes the needs of those who are hungry, homeless, without jobs, or sick. Therefore the Conservative society as against others enlarges the total of what is distributed according to ability to pay, and decreases the total of what is distributed according to need. It favours to a greater extent individuals of the given ability, and hence to an extent certain other personal abilities and inclinations. It gives less help to individuals with needs.

It would be possible, with respect to those in need and unable or less able to help themselves, to give them the means – money or the like – to enable them to make necessary purchases from the large private sector. It would be possible, that is, to have a large privately-owned sector without giving the particular greater advantage to entrepreneurial and suchlike individuals. Conservatives engaged in enlarging the privately-owned sector do promise or purport to do something effective along these lines. What they do is not effective, partly because to do something effective would affect the third element of the property-freedom they favour, notably the extent of taxation.

The third element of the sort or sorts of property-freedom favoured by Conservatives, to repeat, is a matter not only of the non-legal means to private ownership we have been considering. It is also a matter of a choice of particular legal rights of owners, and particular legal duties that are to fall on others in virtue of the legal rights of owners. Most sorts of property-freedom, Conservative and otherwise, involve some or all of the following related but distinguishable legal rights of owners: (i) some right of possession, usually in the form of physical control; (ii) a right to the capital, including a right of sale; (iii) some right to use; (iv) a right to manage; (v) a right to income; (vi) a right to security or immunity from expropriation; (vii) some right to bequeath; (viii) a right to more than a limited time or term of possession and the like.[13] The particular sort or sorts of freedom to acquire and hold private property favoured by Conservatives, in brief, include *stronger* or *more extensive* rather than weaker or limited versions of all these legal rights.

The right to *possess* an estate or farm, in a Conservative way of thinking, ought to be unqualified enough to exclude certain ancient claims as to a path across it for walkers or bird-watchers, and the possession of a patent on a new shotgun should really deter would-be makers of similar ones. The right to *capital*, including the transfer by sale or gift of a thing, or its consumption, waste and destruction, should be more or less untrammelled. The right to *use* the river running through the chemical corporation's property, diminishing or polluting it, should be such as to keep at bay government inspectors and self-appointed defenders of the environment.

The right to *manage* should be such as to keep in their places the accursed unions, and also governmental regulators, local safety officers and health researchers. No doubt owners of properties should be subject to some duty not to use them in ways harmful to others, but no one should be allowed to run riot in enforcing this duty. The right to *income* should, of course, involve at most only sensible taxation, not taxation named as confiscatory, punitive or ruinous. For some Conservatives, incomes should be as good as untouched by taxation, since, as noticed earlier, Robert Nozick has proved to us all that taxation on earnings is forced labour. With respect to the right of *security*, it ought to enable industries to resist nationalization and the like. With respect to *passing on one's worldly goods*, that should not be made more disagreeable in prospect by the fact of death taxes. Finally, and relatedly, these various rights should *not* be as the rights of one's tenants, lessees, renters and the like, which come to a preordained end.

The third element of Conservative property-freedom, in so far as it has to do with what other means individuals are to possess in order to act on their ownership-desires, is in one small way not unique. That is, those political traditions different from Conservatism with respect to what things can be privately owned do none the less require that individuals have ability to buy what they are to own. But this, of course, is not the whole story. In fact the similarity between Conservatism and other outlooks, that all require property to be paid for, is wholly overshadowed by a further difference having in part to do with ability to buy and in part with other things about Conservative property-freedom already noticed, including the stronger legal rights. This is not the difference that it favours entrepreneurial and like persons, but that it favours a second class of individuals.

As a result partly of the stronger legal rights favoured by Conservatism, those individuals who are *already owners*, and, at least as important, *their children and others they choose to benefit*, have more or vastly more than other individuals of the other means – money – which is needed in order to come to own more property or to own a first amount of it. To put the matter one way, the financial distance between the class of *owners and their beneficiaries* in a Conservative society, and others in that society, is greater or vastly greater than the financial distance between owners and beneficiaries, and others, in other societies. Each of the eight stronger legal rights makes a contribution to this state of affairs. In the case of the preferred rights to capital and income and several others, this is obvious. If I can sell more things profitably, and am taxed less, I can buy more. It is not much less obvious with the remaining rights. The right to manage, used against collective bargaining by employees, is in fact like others in contributing to greater profits for owners.

The state of affairs which results importantly from the Conservative choice of legal rights and duties, indeed, will be one where much property is such that many non-owners have no chance whatever of acquiring the means to possess it. They may be candidates to own property, given the first element of the property-freedom favoured by Conservatives, but with respect to much property they are candidates with no chance of success. They will not become newspaper proprietors, certainly, or significant shareholders in any enterprise. They will not have the power which goes with those roles. If their counterparts in certain non-Conservative societies do not have much chance, they do have more.

This benefiting of some people and depriving of others, if it is owed importantly to the stronger property rights favoured by Conservatives, is owed about as much to the first element of Conservative property-freedom. That is, a society which allows *more* of its resources and services to be privately owned is one which, when compared with others, allows to its well-off owners and those close to them a greater or far greater share of other means to the possession of more property. Other things being equal, I and my son or daughter will be better off in a society where the means of my wealth are effective with respect to more things – where I can buy shares not only in breweries, computer companies and chains of stores, but also railways, electricity supply, hospitals, local swimming pools or the army.

We now need a summary of the particular freedom to acquire and hold private property favoured by Conservatives. It is a freedom which when compared with other such freedoms (i) allows more or greatly more things to be privately owned and (ii) accords stronger legal rights to property-owners. It thus (iii) gives a greater advantage to the class of entrepreneurial and efficiently acquisitive individuals and also (iv) enables a second discriminable class of individuals – existing owners and those they benefit – to possess yet greater opportunity for the realization of their desires for property or more property, and what goes with it, including greater power. That the two classes have some members in common does not make it mistaken to distinguish between them. Finally (v) Conservative property-freedom greatly reduces the chance or in fact actually deprives other members of a society of any chance to realize many of their desires for property, since they lack the means other than legal opportunity and help. This fact is not much touched by Conservative willingness, indeed the Conservative desire and strategy, to increase to a limited extent the number of holders of some small amount of property, notably a home or a few shares, neither of which carries the great benefits of other amounts and forms of property.

As implied already, Conservatism's commitment to the given freedom to acquire and hold private property does indeed distinguish it. We here come upon a further mark of Conservatism, perhaps more indelible than the others so far noticed. It is more effective than the other distinction in terms of freedom – a commitment to freedom from social persuasion (p. 71). Burke, whose opinions are not so lovely as some of his sentences, advised Pitt that his government should have no concern to make food available to its people by other means than through sale for profit, no concern to take other steps to alleviate suffering and death caused to its own people by famine.[14] He expressed a reality of Conservatism. So too did Hugh Cecil in 1912 when he limited state intervention in the lives of the people, including those of them in need, to the provision of streetlights and the like.[15] But let us come up to date. Enoch Powell, MP, is near the truth in this declaration: 'Whatever else the Conservative Party stands for, unless it is the party of free choice, free competition and free enterprise, unless – I am not afraid of the word – it is the party of capitalism, then it has no function in the contemporary world.'[16]

We now have a general but adequate grasp of the particular sort of freedom to acquire and hold private property which is one distinction of Conservatism. In the course of getting that grip we necessarily have encountered or come near to certain related freedoms. In fact we have encountered or come near to an indeterminate number of related freedoms. This is so since almost any feature or facet of an ideology – certainly including those of the part of Conservative ideology which has to do with property – can be regarded as giving some freedom or other to someone (cf p. 83). The particular sort of freedom to own property which is a distinction of Conservatism, together with these additional freedoms, make up what might be called *Conservative economic freedoms*, or the *freedoms of the Conservative economy*. It will be best to notice something of the additional items explicitly before considering together the arguments advanced for freedom of property and the other freedoms of the Conservative economy.

One such other freedom or group of freedoms is most closely related to a part of one of the rights involved in almost all private property, the right to capital (p. 90). The part in question, which can be spoken of as a right itself, is the right to sell one's property to whom one chooses, most likely someone who can buy it at an agreed price, typically the highest price the seller can get. Almost any society's institution of private property, then, carries with it the possibility of a system of exchanges or transactions of a certain kind, which is to say a *market* or a marketplace. What is sold and bought may include natural resources, one's own labour, manufactured products, houses and the like, money itself, and in short any private property.

Clearly a society may have more or less of what can be called *market-freedom* or *market-freedoms* – it may accord to individuals greater or lesser powers, of several kinds, with respect to selling and buying. The particular Conservative commitment to private property carries with it a particular commitment to market-freedom or a set of market-freedoms. As will be anticipated, it is a greater or more extensive freedom than those which go with the institutions of private property favoured by other political traditions.

It is greater in that, first, more of the total goods or resources of the Conservative society, goods and resources of various kinds, are in the private-property sector (p. 88) and hence open to selling and buying. The New Right's policy of privatization, evidently, contributed significantly in this way to the particular market-freedom secured by recent Conservative governments.

Conservative market-freedom is greater than others, second, in that it accords to *more* individuals or entities the possibility of offering things for sale. In place of medical services being provided free of charge by publicly-owned bodies and organizations, such as the National Health Service, they may be offered for sale by privately-owned health schemes or groups of doctors or individual doctors. So with bus services, education and so on. However, an increase in the number of actual sellers is not automatically a result of the greater extent of private property, the larger private sector, favoured by Conservatives – it might be and sometimes is the case that certain property, perhaps once public but now private, is concentrated in the hands of a few corporations. But the increase in sellers does typically go with the greater extent of private property.

Thirdly, Conservative market-freedom is greater than others in that it involves fewer or no constraints having to do with prices. With respect to the price to be paid by an agricultural business or restaurant for labour, a constraint is removed by revoking or not enforcing minimum-wage laws. The work of fruit-pickers and waitresses can be bought more cheaply. The same is to be said with respect to the non-enforcement of laws aimed at protecting women by securing equal pay for equal work. By way of a further example, again involving a benefit to businesses or suppliers rather than employees or consumers, it is no part of Conservatism to have controls or ceilings on the price of goods. Sellers have a greater freedom to make a higher profit. The higher profit may be owed, as well, to lesser constraints having to do with the standard or reliability of goods, say the purity of water or the healthiness of eggs, or the safeness of cars and toys.

Fourth, to make something more explicit, Conservative market-freedom is likely to be greater in that it is likely to offer to individuals a wider choice between suppliers of goods, and indeed goods. To persist with medical care, the replacement of a national health service by private health schemes and free-enterprise doctors does of course give more choice as to suppliers and perhaps as to what is supplied. There may be more of what is called responsiveness to consumer-choice. As already noted, however, there is certainly no guarantee that the privatization of a part of the economy will have this effect. A public monopoly or near-monopoly may well be replaced by a private one. Or, the real departure from monopoly may be small and of no great significance.

Much the same facts can be spoken of in various different ways. It may be said, rightly enough, that Conservatism involves more *competitive freedom*, which is to say more freedom for individuals to compete in the supplying of goods. It may said, perfectly truly, that Conservatism involves freedoms or greater freedoms *from* certain things. It involves *a greater freedom from kinds of state control* or *freedom from regulation* or *freedom from socialism* or *freedom from planning or intervention in the economy*, which is simply to say what we know, that the Conservative economy has a larger private sector, accords stronger rights to property-owners, and so on. To allow that Conservatism involves a greater freedom from state control or the like, of course, is not for a moment to be taken as excluding a proposition, quite as true, that Conservative property-arrangements and economy involve *lesser* freedoms of other kinds, to which we shall certainly come later. Nor is it to be taken as excluding the proposition, if it can be got clear, and whether it is true or false, that Conservatism involves *less freedom in total* than other property-arrangements and economies.

The same comments are to be made of an assortment of other things of which Conservatives speak, such as freedom from coercion by trade unions, freedom of parents with respect to education, freedom to opt out of this or that social scheme, freedom of choice with respect to health. There is no shortage of these items, just as there is no shortage of items on very different lists emanating from other parts of the political spectrum. There are at least as many sorts of freedom to be spoken of in any part of life as there are sorts of desires, and, depending on your method of counting, there can be an awful lot of sorts of desires.

So much for an account of Conservative property-freedom and the other freedoms which typically go with it. The whole account has necessarily been general and impressionistic. The account does not distinguish between parties, sects, tendencies, traditions and doctrines. In particular, it does not give separate attention to sections and cadres of the New Right. Here there were some who called themselves Liberals, some Libertarians, some Republicans, and some economists. Let us pause to give some of them attention.

One messianic part of the New Right was informed by the Anarcho-Libertarianism of Murray Rothbard and others, which doctrine advocates the dismantling of the state, and not only, as was misleadingly said, 'the modern state' or 'the welfare state'. We were to learn to see the state as the 'central, dominant, and overriding aggressor' against individuals, its aggression being carried forward in part by 'the practice of forcible theft which it calls "taxation"'.[17] As remarked earlier (p. 88), we were to get rid even of police and courts, partly by building on the promising foundation of private detective agencies.

It should be noticed that by means of such facts as that they favour certain 'civil liberties', and have an enlightened tolerance of certain sexual oddities, but oppose governmental support of industry and farming by means of subsidies and the like, our remaining Anarcho-Libertarians may take themselves to prove that there is no general distinction between Right and Left in politics, and that it is confused to speak of them as being of the Right. It must be a puzzle to them that they are readily recognized by more traditional Conservatives as kith and kin, if slightly dotty kith and kin, and are in no danger of being invited to socialist congresses. In books on Conservatism they are always ushered onstage, and off, but they never make an appearance in books on socialism. In fact, as is plain, just their fundamental and extreme commitment to private property indubitably locates them within Conservatism, the New Right, and the Right of the political spectrum – of which spectrum a bit more will be said in due course (pp. 231 ff).

The given account of Conservative property-freedom and the like also does not distinguish the thought of Robert Nozick, also of the

New Right. He is attracted to this Anarcho-Libertarianism, which would barely preserve the state at all, but argues himself by stages into acceptance of the Minimal State.[18] We are to wipe away time, put out of mind the transformation of societies, and return to what some represent, by selective quotation, as the political philosophy of President Thomas Jefferson – that we have only 'a wise and frugal government, which shall restrain men from injuring one another, which shall leave them otherwise free to regulate their own pursuits of industry and improvement'.[19] We are to return to the economist Adam Smith's grim little government of three plain duties: defend against invasion, administer legal justice, carry out the public works from which businessmen cannot make a profit.[20] We are, in Nozick's words, to be permitted to keep a state limited to the small functions of protection against force, theft and fraud, the enforcement of contracts, and a bit more along the same lines. In all other respects, individuals are to stand on their own two feet, use their initiative, leave home to go where the jobs are, and so on. Is it unclear or unsettled in this doctrine what is to happen to them if they cannot? It is not. What happens to them if they are in extreme need is that either they get private charity or they die.

Finally, our general and impressionistic account of Conservative economic freedoms does not distinguish the outlooks of such New Right governments as those of Margaret Thatcher and Ronald Reagan, and of the economists and political theorists closest to them. Here, by way of one example, and as a consequence in part of electoral necessity, we have had the promise that a Conservative state and society will maintain a 'safety net' to support those of us not good at making use of our legal right to acquire private property, to compete in the marketplace. Nozick places on a society no general moral obligation to help its unenterprising members from starving to death, but the politicians of the New Right have been more circumspect.

If it would be agreeable to characterize fully these and other strands of feeling and thought, and to look further at the division in the new Right between the Neo-Liberal and Neo-Conservative sections, it is unnecessary to go further in order to establish what we have, which is a further distinction of Conservatism generally. That is its commitment to a kind of property-freedom and certain related freedoms of importance. We need not go further, either, in preparation for the task to which we now turn. That is the attempt to find further distinctions of Conservatism, and above all its rationale, in the battery of arguments used in defence of Conservative economic freedoms.

They are most often defended, if that is the word, by declaration. This is the standard method of politicians and a goodly number of economists whose 'science' moves in the direction of ideology aided by a pretence of objectivity. But no one's *declaring* some policy or state of affairs to be one which realizes a freedom goes anywhere towards providing a significant argument for it – if only for the reason that a contrary policy or practice can almost always be declared to realize or secure some other freedom (cf p. 83). In the case of the particular property-freedom defended by Conservatives, there are the alternative and conflicting property-freedoms defended by other political traditions, say the socialist ones.

Further, there are things not having to do in the first instance with property which conflict with Conservative property-freedom and cannot be *ignored*, whatever weight is given to them in the end. They can be described in terms of freedoms, certainly, but they can be as well described without recourse to talk of freedom. Conservative property-freedom conflicts with fundamental human desires, desires whose legitimacy is beyond all question, desires shared by all of us and a condition of our humanity (p. 60). It is perfectly possible that the right course of action, given a conflict between your desire and what it may be conventional or even natural to call my freedom, is to satisfy your desire. So too, of course, with a conflict between need and freedom.

Thus the particular freedom of property favoured by Conservatives needs to be defended by argument. Reflective Conservatives, of necessity, have on the whole felt the need to argue for their property-freedom, and, they will certainly say, we can advance our present inquiry into their politics by considering their arguments. There are a number of them.

To begin by glancing back to our inquiry into human nature, we did not spend time over the proposition that it is our human nature to have a deep desire or need for private property (pp. 53, 63). Is there an effective argument for Conservative property-freedom to be based on the proposition that *all of us, or very nearly all of us, are alike or equal in having such a deep desire or need*? Shall we look into sociobiological claims as to genetic bases of territorial demands by various species of animals? Or, as some deep theoreticians do, look into our own primal impulse to keep other individuals standing 2′ 3″ away in cocktail party conversations? Shall we set about the deciphering of Roger Scruton's deciphering of Hegel? I have in mind their various thoughts on our common, absolute and ineradicable need to imbue our worlds with will, to rescue things from 'thinghood', to discover ourselves as social beings, to awake into true self-consciousness, etc.[21]

Shall we spend some time, before hunting up such evidence for it, in trying just to clarify the given proposition about human nature, and in particular the ideas of deep desire and need? There might be reason to do so if we were in search of an argument for some other conclusion than the one we are considering, that our societies ought to secure *Conservative* property-freedom. The human-nature proposition, taken by itself, might give support to the proposal that there be *equal* property freedom, that *all* of us should in fact be equally able, or something like it, to acquire and hold private property.

But *that* conclusion is nowhere near the Conservative one. The property-freedom supported by Conservatives most certainly does not accord an equal freedom, but rather involves greatly more freedom for two discriminable classes – entrepreneurial and similar persons, and existing owners along with those they benefit. It is no surprise that Burke, defending not only unequal amounts of property, but 'great masses of accumulation', delivers himself of this declaration: 'the characteristic essence of property, formed out of the combined principles of its acquisition and conservation, is to be *unequal.*'[22]

It is possible, of course, to characterize Conservative property-freedom in ways which bring in or drag in an idea of equality. Conservatives are not loath to do this, despite the great aversion they may have to talk of equality elsewhere. Thus David Green of the New Right, whose research fellowship at the Institute for Economic Affairs seems not to have given him too much time to read Burke, has it that 'property is the right of everyone who is prepared to work, not the privilege of a few'.[23] What that unhappy sentence must come to, and indeed the only thing it can come to, is that all persons, *if* they satisfy certain conditions, one of which has to do with working, can actually have legal rights to certain property – actually possess property. (The sentence cannot be about just the *opportunity or help* which the law will provide to all of us without exception – *that* is on offer whether or not we are prepared to work.) David Green's reassurance for us, his stout egalitarianism, has a parallel in this: 'Climbing the north face of the Eiger or absailing down the Empire

State Building is the right of everyone without exception who happens to be stunningly good at mountaineering, not the privilege of a few.' Let us not lace on our boots just yet.

Or, of course, Conservative property-freedom can be given an egalitarian disguise in another way. It can be spoken of in such a way as to bring to the fore that one part of it is *equal* legal opportunity or help. It is very clear, however, that a human-nature proposition to the effect that we all want or need property is most unlikely to support a commitment which in sum is that we are to have greatly unequal property-freedom, with some of us having none at all, which inequality is the result of the non-legal means that are also required.

Exactly the same point can be made, as anticipated earlier (p. 85), if we state the Conservative view of property in terms of the ideas that freedom to acquire and possess it consists in only the law's equally offering legal rights to all, and that other means, very unequally distributed and having nothing to do with freedom, are also required. The view so expressed is exactly as unlikely to find support in the proposition that we all have a deep desire or need for private property. Very clearly such a proposition is more likely to support certain socialist ideas about private property, for example that there should be a sharing of it that gives a significant amount to everybody.

Our inquiry into Conservatism and human nature attended to something more substantial, the general argument about our low natures and incentive. The argument proceeded from premises about (1) a goal of economic well-being or of a standard of living in a society, (2) the need for or desirability of what is called social freedom in pursuing the goal, (3) the result that individuals will contribute only out of self-concern or altruism, and (4) our being primarily self-concerned rather than altruistic. The conclusion was (5) that external incentives are to be offered to individuals, perhaps through privatization (pp. 69 ff).

In the course of considering this argument we took ourselves to have found several distinctions of Conservatism, but not a rationale. Partly because our concern was what it was – human nature – we did not pause to consider a more specific form of the general argument, one which draws a more specific conclusion about incentives. The argument in that form concludes that incentives *in just the form of Conservative property-rights* are necessary – that members of a society are to have just the particular freedom to acquire and hold private property, and to engage in a market, that is defended by Conservatives.

Do we conceivably get *more* light shed on Conservatism by this specific argument? Might we here come to a *clear and strong* argument that constitutes or gives us a greater distinction, perhaps gives us even the rationale of Conservatism, or an indication of that rationale? Certainly the general argument was no clear and strong argument. Its obscurity was a matter, above all, of the first premise, having to do with some goal or end given the name 'economic well-being' or the like but not explained (p. 70). It was also a matter of the second and fourth premises, about the need for social freedom so-called and not relying on social altruism, and also the disregarding of intrinsic as against extrinsic incentive. The ground for these latter three judgements or attitudes remained as obscure as the goal of well-being.

Shall we now become more amenable and less demanding – become, as some might say, more open-minded, perceptive or reasonable? Shall we, as we might have with the general argument, try harder – try harder to see how the specific argument *does* constitute a clear and strong argument even if it lacks, above all, what we have been calling an explicit idea of the goal of economic well-being? Shall we consider how it could be true that the specific argument does not really need so explicit an idea of the goal?

Certainly it is common to make the assumption that the specific argument is respectable. It is no less than the customary practice of Conservatives, and others have come to accept that practice. In fact this carelessness, if that is what it is, can be no part of serious inquiry. No amount of charity can make it possible to take seriously the line of argument with which we are now presented: in short that Conservative property-freedom and nothing less than this is necessary to some end or other named 'economic well-being', 'prosperity', 'a rising or maintained standard of living', 'economic growth', 'the creation of wealth' or whatever. It is perfectly impossible, with the best will in the world, to believe that the very specific freedom *is* a necessary means to an end-we-know-not-what, and hence that we actually have an argument for that freedom.

It may be that it is sensible to think that *some* freedom or other to acquire and hold private property is necessary to various goals of the kind suggested by the various names, but that is nothing to the point. It could turn out that the only specific goal which Conservatives are capable of defending, and thus the only one that presently matters, is one to which Conservative property-freedom, an extreme property-freedom, is not necessary. It could turn out, differently, that this extreme property-freedom *is* the only means to a certain goal, but that that goal, when clearly perceived, is indefensible.

Will someone, perhaps a thinker in one of the institutes, save us from our confusion? Will he say that it is clear what the goal is, that it is the economic well-being that is *the result or upshot of a society's having the property-freedom defended by Conservatives*? And hence that it is clear that what we need as a means to it is exactly Conservative property-freedom? I believe I can hear him now. He is, alas, to be thanked and returned to his researches.

If I encounter a man diligently arranging small Latvians in straight lines, and ask him to explain why it is worthwhile going to all the trouble, I am no further ahead when he points out that the result is straight lines of small Latvians. I need, in order to understand that he is up to something sensible, or anyway sane, to have an idea of what *recommends* the upshot. Similarly, we need to have an understanding of what recommends the upshot of Conservative property-freedom if we are to judge that it can be defended by that upshot. We are given no such understanding, which would give us a good idea of a rationale of Conservatism. As noticed in our earlier inquiry into incentive (p. 70) we are given no understanding, for example, by the politicians' proposition, even if it is true, that the goal is to make everyone better off – or to preserve the economic state of affairs summed up in the declaration that 'you never had it so good'.

Let us persist a bit longer, and run no risk of missing anything of importance. We are, after all, dealing with something that is commonly taken as fundamental to the whole ideology we are considering. If the tradition of Conservatism seems to contain no clear and strong incentive argument for Conservative private-property-freedom and market-freedom, might it be that it does have in it propositions about incentive and the like that serve to characterize the tradition further?

Conservatives remain fond of Adam Smith's pious discerning of a hidden hand in our affairs. This is the speculation, particularly congenial to Conservative economists, to the effect that if each of us seeks selfishly our own personal profit, this may somehow and mysteriously serve a general end, the good as it is somehow conceived of society as a whole. (Smith himself sometimes speaks of 'the public interest', sometimes of 'the annual revenue of the society'.) There is this happy consequence, he observes, where a manufacturer supports his own domestic or national industry as against a foreign industry, and seeks to maximize his own returns from it.

By preferring the support of domestic to that of foreign industry, he intends only his own security; and by directing that industry in such a manner as its produce may be of greatest value, he intends only his own gain, and he is in this, as in many other cases, led by an invisible hand to promote an end which was no part of his intention. Nor is it always the worse for society that it was no part of it. By pursuing his own interest he frequently promotes that of the society more effectively than when he really intends to promote it. I have never known much good done by those who affected to trade for the public good.[24]

To see the content of this utterance, and thus to come to see what might be called the Hidden-Hand Vindication of the property system favoured by Conservatives, we may be invited to concentrate on sides or aspects of the general fact that Conservative market-freedom involves a larger private sector. More of the activities of the society are a matter of buying and selling, and of buying and selling competitively. In the place of the state's supplying me with fillings for my teeth free of charge, a private dentist sells them to me, at a price which is supposed to take into account that other members of his profession are also seeking my business.

One side of the general fact is that *more* individuals are *motivated* to work hard. Teeth are better filled, streets better cleaned, sicknesses better diagnosed, pupils better taught, parking regulations better enforced and consumer products improved if those who do the filling, cleaning or whatever can by greater effort earn more money or enjoy a greater profit – and need to try harder, given conditions of competition, in order to have the earnings or profit. Public servants are inefficient or slothful; private companies and their employees are efficient or energetic. We are all better off with more of the latter and less of the former. (So are our houses, by the way. Lincoln Allison records, finding in his own life a reminder of all our natures, that he once lived in a university house, and laughed when water came through the ceiling.[25] He is now a home-owner, and does not laugh, but engages in good husbandry.) This general consideration about motivation resting in part on a view of human nature, is one to which we have already paid some attention, although not precisely in terms of public and private enterprise.

A goodly number of closely related propositions may be added. One is that self-interest and competition foster creativeness. It is not merely that a larger private sector gives us, more cheaply or quickly or effectively, what we had before, but that it gives us new ideas, new ways of doing things, new things. We get that splendour, technological progress, a kind of ongoing Renaissance. This is the work of those heroes of Conservatism noticed earlier, entrepreneurial persons.

The larger private sector has a second side. It brings to bear a greater *knowledge* on every aspect of the devising, manufacturing and distributing of goods. In place of the limited knowledge of a central agency, the government ministry or department of this or that, we have the great sum of diverse intelligences involved in the Conservative economy. This is a yet greater boon than might be expected, since we are inclined to overestimate the knowledge of any particular individual. In some typical although unfortunately self-referring words of Friedrich Hayek, 'It is because every individual knows so little and, in particular, because we rarely know which of us knows best, that we trust the independent and competitive efforts of many to induce the emergence of what we shall want when we see it.'[26]

Third, a larger private sector involves less of the *waste* which results from producing what no one wants. We have supply and demand more in equilibrium. There is not the awfulness of a Soviet civil servant, lately back from a tour of the English shires, overestimating the demand for green rubber boots, ordering the production of some millions of pairs, and then discovering he cannot shift them. In the Conservative economy, in so far as it consists in suppliers not at a great height above the market, or suppliers well informed by market researchers, a persistent preference for black is not disregarded. There is waste neither of rubber nor of labour.

Those three are by no means all the propositions of economics that are added to the basic idea about incentive in the Hidden-Hand Vindication of Conservative freedoms of the economy. We are told that those freedoms prevent to a greater extent the depletion of natural resources, which claim has to do with private owners having in mind their children and further descendants. It is said of the Conservative economy that it minimizes a society's administrative or decision-making costs – it involves fewer governmental planners and administrators. It is said that the Conservative economy is a more efficient machine for the distribution of incomes.

Friedrich Hayek, incidentally, is aware that the more efficient distribution of incomes may be regarded, indeed for long has been regarded, as unfair or unjust. He instructs us that there are many replies, one being this: 'It has of course to be admitted that the manner in which the benefits and burdens are apportioned by the market mechanism would in many instances have to be regarded as very unjust *if* it were the result of a deliberate allocation to particular people.'[27] But let us not delay – it may appear to be an enormous fact, as clear as daylight, that the 'market mechanism' is deliberately sustained by Conservative governments, that Conservative governments do secure predictable allocations to predictable people, indeed that these governments claim credit for doing just this. A sustained study of the works of our instructor would no doubt reveal this to be an unfortunate illusion.

We now have before us the Hidden-Hand Vindication, a somewhat changing bundle of Conservative economic propositions, tied to some central declarations about incentive and competition, and in particular a large private sector. That the bundle is a changing one is indicated by the fact among others that it recently had in it, to the fore, the prophesy of monetarism. That is to the effect that it is plainly proven that if we are all to prosper, and in particular if we are to escape inflation, all that governments need do is to control the supply of money: print less of it, have less of it in any form. This item in the bundle, to the extent that it persists, is no longer a matter of living faith.[28] Milton Friedman is no longer counted on except by himself to lead us into the Promised Land.[29]

To remember the recent course of our reflections, we allowed that Conservatism's commitment to a greater property-freedom and a greater market-freedom is an indelible distinction of it (pp. 93, 97). We earlier found other distinctions in a general argument about the need for incentives (pp. 71–4). We have lately failed to find, in a specific argument about incentive, any further distinction of Conservatism, and again nothing of its rationale. Do we now make an advance by way of the Hidden-Hand Vindication? Do we find something *new*? It needs to be said, and it will not have escaped the sensible reader, that finding or not finding distinctions with respect to a political tradition is in part a matter of judgement, and that sometimes there is room for respectable disagreement. Is the latter the case here? Is it arguable that we have something new?

I doubt it. It is true that what we have in the Vindication does contain what has already been allowed as a mark of Conservatism, its preference for incentive systems as against encouragement of social altruism (p. 73). That preference was also a part, although not one noticed explicitly, of the specific incentive argument for exactly Conservative property and market. The Hidden-Hand Vindication, putting aside this basic part of it, consists in the variable group of

further propositions, which is our only hope. It is not much of a
hope. Conservatives are not much identified by this assortment of
disputable propositions culled from the past and present of economics.
The reality of Conservatism is open to better definition.

It is beyond question that the propositions of the Hidden-Hand
Vindication as given, and more technical and theoretical variants of
them, are disputable. The high incidence of disagreement in this part
of economics is most of the explanation of the subject's uncertain
claim to the name of science. By way of just one or two indications
of disputability, there *has been* great technological progress in societies
not blessed by Conservative property-freedom, including our own
societies at certain moments. Further, the absence of technological
advance in various societies cannot be assigned quickly to just their
more limited property and market systems. With respect to the
proposition having to do with supply and demand in equilibrium, it
concentrates on but one aspect of the general question of waste in
economic systems – to perch on this proposition without turning an
eye to great and surely endemic facts of waste in Conservative pro-
perty-concentration is remarkable. Also, it will take a truly single-
minded thinker to praise the preservation by families of some natural
resources, say kitchen gardens and the private parks around stately
houses, and ignore the depletion of such natural resources as rain-
forests by corporations. Finally, none of the economic propositions
takes into account the diversity of alternatives to Conservative
market-freedom. It is not as if there were but one alternative, say the
bogey of 'nationalization'. Proponents of the propositions in the
Hidden-Hand Vindication are not guilty of making too many distinctions.

I cannot claim them as allies in argument, but it is no surprise that
Conservatives are readily to be found who readily agree that their
tradition is not to be identified with what they sometimes call marketism. Lincoln Allison is on surer ground here than with compulsory
cricket, but perhaps not wholly at one with himself as an exemplary
home-owner. He regards marketism as a fundamentalism which has
taken a hold on Conservative politicians, above all American ones,
despite 'the complete absence of any real rebuttal of the arguments
against markets'. He does not regard it as a fundamentalism fundamental to true Conservatism.[30] Roger Scruton is of something like
the same mind. He is aided in that by his general insight that
economics stands to politics in much the same relation as neurology
stands to personal affection. Be that as it may, and whatever further

reasons he has, he takes the recent economizing of the British Conservative Party as merely a case of succumbing to a passing fashion,
a temporary confusion, after which eternal verity will reassert itself.[31]

It would be agreeable to press on, to cast further doubt on the
Hidden-hand Vindication as a source of enlightenment, perhaps by
reflecting on a concept that is central to it but not much explained,
that of *efficiency*. What is it? As used in Conservative ideology, this
idea of efficiency is certainly not to be identified with any well-
defined notion or term of art in economics (cf pp. 70 ff, 41). It would
also be agreeable to ask whether it is true, in certain clear senses of
the word 'efficiency', several of which actually light up parts of the
Dismal Science, whether privatization is in fact efficient. But let us call
a halt, with one final and now familiar reflection, about something we
have latterly put to one side.

The Hidden-Hand Vindication, like the arguments considered
before it, is a defence of certain economic freedoms as serving a
certain end, which end is taken to justify those means. The end is all-
important. We shall not find the rationale of Conservatism in this
argumentation, try as we will, if we do not know the end. Nor, if we
do not know the end, shall we know the worth of the Vindication as
an argument. As remarked about its predecessor, there is the possibility that Conservative economic freedom *is* a means to the end, but
that the end is indefensible. Or, it might be that the end *is* defensible,
but there are means to it other than Conservative economic freedom.
We shall in due course come to see for ourselves that Conservative
economic thinking, like its other thinking, is governed by or is the
product of a certain commitment. We are not helped in this enterprise
by what Conservatives supply to us when inspired by Adam Smith.

There remain non-economic arguments for Conservative economic
freedoms. Some of them are of precious little use, and of precious
little use to us in our inquiry. One sort has to do with non-legal
rights. It was noticed earlier that while Conservatives are on the
whole antipathetic to talk of Natural Rights, human rights and so
on, they are no more consistent than other mortals, and do fall into
such talk themselves (p. 42). They do so in connection with property.

Their argument in one form, freed of encumbrances and distrac-
tions, is that certain individuals have a non-legal right, presumably
a moral right, to Conservative property-freedom and what goes with
it. They have a moral right to what that freedom consists in, which
is legal opportunity or help and also other means to the possession of
goods. These individuals have a moral right to acquire extensive

legal rights over many things. This doctrine is traced to the seventeenth century and the philosopher John Locke, and appears to be
involved in Robert Nozick's conclusion, noticed above, that the most
that can be justified is the Minimal State.

What was once meant by claims of the form '*A* has a moral right
to *X*' was roughly this:

> As follows from God's law or some 'law' which is both a matter
> of morality and also like the Law of Gravity in that it is true of
> nature or reality, or anyway as follows from a law which is
> fundamental and universal in that it is 'writ in the hearts of
> mankind', *A* ought to have *X*.

What can be meant now by those who cannot be stopped talking of
the moral rights of individuals, but mercifully have stopped proposing
the Divine to us, and funny laws, is no more than roughly this:

> As follows from some certain or formidable moral principle, *A*
> ought to have *X*.

But nothing effective is said of what the principle is, nor anything
enlightening about its special character. About the best that has been
done is to nod in the direction of the philosophy of Immanuel Kant,
and produce the sentence that each of us is to be treated as an end,
never as only a means. As an acquaintance with the struggles of
Kantian moral philosophers shows, any clear understanding of the
sentence – for example that each person's chosen end or desire is to
be taken into account in deciding what is to be done – makes it pretty
well useless as a source of moral direction. It is certainly useless in
connection with justifying a system of property.

Thus to say that a society ought to have Conservative property-
freedom, or in no more than the Minimal State, because some
individuals have moral rights, is at bottom to say that the society
ought to be that way because that is the way it ought to be. This
does no more than beg the question, if it is pretended that an
argument is being advanced, or reduces to no more than declaration.
I can as readily declare that all societies ought without further ado
to embrace socialist property-freedom, somehow defined, because
some or all individuals have moral rights.

Others have spent more time in coming to such a sceptical conclusion on this sort of ineffective use of talk of rights.[32] Given the

extent to which the pointless can be prevalent, it was time well spent. The kind and discerning reader will not call for further labour.

The kind and discerning reader will also excuse my not lingering over, or, in the words of Burke in another connection, not complimenting with long discussion, certain other arguments for Conservative economic freedoms. One is that they produce stability in a society. A brief reply is that they may produce or anyway be followed by the opposite, including bloody revolution, that other kinds of freedom may produce or be followed by stability, and that stability is not in its very self worth having (cf pp. 2 ff). A second thing that need not detain us, in Clinton Rossiter's brisk formulation, is 'that property is essential to the existence of the family, the natural unit of society'.[33] That, plainly understood, is false. Understood as a proposition to the effect that property is good for families, all families, it may be true, but does not lead towards a recommendation of Conservative property-freedom but away from it. Third, there is the sonorous line produced by Paul Elmer More but certainly not peculiar to him, that Conservatism about property preserves nothing less than 'civilization'.[34] Nor is it peculiar to Paul Elmer More to leave civilization in the intended sense undefined, except for an intimation or two, perhaps the intimation that it may encompass dealing with strikers by shooting them (p. 86).

There remain only three arguments for Conservative economic freedoms that can do with more attention. The first may seem like, but can be distinguished from, the futile policy of mere declaration – the policy of purporting to justify something by declaring it to *be* freedom. The argument is to the effect that Conservative economic freedoms are more to be prized than any alternative set of such freedoms. Considered in itself, and without taking into account any effects, the first set of freeedoms is to be preferred to any more limited set, also considered in itself. This comparative proposition, like the policy of declaration itself, has often seemed fundamental to what New Right politicians were inclined to call, having no great acquaintance with that inquiry whose name they appropriate, their philosophy.

One may be tempted to speculate that what is intended is just that the Conservative economy involves *more* market-freedom. But that speculation would do no justice to the tradition of Conservatism. *Of course* the proposition is true. What has just been called the Conservative economy does by definition involve *more* market-freedom: a larger private sector and so on. We know that, and are asking why more is better – we get no sensible answer by being told it is more. Certainly there can be no sensible presumption that more of anything whatever, or any freedom, is better than less. For a Conservative to say so, further, would open him or her to the waiting embarrassment that *more* of what we might now set about defining, what Socialists call *social responsibility*, is better than less. Or that it would be better to have more freedom rather than less for bank robbers and tax inspectors, less constraint rather than more.

What must instead be intended in the comparative proposition is something along the following lines. Economic freedon in general, in all its different extents, and unlike almost all other things of which we can have more or less, has some particular value or recommendation, such that the greatest extent of that freedom, when compared with other lesser extents of it, is to be preferred. Buying and selling, having rights over what is possessed and so on – these things have a particular value or recommendation such that we ought to have the greatest possible extent of them. By contrast, social responsibility, bank-robbing and tax-inspecting lack this value or recommendation, and so less of them is better than more. Here, more constraint is what we want.

Burke in much of his denunciation of the confiscation of corporate property by the French revolutionaries seems to be engaged in this enterprise of argument, and many have followed him. Milton Friedman, he who discovered or rather rediscovered monetarism, comes to mind. He has it that Conservative economic freedom is valuable not only as a *means* to something else – as we shall see in a moment – but that it is also *an end in itself*. He is likely to be taken as supposing that economic freedom, as a type of thing, is such that having more of it is better than having less. As he would no doubt say, a greater rather than a lesser diminution of economic coercion is better. But *what* is the particular value or recommendation of economic freedom generally? What is it of which we cannot have too much? Not to have an answer is not to have an argument. It is not to have part of one either, but to have no argument at all. To have the answer, no doubt, would be to have the rationale of Conservatism.

The second argument for Conservative economic freedoms is that they have the overwhelming recommendation that they secure or preserve other freedoms, these including political freedoms and civil liberties, and that alternative kinds of economic freedom limit or reduce these freedoms and may lead to their entire destruction.

Milton Friedman, as remarked, is of this opinion. He expresses a

version of it after first advancing the comparative proposition at
which we have been looking, when he writes: 'On the one hand,
freedom in economic arrangements is itself a component of freedom
broadly understood, so economic freedom is an end in itself. In
the second place, economic freedom is also an indispensable means
toward the achievement of political freedom.' It is the indispensable
means of avoiding something that can be called 'totalitarian socialism'.[35] Noel O'Sullivan remarks that some such idea, which he
takes to be a new one, has recently come to occupy an almost
unchallenged ascendency in Conservative thought.

> In its simplest form the new doctrine consists of the proposition
> that liberty is indivisible. The idea behind this seems to be that
> men forget that they must take the rough with the smooth, and
> assume too readily that they can have the smooth by itself.
> 'The smooth', in this context, means limited government, indi-
> vidual liberty, and a pluralist social order, whilst 'the rough'
> is identified with the hardships and inequalities associated
> with a capitalist economic system. The proposition that liberty
> is indivisible may therefore be translated into the assertion that
> too much state intervention in social and economic life is in-
> compatible with a liberal-democratic political order, and will
> end by creating totalitarianism.[36]

O'Sullivan is as good a sympathetic guide to Conservatism as we
are likely to find, but here he inclines in the direction of a carelessness.
It is a carelessness which has bemused others into thinking they
possess more of an argument than they do. He speaks of a 'capitalist
economic system' being needed for, among other things, 'limited
government'. Indeed it is, since, for present purposes, they come to
one and the same thing. Liberty is indivisible, and no doubt about
it, if that means we cannot separate the Conservative economy from
the Conservative economy. But our concern is whether liberty is
indivisible in the sense that we cannot divide the Conservative
economy from *political* and like freedoms.

That we cannot is certainly the theme of at least one of Friedrich
Hayek's works, whose title brings to our attention that if we have
anything less than Conservative economic freedoms we are on *the
road to serfdom*.[37] His predecessor in the Austrian school, Ludwig von
Mises, was as certain, and yet more particular in his forecast. The
end result of the bureaucratic planning mentality, if it were to take

hold, and to overcome sound judgement about property, would be that 'nomad tribes from the Eastern steppes would again raid and pillage Europe, sweeping across it with swift cavalry'.[38] A more restrained version of the view is supplied by Anthony Quinton, who says socialism 'tends inevitably in a totalitarian direction by reason of its project of absorbing the economy within the state'.[39] Robert Nisbet, who is wisely allowed by some of his fellow Conservatives to show a tendency to exaggeration, suggests that the New Deal, the policy of governmental intervention which helped America out of the 1930s Depression, was the West's first taste of Fascism.[40]

We cannot deal well with one part of this argument until we know what political freedoms are actually favoured by Conservatives – what the political freedoms are which they take to be secured by the Conservative economy. These are part of the subject of the next stage of our inquiry. We do not get a clear idea of them by hearing only of 'a liberal-democratic political order'. Let us then postpone certain considerations until later (p. 145).

Let us at this point look only at the claim that to abandon or to lack Conservative economic freedoms is to be in danger of *totalitarianism*. That is, it is to be on a road, or slippery slope, to the kind of modern dictatorship or tyranny which transcends earlier dictatorships or tyrannies, its greater capacity being partly owed to industrial, technological and other features of modern society. There is a single political party and ideology, and complete regimentation of all of political, social and intellectual life, including the law, trade unions and so on. As in the case of Nazi Germany and Stalinist Russia, there is likely to be a single and overwhelmingly powerful political leader, and coercion and terror of much of the population by such means as a secret police.

It is important to keep the right argument in view. Conservative thinkers seem not to be careful about keeping in focus what they are attempting to defend. That is a certain commitment to economic freedoms distinguishing them from, among other things, other political traditions within what are called the Western democracies. It is a commitment which distinguishes, say, the British Conservative Party from the Labour Party. The aim of their exercise is not a defence of the whole spectrum of non-Communist economies against Communist economies. It would be *easier* to argue about *these*, however well, that giving them all up would be to be in danger of totalitarianism. To abandon all of these would be to embrace an extent of government which, it might be argued, *would* readily allow for a transition to totalitarianism. Be that as it may, it is the intention of Milton Friedman and his associates to defend *Conservative* economic freedom. That is what we need to keep in mind, not something which includes Sweden and its ways.

It is usually less than clear what connection is taken to hold between Conservative economic freedom and the avoidance of totalitarianism. It may be that some Conservative doom-singers, perhaps several of those mentioned, take it that any sizeable want or decrease of Conservative economic freedom is *enough by itself* to ensure our arrival in a police state. To put the point differently, Conservative economic freedom is *the one sufficient condition* for our avoiding that fate. Friedman, as noticed above, is more cautious. He looks to the record of history but cannot bring himself to say that it shows that having Conservative economic freedom is a sufficient condition of avoiding totalitarianism or something like it. However, he can discern from history that having such freedom is a *necessary condition* of avoiding it. Such freedom is part of what is needed. History shows that to avoid totalitarianism, a nation needs to be one which has such freedom.[41]

This conclusion, that Conservative economic freedom is causally essential to avoiding totalitarianism, goes far beyond anything that might be believed to be part of the historial record. Suppose for a moment that the desired historical belief *is* true: *all nations which avoided totalitarianism were indeed nations which enjoyed, if that is the word, Conservative economic freedom*. It needs saying, it seems, that there is the difficulty that exactly this could be so without its being the case that the freedom had anything significant to do with the avoidance of totalitarianism, or indeed anything at all to do with it. That X-type things have always preceded Y-type things certainly does not establish that X-type things are necessary to Y-type things. They might have had nothing at all to do with them. Does our economist think otherwise with respect to Conservative economic freedom and no totalitarianism? He might as well suppose that since all non-totalitarian societies have earlier had bad arguments in them, maybe economists guilty of the fallacy of *post hoc ergo propter hoc*, we can conclude that bad arguments are a necessary condition of avoiding the police state.

No doubt it would be kind to allow that he recognizes that things going together is no proof that the first is sufficient or necessary, all or part of a cause, of the second. He himself, after opining that history shows that capitalism is a necessary condition of avoiding fascism and the like, allows that 'historical evidence by itself can never be convincing'.[42] Let us assume that he recognizes what is true, that a run of things going together is no proof of real connection but is some evidence for it.

If so, he will also allow that an argument for a connection between Conservative economic freedom and the avoidance of totalitarianism – still on the brave assumption that its historical premise is true – is at best something uncertain and disputable. Certainly it is possible to adduce evidence pointing the other way. It is possible to have the idea that Conservative economic freedom, given its perceived injustice and unfairness, was a necessary condition not only of avoiding totalitarianism, but of coming to have it. The idea, of course, is perfectly consistent with the general proposition, still taken as true, that all nations which avoided totalitarianism were nations which enjoyed Conservative economic freedom. The idea is that nations which *did* suffer totalitarianism did so as the result of the operation of causes which included Conservative economic freedom. There are other embarrassments for the argument we are considering, and variants of it. One is that Nazi totalitarianism was very definitely not owed to the socialist planning mentality, and something the same can be said of Stalinist totalitarianism.[43]

But I indulge myself in chinking, and may cause annoyance to others than Burke's great cattle reposed beneath the shadow of the English oak. There is no real need for these reflections on the argument in question, since its historical premise is false: it is not true that all nations which have avoided totalitarianism are nations which have always had, or even mostly had, Conservative economic freedom. Neither America not Britain, to say nothing of Sweden and other more Leftward nations, have consistently enjoyed or suffered the given economic freedom. The New Deal did happen, as did the Welfare State. Of course it may now be said that these are really not exceptions to the intended historical generalization, to exactly the generalization which Friedman *et al.* have had in mind. It may be said that the generalization we have been considering is not sufficiently precise. Plain words will not do.

There is always the possibility of such a recourse or resort. It is hardly persuasive in the present case. We *did*, after all, begin with the words of advocates of the given argument. How is it that those words are precise enough in their books but not in others?

Let us leave to others the endeavour of trying to find a more defensible historical generalization and, if they do, the yet more difficult task of showing it will do what is desired as a premise in the given argument. They are unlikely to get what they want, for example, out of the generalization that all nations which have avoided totalitarianism have sometimes had Conservative economic freedom – that would allow us to have safe periods of socialism with respect to property. What is plain is that we have no clear and good argument having to do with totalitarianism, and precious little hope of finding one. If it is our hope to find further good distinctions of Conservatism, and above all its rationale, we do better to save our energies to look elsewhere.

We do better to look to the third and last piece of argumentation we shall consider for Conservative property-freedom and what goes with it. Or, more precisely, we do better to look at what has been considered as a principal justification of private property generally, in its various forms, and has often been taken up as a justification of the Conservative form in particular. It is owed in the main to John Locke, the seventeenth-century philosopher who is counted as the first if not the most acute of the British Empiricists, and it has been refurbished often enough, most recently by Robert Nozick as part of his contribution to the mission of the New Right. It is no clear and simple thing, as several kinds of good accounts of it demonstrate.[44] Its familiar rudiments are as follows.

(i) Each of us owns his or her own body, and hence each of us owns his or her own labour. (ii) This labour we may mix with things. We may mix it with things owned by no one, or by all in common. Our ancestors, or some of them, did this with land, often by tilling. (iii) It may be, further, that a man's coming in this way to own a thing, to have it as private property, will satisfy a certain proviso. That is to say in part that his coming to own it will leave as much and as good for others, or, if that is not so, will not worsen their situations. (They might, for example, be better off as a result of being employed on his land.) The proviso in its other part is that his ownership will not result in the wasting or spoiling of the thing.

If all this is so, he is justified in having the thing in question as private property. There is more to the story, however, and in a certain sense we have not yet got to the main part of it. I may certainly be as justified in the ownership of a thing which involved no initial labour-mixing by me. In fact, if I am a typical twentieth-century person as far as ownership goes, nothing or hardly anything of what I own will be owned by me as a result of my mixing my labour with an unowned thing and satisfying the proviso. Rather,

(iv) my ownership of a thing is owed to the fact that it came to me by a voluntary act on the part of the original labour-mixer, or else someone who was in the last link in a chain of voluntary transactions going back to an original labour-mixer. Such voluntary transfers are most importantly sales, bequests and gifts. They are distinct from transfers made under force or duress or anyway without willingness or agreement – say by robbery or extortion. This latter and main part of the story is in fact more or less implicit in the midway conclusion that by mixing labour with something an individual may rightly have it as private property – since private property, by definition, has the feature that its owner may transfer all or most of his or her claim to it (p. 90).

It would be very strange indeed if there were no sense in this frayed and battered doctrine – it must have something durable in it – but the sense is not easy to state.

No doubt we can take the very beginning, about the unexplained ownership of one's body, to amount to certain moral claims that each individual has a right to life and not being injured, and to direct his or her own activities, to enjoy a general freedom of some sort. It would be agreeable to have these moral claims set out, since they will need careful drafting if they are to be acceptable to their proponents – who *do* want to put people in gaol in certain circumstances, may want to send them to war without their agreement, and so on – and also not make trouble for the argument later. To come on to the second step, what is it to mix one's labour with something? The short answer is that it is to work or labour on it, or, as Locke says, to take pains with it. That gives us a first large question. Why should work – supposing the proviso is satisfied – issue in the conclusion that it is right that the worker should own the hitherto unowned thing?

Some, as it seems, have been bemused by the metaphorical talk of mixing labour with a thing, and taken the answer to be that the labour has got into the thing inextricably, like the heaped tablespoon of plain flour into the *boeuf bourguignon* or the Worcester sauce into the Welsh rarebit, and so the owner of the labour gets the whole thing – which he needs to get in order to hang on to his labour. But why, as Nozick has the credit of asking, should the labourer not be regarded as careless? Why, careless or not, should he not lose his labour since he has gone and mixed it up with something else?

Suppose we escape the tedious metaphor, and keep in mind that all that is in question is the plain proposition that someone works or labours on something. Why, to repeat, should that make it into his property? Some have thought that it is because he has improved the thing, added value to it. But consider the toiler who arrives on the desert island and gives over the best years of his life to improving some acres. In fact, through bad luck, he worsens them. They used to grow shallots but now will grow nothing at all. Does he not have *as much* claim to the acres as his luckier neighbour has to the acres he has worked on? Most of us would say that if the second toiler does have a claim, so too, it seems, does the first. There is another problem waiting, of course. Supposing that we do arrive at a reason for property rights going to individuals who have worked on hitherto unowned things, will it really be possible to prohibit its use on behalf of subsequent individuals who work on things already owned by others? Should they not get at least a part of those things? That, I am reliably informed, was one of Karl Marx's better questions.

In any case, there is also what was called the proviso: that the result of converting a thing into private property must not have resulted in waste or in the situation of others being worsened. Was that always true? Was it often true? Was it *ever* true? Only rather conventional and unreflective thought about the wide benefits of wealth, or the enriching of a society by industry, is likely to seem to make those questions seem easy.

There is still a larger question, having to do with the voluntary transfers. One fact often remarked upon is that the history of very much property includes episodes from which pious eyes need to be averted: involuntary transfers, transfers that broke the sacred chain of voluntariness. This may be true of the wealth of most great families. If they do not all have robber-barons in their histories, those histories are very likely to have had transfers in them which do not strike one as paradigmatically voluntary, say the expropriation and reallocation of land by a royal house.

To retreat to still safer ground, questions arise about the very conception of a voluntary transfer. No doubt we are all inclined to feel happy about the transaction in which A wants to transfer X to B, and has satisfactory or tolerable alternatives to doing so, and knows what he is doing, and will not be injured or will be benefited by the transaction – and B is in a like situation. But that preliminary and vague idea of a voluntary transaction will certainly not begin to enable us to sort all transactions into the voluntary and the involuntary categories. Arriving at a really effective conception of the kind of transfer which we would always take to be defensible is no easy matter. In fact, I think, none is available, partly because arriving at one will involve moral and political inclinations and commitment.

Suppose, against the odds, that we do arrive at an effective conception of a voluntary transfer, one whose voluntariness justifies or recommends it to us. The question noticed a moment ago will certainly arise. Will there be much of the history of owned things that consists *only* in such transfers? The answer will involve, certainly, not just robber-baron episodes, but vastly more common episodes. It will involve those common episodes in which a man sells his labour or produce to another and it is natural to say that he has little choice in the matter.

If we now add what is inevitable, that there can be no guarantee that a completed account of labour-mixing and voluntary transfers would justify Conservative property-freedom in particular, as against some other form of property-freedom, we certainly come to a familiar kind of conclusion. It is that commitments to this sort of argumentation, if they may perhaps be argued to distinguish Conservatism from other political traditions, do not at all clarify a rationale or underlying principle. They do not show us, as some say, the fundamental nature of Conservatism.

The sceptical reader may wonder if the piece of argumentation we have been considering is in good part philosophers' or logicians' work, a kind of embroidery or clutter that conceals what is plainer and stronger. I own up to being tempted to something like that myself. What comes to mind is that Locke's reflections on labour-mixing come to this, that those who labour *deserve* the reward of ownership. What also comes to mind is that the voluntary transfers which Conservatives favour are those which can somehow be said to reflect the *deserts* of one or both participants. More generally, can it be that what is in question is the proposition that Conservative property-freedoms are justified by desert somehow conceived? That would be well connected, incidentally, with the Conservative attachment to the doctrine of Free Will and rejection of Determinism.

If one looks to Conservatives who depend on the doctrine of labour-mixing, however, one finds no idea of desert ever explained. One does not often find it stated. Sometimes one finds it denied. Nozick himself is very very much against the idea that the distribution of things ought to be according to the characteristics or properties or natural claims of individuals themselves, including their characteristic of deserving rewards for labour.[45] No doubt he supposes this may have results or corollaries uncongenial to him. Rather, he burkes the question of why we are to own what we have mixed our labour with, or have had voluntarily transferred to us. He says, in effect, just that we *ought* to own what we have had voluntarily transferred to us or have mixed our labour with under certain conditions (cf pp. 43 f). He does not say *why* that is so, what justifies this state of affairs. If he had done so, he might have supplied to us what we seek, and still have not got, which is the rationale of Conservatism.

What remains in this part of our inquiry can be only a glance at certain other freedoms. What we have been considering so far in looking at economic matters are the most important freedoms, *for a study of Conservatism*, within the large category of non-political freedoms. This large category has in it all freedoms other than those – political freedoms – which can be said to be part of the choosing and influencing of governments (p. 83). That we have given so much attention to economic freedoms should very certainly not be taken as implying that they are the most important freedoms in the category from any political point of view. They are not. It may come to mind, by the way, that Conservative economic freedoms, if they can be said not to be part of the practice of choosing and influencing governments, none the less have very much to do with that choosing and influencing. That is certainly so, and a fact to which we shall be paying attention in due course.

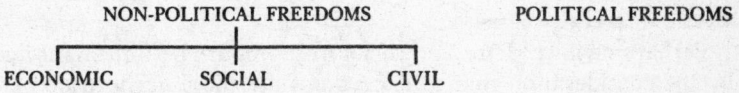

For now, there remain to be noticed the two other sorts of non-political freedoms, the social and the civil. We shall take it that they are in one part a matter of social and civil rights, which is to say certain legal rights. The particular civil freedom which is a freedom of speech is to be taken as consisting in part in a legal right. The other part is the ability or power to act on the right. The situation here is thus the same as with the freedom to acquire and hold private property (pp. 83 ff). By way of a further introductory remark, it is true that the two terms 'social freedoms' and 'civil freedoms' do not suggest a sharp distinction. That is no bad thing, since there *is* some arbitrariness in assigning certain items to one or the other of the two sorts.

Social freedoms may be characterized as being mainly those associated with certain twentieth-century advances. These advances include reforms of the Poor Laws in England by the Liberal Party government of Herbert Asquith (1906–11), the construction of the Welfare State by Clement Attlee and others in the Labour government after World War Two, the lesser provisions of the New Deal in America (1932–7), and, perhaps, President Johnson's 'War on Want' (1964). Social freedoms involve what are called welfare rights, social security rights, health and educational rights. Social freedoms include what can be named, with absolute propriety, freedom from poverty, freedom to work, freedom to develop one's capabilities by way of a university education, and freedom from want in old age. They also include freedom from racial and other discrimination. That the names are not so familiar as others makes no difference whatever to their use, which involves no contentiousness whatever.

Civil freedoms are not so tied to large and specific twentieth-century advances. They include the freedoms suggested by the principles of equality before the law and the rule of law, in particular the freedom to use and be defended against the law and freedom from arbitrary arrest and certain police powers. They include freedom of speech, freedom of information or the freedom to know, and freedom of the press. They also include freedom of association and of organization, essential to trade unions, freedom of privacy, cultural freedoms and in particular religious freedom, freedom of movement, and a good deal else.

Perhaps civil freedoms and social freedoms are best distinguished by the consideration that civil freedoms are those likely to be perceived as open to being infringed by governments and other authorities, and social freedoms those likely to be perceived as frustrated by the social and economic natures of societies, natures which governments may or may not attempt to alter.

It is possible to fall into supposing that Conservatism has some commitment to the securing or defending of social and civil freedoms. This idea is likely to be owed in part to a history of general effusion by Conservatives, to the effect that *they* are the defenders of liberty, all true liberty. Burke may be taken to have begun that history with such declarations as the one noticed earlier in support of all manly, moral, regulated liberty (p. 82). It has repeatedly been said, too, that Conservatives defend all freedom which is short of being licence. More recently, Conservatives have been persistent in announcing a conflict between what they call equality and liberty, neither of them clarified, and affirming that they embrace the latter. We shall spend a good deal of time on that (pp. 188 ff). We have had, too, the declarations of the Libertarian strain within the New Right, also noticed earlier (p. 82). Some of these thinkers, indeed, take the name of Civil Libertarians. Keith Joseph also comes to mind. It was he who managed to suggest in 1979, just in time, that his Conservative Party would give the United Kingdom greater intellectual freedom, and rescue its universities from a prevailing orthodoxy.[46]

It is nonsense to suppose that the tradition of Conservatism, or Conservatism today, seeks to secure anything remotely like the social and civil freedoms. In fact, as we have already seen, the Conservative commitment to certain economic freedoms is *in itself* nothing other than opposition to most of the social freedoms listed above. To secure or maintain what is indeed called freedom from state control, freedom from coercion by trade unions, freedom from the dependency-culture, and so on, is precisely to reduce or destroy most of the social freedoms as defined or to prevent their realization.

To remember again the England to which I came in 1959, it was above all the England which looked after those of its people less able to look after themselves. It accorded to them large things whose importance we do not bring into clear view by talk of social freedoms. The general and abstract term 'social freedoms', however justified, distracts one from the realities in question. England accorded to all its people the effective help of doctors, and of other professions on whom we rely in adversity or just in the ordinary course of life. England was determined to enable men and women to have work and its rewards, determined that there should not be poverty. It acted on the moral truths that all the young should be able really to learn, and all the old should at least have succour. It sought not to denigrate those who came to it from elsewhere and brought little with them, or were not white-skinned.

England was then closer than at any time in its history, or its history in peacetime, to being a decent family. Like any decent family, it had a special concern for those of its members in need of that concern. England then had a moral standing to which, it is fair to say, and to make but one comparison, the United States has never raised itself. To join it was to acquire a kind of honour.

England now, after ten years of government of the New Right, is different. If it is a family, it is a degraded one, one in which the father, if he helps the son, charges interest. It is a family in which large promises, in retrospect, are hard to distinguish from lies. I do not engage in party politics, but rather record a grim truth in

remembering that the leader of the Conservative Party promised
those who would need it that 'The National Health Service is safe
with us.' England now is a family with beggars in it, living in filthy
streets. It is a family some of whose members are more likely to fall
into kinds of moral degradation as a consequence of having nothing
worthwhile to do. It is a family whose elected leader, on being chided
by some of its more fortunate members for disregarding the less
fortunate, seeks to silence them by the vulgar reprimand that they
themselves have done very well out of the way that things have been
arranged.[47] It is a family more concerned to apprehend and to punish
those who offend than to do what would make less likely those
offences. It is a family not united by concern but divided by what it
is too kind to call competition.

What of civil freedoms? Let me again restrict myself to the New
Right in Britain. In the decade after 1979, Thatcher governments
reduced civil liberties significantly, and to an extent to make reasonable men and women uneasy about the future of the society.

Equality before the law was reduced by influences and pressures
brought upon a judiciary which in good part became, if not supine,
not noticeably erect. Equality before the law was also reduced by
such particular measures as an effective reduction in legal aid to
those unable to pay. With respect to the rule of law, there were lesser
restraints on those particular servants of the state above the law to
whose counterparts in other societies we give the name of secret
police. Also with respect to the rule of law, there occurred in 1988
what everyone who could read, or, if not that, watch television,
rightly understood to be murder by the state. Whether or not many
chose to utter such hard words is another and smaller matter. It is
not so small a matter whether the British government, desirous of
retaliating sharply against terrorism, and being seen to retaliate
sharply, was prepared to contemplate in advance that its action
would be seen as murder by the state. I refer to the killing of
three unarmed and at the time unthreatening members of the Irish
Republican Army in Gibraltar. It is no surprise, to put aside the
IRA, that police powers over ordinary citizens increased significantly
in the decade. With respect to freedom of speech, it was further
reduced by facilitating a greater concentration of press control.
Rupert Murdoch's two varieties of newspapers, the gutter variety
and the variety with somewhat greater pretensions, opened their
columns to fewer kinds of speakers. Freedom of information was not
increased, to say the least, by legislation on government secrets.

Nor was it increased by the conversion of the British Broadcasting Corporation to what, if it were elsewhere, would have been in danger of having the name of being a voice of government, or at any rate a very good listener to it.

What else can be said of civil freedoms does not need to be said here. Peter Thornton, however suspect he may be as a former chairperson of the National Council for Civil Liberties, tells the story very plainly.[48] The New Right has been no friend to civil liberties, but a resolute adversary. No amount of stuff about the demands of national security, no redefining of terms, and no sanctimony about the preserving of real principles can conceal the fact. In particular there is no concealing the unique extent to which Thatcher governments have been found by the European Court to have contravened the European Convention on Human Rights. Nor, ever, have Conservatives of whatever species been friends to civil liberties. That generalization easily withstands a certain refrain in Conservative writing, to the effect that liberty is protected by those who have property or wealth and have an ability to resist an encroaching state. It was indeed notable, in connection with the Gibraltar murders, that commercial or independent television sought to tell the truth, thereby giving credence for a moment to the refrain that wealth makes for resistance to over-mighty governments. It was as noticeable that singularly effective steps were taken by the Conservative government to minimize the chance of a repetition.

Our earlier conclusion was that Conservatism's support of certain economic freedoms distinguishes it (pp. 93, 97, 105). Its opposition to social and civil freedoms is a further great distinction of it. The support of the economic freedoms is simply inseparable from the opposition to social freedoms, and it is in some good linkage with the opposition to civil freedoms. We have assumed that these distinguishing features are owed to some principle or rationale. Such a rationale, if it is perceived by Conservatives, is left inexplicit. If it does not come to light before then, we may discover it on returning to the subject of social and civil freedoms, in connection with equality.

– 5 –
Government

> ... this outstanding minority should exercise more influence over public affairs than the untalented majority: should form, that is to say, a ruling class.
>
> Peregrine Worsthorne

In his great diatribe against the French Revolution, Burke found as much time for the abuse of persons on his own side of the English Channel as for the wretched revolutionaries. Indeed it was his perception of the treachery and dangerousness of his own countrymen that stirred him to put pen to paper. One of these was the dissenting preacher, Richard Price, who offended against Burke's dictum that 'No sound ought to be heard in church but the healing voice of Christian charity'.[1] In particular, and as we have already noticed, Price had had the wonderful impertinence to assert on behalf of Englishmen these freedoms: 'To choose our own governors', 'To cashier them for misconduct', 'To frame a government for ourselves'.[2] These democratic sentiments, to Burke, were a mad fiction flung in the face of the sacred history of the English people. Elsewhere, somewhat calmer, he still will have none of the idea that 'a majority of men, told by the head', rather than a minority, should lay down law for a nation.[3]

Burke's resolute opposition to democracy has been carried on by his many successors. Conservatism has had to make compromises with the ongoing if uncertain historical movement towards democracy, but it has never or very rarely indeed been democratic by choice. It has always sought, with some good success, to delay or stop or reverse that historical movement.

Fisher Ames of Massachusetts was noticed earlier for his diagnosis in 1807 of the disease which was American democracy, affecting skin, bones, marrow and all (p. 3). John Randolph, speaking at Virginia's constitutional convention in 1829–30, was as appalled by the monstrous tyranny of King Numbers.[4] He could, it seemed, hardly have feared anything more than the 'deadly principle' whereby 'a bare majority may oppress, harass, and plunder the minority at pleasure'. Benjamin Disraeli is forever remembered by his fellow Tories for widening the voting franchise as an electoral ploy and thus dishing the Whigs, and also for trying to persuade the English that they were One Nation. But he was under no illusion, as we shall see, that the elected House of Commons was to be regarded as itself speaking for or deciding things for that nation.[5]

Lord Macaulay, a few decades later, reminded an American correspondent, who innocently thought he might have a good word to say for the democrat Thomas Jefferson, that he had never in Parliament or even to voters on the hustings uttered a word 'indicating an opinion that the supreme authority in a state ought to be intrusted to the majority of citizens told by the head, in other words, to the poorest and most ignorant part of society'.[6] In 1883 Lord Salisbury asserted the idea that increasing democracy spelled the end of what he succeeded in perceiving as 'impartial' government, and moreover, would bring about the whole disintegration of society.[7] He was not the first and certainly not the last to announce that since more democracy was in prospect, the end was nigh.

In 1912 Lord Hugh Cecil, fearful of an increasing number of socialists in the House of Commons, proposed to weaken that chamber's power. His idea, perhaps not too wild, was that there should be a constitutional means whereby the House of Lords could appeal directly to the people, by way of a mass referendum, and count on their 'natural conservatism' to deal with the socialists.[8] Over succeeding decades there was no shortage of other ideas for dealing with the advance of democracy. There was also no shortage of dismay, leading in the direction of what can be called a kind of cultural fascism, on the part of those who linked rising democracy with a decline in culture.[9] T. S. Eliot was all too aware that the common man was interested in 'balls propelled by hand, or foot, and by engines or tools of various types; in playing cards; or in watching dogs, horses or other men engage in feats of speed or skill', and thus was not wholly engrossed in reading *The Wasteland*.[10]

To leap forward to the present, to a day when there is not much prospect of achieving more democracy, we are taught by Roger Scruton of the New Right that democracy is dispensable. 'In politics the Conservative attitude seeks above all for government, and regards no citizen as possessed of a natural right that transcends his obligation to be ruled. Even democracy – which corresponds neither to the

natural nor to the supernatural yearnings of the normal citizen –
can be discarded without detriment to the civil well-being as the
conservative conceives it.' Still, our teacher is perhaps not without
hope for an end to 'the contagion of democracy, now raging so
wildly', since 'it is possible to mistake its high flush of fever for the
light of health'.[11]

Clinton Rossiter, no enemy of Conservatism, and a plain-speaking
American of other than the innocent variety, provides another
summary. He assigns it to an imagined critic but does not strenuously
dissent from it himself.

> Conservatism is anti-democratic. It is hard not to be skeptical
> about the Conservative defence of constitutional democracy.
> Conservatism fought it savagely at every stage of its development
> and never embraced it until compelled to choose between sur-
> render and oblivion, and even now the embrace is more forced
> than fond. The Conservative's opinions and assumptions about
> liberty, equality, progress, individualism, authority, class,
> suffrage, and education are all at odds with the democratic faith.
> Enough Conservatives remain bluntly honest in their distaste
> for democracy to bring this whole faith under a deep suspicion.[12]

Robert Nisbet gives us another summary.

> One will search the history of Conservative thought in vain for
> anything resembling a 'one man one vote' philosophy. Con-
> servatives fought hard in the United States for indirect elections
> of officials, in the local communities and the states as well as the
> national government, as English Conservatives had fought for
> 'rotten' boroughs and the strength of the House of Lords. The
> highly democratic measures of initiative, recall and referendum
> which came into being in the American states around the turn
> of the century were opposed every step of the way by con-
> servatives – whether Democrat or Republican.[13]

Our present subject is Conservatism and government, including
Conservatism and political freedoms. It will be best to deal with it
mainly by first getting clearer about Conservatism and the forms of
government which have the name of democracy. To that end, we
need what is not often offered by Conservatives when they are drawn
to the subject: a tolerably clear conception or definition of democracy.

In getting one, incidentally, we deal in passing with an occasional Conservative inclination which serves the end of avoiding an uncomfortable issue. It is the inclination to suppose that the term 'democracy' is so variously used that nothing sensible can be said by way of it. Lincoln Allison is to the fore here, with the proposition that 'democracy' is an emotive term or a term of praise of no descriptive meaning at all, which is to say no meaning at all in the ordinary sense, and hence that serious discussion about democracy as such is not possible.[14] He is fortunate to be of a different view about 'participation', which word, you will be reassured to hear, remains serviceable, and enables him to express certain Conservative sentiments usually expressed by way of the meaningless term he has given up.

There is no great mystery about how to proceed. What we need, evidently, is not some agreed idea which is so abstract or general as to cover all the forms and instances of government that have been or are called democratic. We need instead a clear conception of one possible form of government in terms of which actual forms of government and political traditions can be discussed. Conservatism will be clarified by its attitude to this form of government, and by the contrasting attitudes of other political traditions. Something like this has been the implicit and sensible procedure of all those, including many Conservatives, who have considered democracy in a general way. This way of proceeding involves a certain amount of decision or stipulation as to the use of the term 'democracy', but that is familiar, and no shortcoming. Of course we might instead single out and describe one of the actual forms of goverment called democratic, the contemporary British, American or Soviet, and clarify Conservatism by setting out its attitude to just that. There is greater simplicity and less room for confusion in proceeding more generally, by way of a possible type, or what some call an ideal type.

Democracy, by way of a first approximation, is *a possible form of government such that in virtue of certain features all of the people choose and then influence those who govern the nation and control its relations with other nations*. It is, then, although more needs to be said, not rule by the people, which thing must now be regarded as what perhaps it always was, a utopian dream. It is rather the choosing and influencing of rulers by the ruled. This possible form of government is to be clarified by specifying or separating out three groups of the mentioned features. They have to do with the choosing and influencing being free in the sense of being voluntary (p. 76), with there being an equality of opportunity in the choosing and influencing, and with there being both voluntary and effective decision-making by the chosen rulers.

(i) This democracy involves regular elections with short intervals between them – elections at which all those adults who live in a society, with some few exceptions, can vote secretly for a political party. Their votes are voluntary, not coerced by an army, police, thugs, employers, bishops or an ascendant class. As important, voters are voluntary in their votes in the sense of not being constrained by ignorance, confusion or the manipulation of feeling. They are not in their votes the creatures of propaganda machines, called by whatever respectable name (p. 82). Their votes are thus minimally rational, at least in the sense of being sensibly self-interested, and, being so, confer a rationality on the outcome of the election.

To turn to those for whom they can vote, there is no significant legal or other barrier to individuals and parties presenting themselves as candidates for election. Further, these individuals and parties are not in their campaigning subject to coercion by an army, the police or whatever. None, certainly, are excluded from offering their services by the provisions of a constitution.

After an election, and until the next one, those who live in the society are able to bring influence to bear on the elected government. This is a matter of a number of things, including the absence of coercion of the sorts already mentioned. It is also a matter of free speech and platforms for it, the availability of information as to the government's activities, local elections and by-elections, the possibility of demonstrations in the streets with respect both to particular issues and also the continued acceptability or want of it of the government itself. These freedoms, in effect, enter into the campaigning for the election to come.

Each of these mentioned features having to do with voluntariness might have closer definition. Given what has been said, it is conceivable that some resolute defender even of the Soviet political system of the past, by defining terms to suit himself, will argue that that system was an instance of the possible democracy, or an approximation to it. Certainly others will say that British or American democracy is of this kind. My understanding of what has been said is such that the Soviet defender would be engaged in a hopeless endeavour, whatever is to be said in sum for or against the system of government in question, since it did not allow any party to present itself for election. Also, given my understanding, the defenders of the

Western democracies will be hasty indeed to suppose that their chosen systems, whatever can be said for them, can be demonstrated to fit the bill. This is a matter in good part of the fact of propaganda in those systems. For several reasons, there is no room at all for argument to the effect that the bill is filled by contemporary South Africa, say, or the Greek city states of antiquity, given the place of women and slaves in them, or the many contemporary societies where the generals or the lieutenants of an army are in control.

(ii) Some of the second group of features of democracy, having to do with equality, will have been taken as bound up with or pre-supposed by features in the first group. They are, but they need to be made explicit. In this democracy each voter has one vote – the rule, stated as we now must, is 'One person, one vote'. In order to avoid what would take much time, a consideration of alternative voting systems and in particular systems of proportional represen-tation, let us not require that each vote be of equal worth or effect in electing a representative. We do require, as implied by what was said of ignorance, confusion and manipulation, that each party at an election – or each party that passes some test of minimum support – has an equal opportunity to lay out the truth as it sees it or pretends it to be.

It is not the case, in this democracy, that one party or group of parties has any greater means, other than argument itself, of overpowering the reasoning of the electorate or any significant part of it. It does not have greatly more money, or the support of most of the press. It does not have a hold on the priorities, or the usages, of those who give us the news on television. It does not, in virtue of being in power, use the national exchequer to employ advertising agencies to spead its politics under the guise of giving out official information. It does not, as it comes to mind to remark in this day of privatization, arrange to have the gullible influenced into supposing that the drinking water will be made safe by first sub-tracting large profits from the budget for doing so.

Much of this will be taken as most pertinent to elections. It evidently applies as well, and nearly as importantly, to the influencing of government between elections. It is not the case that there are the mentioned equalities in some short pre-election period, but that such equalities are lacking for the remainder of the time between elections. This democracy does not allow for a government coming to power as a result of an electoral process of equality, and thereafter being open to persuasion by only a part of the society, for whatever reason.

Again what has been said is impressionistic and open to somewhat divergent understandings. My own is to the effect that it would show a kind of partisanship, not to say zealotry, to claim that the Western systems of government are instances of or very close approximations to this democracy considered in terms of its specified equalities. Any attempt to advocate that the Soviet system has been an instance or close approximation would be pointless. There has been no approximation to equality, whatever may be true in the future, with respect to the freedom of alternative parties to seek election.

(iii) To come to features of this democracy having to do with legislating and governing, it is again true that some of them are implied by what has been said already. If this democracy involves no limit on the range of political parties, it equally involves no final limit owed to a constitution on the powers or scope of decision of the elected government. The government may be subject to constitutional restraints, and impeded by constitutional procedures, but it is not prevented from deciding to do, above all, what it was elected to do. Second, the decisions of government, arrived at by majority vote in the assembly or chamber, are as free from the kinds of coercion mentioned above in connection with voters and candidates. It is not the army or church or an ascendant class that limits or determines what the government decides. Third, as will have been assumed, the decisions of government are effective. They are translated into fact, not thwarted by other institutions. They are not thwarted by the courts, or such upper chambers as the British House of Lords, or international corporations, or arms of governments such as the security services, or recalcitrant bureaucracies, or organized social classes. What the government decides does not fail to happen as a consequence of activities by these bodies and groups. It is not a debating society. If it decides that oil is not to be exported to South Africa by national corporations, it does not turn out that it is, since others decide differently.

It will rightly be anticipated that I take this third group of features of the possible form of government, having to do with voluntary and effective rule, to be such that Western democracies are certainly not actual instances of it, however closer they may be than certain other existing governments. Something the same has been true of the Soviet political system.

We have a further distinction of Conservatism, at least when compared to democratic socialism and traditional liberalism, in its opposition to development of particular political systems towards democracy as defined, and it is not a distinction only of Conservatism past but also of Conservatism present. It is a piece of naivety to suppose that Conservatism is less serious or resolute now than in the past in its resistance to progress in democracy. It would, if it could, reverse that progress, and does in politic ways attempt to do so. The New Right has had some success. This conclusion about Conservatism in general, that it is by nature anti-democratic, needs to be enlarged and made more specific. We can do that by asking what kind of government, different from democracy as defined, is favoured by Conservatives.

We already have a substantial part of the answer. Our inquiry into non-political freedoms clarified the fact that Conservatives are committed to certain economic freedoms. They are committed to Conservative property-freedom and Conservative market-freedom. This, indeed, is what we have so far found to be their tradition's most telling distinction. It follows as the night the day that they favour a kind of government which defends or would secure these freedoms. They favour a government which protects property and market, and hence opposes social and civil freedoms.

Burke, to remember, lets us know on one occasion that the state exists only for the conservation of property (p. 86). If it does, it is inconceivable that it should be capable of confiscating or redistributing it. Was Burke on that occasion overstating even his convictions? No matter. Elsewhere, in the course of inveighing against the moral or natural rights claimed by the French revolutionaries, and defending established legal rights, he makes certain feelings evident. He takes it, no doubt rightly, that society is importantly a matter of established conventions, and that those conventions are a matter of its law, above all its law protecting property, and he draws a certain consequence. 'If civil society be the offspring of convention, that convention must be its law. That convention must limit and modify all the descriptions of constitution which are formed under it. Every sort of legislature, judicial or executory power are its creatures.'[15]

This commitment to government of a kind which protects property-rights has continued to be essential to Conservatism. It was the prime motive of the long resistance on the part of Conservatives to extending the vote to those who lacked property, or enough of it. That same commitment is evident in the little miracle often remarked upon whereby certain Conservatives, American Conservatives above all, manage to perceive no difference at all between the form of government to which they swear allegiance, of course named democracy, and the spirit of free enterprise.

It is worth noticing, finally, that the commitment to government of the property-defending kind is implicit in an argument of importance noticed earlier. That is the argument to the effect that Conservative economic freedoms have the recommendation that they preserve other freedoms, notably political freedoms that enter into the choosing and influencing of government (p. 110). If the economic freedoms are praised as the means to preserving certain favoured political freedoms, it cannot be that the political freedoms are taken by the praiser as being in any way inimical to the economic freedoms.

The conclusion we have, then, is that Conservatives are for a form of government which is prevented, either as a result of a written constitution, or by other means, from interfering with property and what goes with it. With respect to the fundamental feature of democracy that it involves no final limit on the scope of legislation, Conservatives would certainly subtract such a feature from existing governments that have it or come near to having it. They indubitably resist existing governments coming to have it. Would some or many of them dissent from this conclusion? Would they proclaim some commitment to democracy, perhaps even to progress towards the possible form of government sketched above, and thus, in part, declare themselves opposed to a constitution which expressly limited the power of government so as to exclude interference with property? No doubt some would take this wise line, given the political importance of being on the side of democracy, or anyway presenting oneself as being so. This matters little. It is at least true that Conservatives are for government which either by constitutional or by other means is prevented from interference with property and what goes with it.

These means come into view by way of several other features of the government favoured by Conservatives, to which we now turn. Some of these features, however, are important themselves in the enterprise of specifying the government favoured by Conservatives.

Conservatives have always had among themselves those who would speak out for what all of them may be thought to be inclined to, given their disinclination to democracy. That is government by élite, or by some species of aristocracy, or, in some sense, by the best. Peregrine Worsthorne: 'In any society, at any time, there are some citizens who have more to contribute than others, and it is everybody's interest that this outstanding minority should exercise more influence over public affairs than the untalented majority: should form, that is to say, a ruling class.'[16] Kenneth Minogue of the New Right, as noticed earlier (p. 24), would have government carried forward, to a greater extent than it is, by those who truly have the capability of ruling, which capability is most likely to be found among the members of a long-established ruling class.

Burke spent many words on the theme. What we must have is a society 'in that habitual state of discipline in which the wiser, the more expert, and the more opulent conduct, and by conducting enlighten and protect the weaker, the less knowing, and the less provided with the goods of fortune'. This 'true natural aristocracy', having seen nothing low or sordid from infancy, having had leisure to read, reflect, converse, having been taught to despise danger in the pursuit of honour and duty, having been among rich traders who from their success must be presumed to have sharp and vigorous understandings – this aristocracy is the soul to the body of society, and must rule. Those who would deprive us of their service to society must, according to Burke, have war proclaimed against them.[17]

There must be some doubt as to exactly who these worthies are, and more doubt about a characterization of the leaders favoured not just by Burke but by Conservatives generally. Burke elsewhere strikes a note perhaps somewhat different from the one we have been hearing. 'There is no qualification for government, but virtue and wisdom, actual or presumptive. Wherever they are actually found, they have, in whatever state, condition, profession or trade, the passport of Heaven to human place and honour.'[18] With other Conservatives the proposition that a true natural aristocracy ought to govern is run together with something different and of little or no political content, that in any political system whatever, the most able will come to be in command. Yet other Conservatives, including several who have had attention in other connections, have had in mind rather more spiritual or elevated classes of individuals, notably Coleridge's secular clerics and Carlyle's heroic drillmasters (pp. 3, 47). In the day of the New Right, it was sometimes difficult to escape the thought that Conservatives take the view that those who have the passport of Heaven to seats in government are primarily those who have exactly and only the virtue of having made money, or are such that they would choose that line of life above all if they could. They need not be notably couth.

It is not essential, for what follows, that we arrive at some really effective definition of what can be labelled the 'true natural aristocracy', which, for Conservatives, is at least to be to the fore in government. It is not open to dispute that this aristocracy will have among its members a predominant number who are possessors of considerable property or indeed wealth, and are likely to be the children of such parents. It is to be allowed that of these well-heeled persons many will have the attributes, not to be disdained, of being entrepreneurial or efficiently acquisitive (p. 89). Others will have capabilities which serve, at least, to maintain and defend inherited wealth. It is to be allowed, too, that those who have had the good fortune to be born into risen families, if they have also had the luck to be able to profit by privilege in education and the like, will have acquired some of the virtues by which Burke was so overwhelmed. It is pretty difficult, for a start, to spend some time with good schoolmasters and decent dons, and not pick up an idea or two. It can be done, of course, and has been, but need not be taken to exclude a sound man from the true natural aristocracy.

To say that Conservatives are not by choice democratic, and are for government that defends private property and gives at least a dominant place to a true natural aristocracy, leaves it pretty much open what structures or patterns of government have their support. It is true that in different times and places Conservatives have complied with or given some kind of assent to different structures of government. These have varied from what can be called, very loosely, limited monarchical to representative. That fact, of which some Conservatives attempt to make a great deal, does not rule out the possibility of a certain generalization. It is that themes of *balanced* or *mixed* government have always been a part of Conservatism.[19]

David Hume, although not consistently Conservative in his politics, may be taken to strike a Conservative note in this: 'If we have reason to be more jealous of monarchy because the danger is more imminent from that quarter, we have also reason to be more jealous of popular government, because the danger is more terrible. This may teach us a lesson of moderation in all our political controversies.'[20]

Burke was for a similar balance of powers, also one that necessarily took into account considerable change and new demands. 'We are resolved to keep an established church, an established monarchy, an established aristocracy, and an established democracy, each in the degree it exists, and in no greater.'[21] Disraeli after him was as firm that the House of Commons should not rule, but that what was required was the balanced government owed to participation in it by the Commons, the House of Lords, and the monarchy. This balance was not to be disturbed by his new electoral arrangement whereby rather more voters had their wills expressed in the House of Commons.

So too, as all know, balance was the aim of very discernible Conservatives among the framers of the American constitution. There was to be no 'excess of democracy', no giving over of the new national independence to 'men without property and principle'.[22] There was to be, rather, a diffusion of power, which would save government and society from the effects of popular enthusiasm and tyranny, including what Conservatives have never been reluctant to call the tyranny of a majority, even a very large majority. In this way of talking, incidentally, it is forgotten that it is what is *favoured*, government which gives great or important power to a minority, which is properly regarded by others as *nearer* to tyranny.

To pass by a great deal more about balance and mix on both sides of the Atlantic, notably much doctrine about what is called pluralism, and to end up with Lincoln Allison, he has it that there should not be too much 'participation' by the people. His cautious and canny prescription for government, as he hopes it is, is for government mixed, moderate and suitable to local conditions. What is suitable to English conditions is, among other things, a hereditary monarchy and aristocracy. This is so, it seems, because they can no longer be rationally defended. 'That is one of their strengths. Because they cannot really be defended, the hereditary aspect of government manages to be, simultaneously, both wonderful and risible; it inspires devotion, but cannot, by its very nature, inspire fanaticism.'[23]

I am not certain that this late-twentieth-century variation on the theme of balanced or mixed government will inspire confidence in all members of the Conservative Party, but let us not linger. Let us rather press on through a survey of other Conservative inclinations and commitments, or at any rate declarations, with respect to government, and then see what the sum of these things can be said to reveal. Some of them, alas, make no great contribution to our understanding.

Nothing is much more often declared by Conservatives to be their ruling idea than constitutionalism. It is usually presented, indeed, as their political shrine. Let us look for a moment to what in our terms counts as pre-Conservatism, and in particular to a figure flawed not only by friendship with Voltaire but by something approximate to atheism – Lord Bolingbroke, he of whom Burke asked, in that early moment of Conservative comradeship, 'Who now reads Bolingbroke? Who ever read him through?'[24] He may be taken to begin a tradition of veneration in Conservatism, if that is not too small a word, for the English constitution. It was, to him, 'that noble fabric, that pride of Britain, the envy of our neighbours, raised by the labour of so many centuries, repaired at the expense of so many millions, and cemented by such a profusion of blood'.[25] To Burke himself, in one of many references, it is verily 'the engagement and pact of society'.[26]

To come to the very late if somewhat cooler celebrator, Anthony Quinton, the English constitution is 'the accumulated and sifted experience of our predecessors as embodied in traditional institutions, laws and customs'.[27] It is what he will have us rely on after he has convinced us that his and our political theorizing and limited intellectual powers are not up to the job of saying how government ought to be organized. For American Conservatives, there is nothing much more sacred than the written constitution of the Republic, at least when properly interpreted by satisfactory members of the Supreme Court.

But we need not pause for more illustration. For one thing, there can be no great need for instruction about the history of Conservative utterance in this connection. For another, no amount of illustration would lead us to a true distinction of Conservatism. The reasons are the same as with what concerned us at the very beginning of this inquiry: the subject of change and reform. It is clear that Conservatism is done no service, done no justice, by identifying it as the political tradition opposed to change in itself, any change, and supportive of any continuation (p. 2). It is not identifiable in this way. If we understand constitutionalism plainly, as *the practice of adhering to constitutional principles or a written constitution*, any such principles or document, it is undeniable that it does not single out the tradition of Conservatism.

If it did, that would reduce a large political tradition to a kind of inconsistency near to nonsense. Conservatives will in fact recommend no adherence whatever to many possible and actual constitutions – however much they may be tempted to say so, or to avoid the question, out of a familiar desire to have the good name of playing by the rules. What they are committed to, and what just such declarations as those already noticed demonstrate, is a *particular sort* of constitution, the sort of which they take it that there are instances which are the foundations of the British and American systems of government. (The members of other major political traditions are about as little or as much constitutionalists. They, like Conservatives, are inclined or committed to one possible sort of constitution, one sort of basis for a system or pattern of government.) When, in a late year of the Cold War, to take a small instance, American Conservatives thought it a worthwhile mission to send some academic persons to sail up and down the Baltic coast, having seminars and lectures on Freedom, their somewhat optimistic intent was not, I think, to uphold the existing constitutions of Latvia, Estonia and Lithuania. They were in favour, perhaps for good reason, of something other than plain constitutionalism ashore.

We might prolong our consideration of this matter by contemplating different concepts of constitutionalism, and matters having to do with duration or age of constitutions, but to no great gain. Nor need we pore over Friedrich Hayek's Model Constitution, which would 'stop' socialism by, among other means, excluding party politics from the legislative assembly, and not allowing anyone in until they have reached the age of forty-five.[28] What we can conclude now is that Conservatism when it adores a constitution is adoring a system or pattern of government which is no more democratic than positively need be, does not disturb or would restore property, is in a sense aristocratic, is balanced or mixed, and so on. The constitutionalism of Conservatives is as good as identical with the sum of their other declarations and commitments with respect to government. Were there any necessity of a further little proof, it could be provided by noting the speed at which praise or discussion of constitutionalism in general transforms itself into praise of local arrangements as distinct from anything alien – however proud that alien fabric, raised by the labour of years, repaired, cemented and accumulated.

These reflections need some supplements which may conceivably strike a rural Conservative reader as perverse, on the subject of revolution. Burke's great diatribe was indeed taken as a manifesto of counter-revolution. His passion against the French Revolution was put to use, not without some absurdity, as Conor Cruise O'Brien notes, by those American Conservatives of another century dedicated to a reversal of another revolution, the Russian.[29] Shall we then say, adding ourselves to an endless line of Conservatives, that theirs is the political tradition that is well identified as being against revolution – against, that is, the alteration of a structure or pattern of government not by constitutional means but by force or the threat of force? It would not be kind to do so. Nor need we exert ourselves to distinguish efficiently revolution and counter-revolution, both of them involving governmental change by force (cf p. 7).

Conservatism, patently, can be said to be opposed to a *kind* of revolution, admittedly the kind that has done much to shape history over several centuries, but still a kind. It is in favour of revolution of another kind, as well as of what would more easily be called revolution if it had other than military origins. Conservatism has often enough sought to instigate these things. It is no more cautious about dealing in blood than the rest of us, and not all that much out of practice. The revolutions it is for, and the counter-revolutions it is for, in so far as these are a matter of government, are sometimes directed to securing systems which are undemocratic or democratic to a lesser degree, sometimes directed to systems which are property-preserving, and so on. As in the case of talk of constitutionalism, so with the Conservative cry against revolution. What it comes to is the sum of its other passions and doctrines about government, that it should be other or less than democratic, property-preserving, and so on.

That is not all. These remarks will have been taken, naturally, as principally concerned with the attitudes of British, American and like Conservatives to revolutions or counter-revolutions in other places. There is also the matter of the attitude of Conservatives towards constituted governments of their own nations. Burke, it is said, anticipated the coming of Napoleon, anticipated that the French Revolution would end in the rule of some popular general who would conciliate the soldiery, possess the true spirit of command, and draw the eyes of all men upon himself.[30] What, we may ask, would he have anticipated if England after 1789 had gone some or all the way in the French direction, whether or not as the result of revolution? Yet more to the point, what would he have *welcomed* had England gone some good way towards democracy of the possible kind indicated earlier? 'A perfect democracy', he wrote, would be despotism, 'the most shameless thing in the world'.[31] Whether or not that shameless thing had in his view been arrived at constitutionally, would he not have welcomed a Napoleon, or at any rate a Cromwell, at least as a temporary expedient?

There is still less room for doubt about some of his successors. Macaulay was noticed earlier for his want of enthusiasm for majority rule (p. 125). In the same letter of 1857 he laid out his convictions about the result of too much democracy.

> ... institutions purely democratic must, sooner or later, destroy
> liberty or civilization, or both. What happened lately in France

is an example. In 1848 a pure democracy was established there. During a short time there was reason to expect a general spoliation, a national bankruptcy, a new partition of the soil, a maximum of prices, a ruinous load of taxation laid on the rich for the purpose of supporting the poor in idleness. Such a system would, in twenty years, have made France as poor and barbarous as the France of the Carolingians. Happily the danger was averted; and now there is despotism, a silent tribune, an enslaved press. Liberty is gone, but civilization has been saved. I have not the slightest doubt that, if we had a purely democratic government here, the effect would be the same. Either the poor would plunder the rich, and civilization would perish, or order and property would be saved by a strong military government, and liberty would perish.[32]

Macaulay was by no means the last figure in the Conservative tradition – he is such, despite having been a member of the Whig party – to have indicated at least an unsettled attitude towards a military government predicted as the result of too much democracy.[33] For the most part, however, Conservatives have taken care not to express anything like a resolution to end, by force, local governments of certain kinds. English Conservative politicians have taken care not to associate themselves with what have certainly existed, minimally ominous corps of patriots discovered by the press to have been presenting arms on a grouse moor to save the nation from socialism. The Conservative policy of embracing constitutionalism has stood in the way of any such support, and, far more important, any open threat to have resort themselves to rather better organized persons, the military themselves, in order to bring down governments of a certain kind.

Still, this politic quiet is no reason for us to fall into a certain piety. Macaulay and those like him are better indicators of truth than their comrades. To keep in mind Conservatism's commitment to private property, its want of enthusiasm for democracy, and its ability to regard itself as a sole preserver of civilization, is necessarily to come to another thought. There is no reason to shrink from it. Conservatism is a political tradition which threatens at least to concur in the ending by force of certain governments, whether or not those governments can claim the support of a constitution. It has on many occasions done much more than just concur.

There is the further and more important question of whether

Conservatives are distinguished by this fact. Those of them who accept it to be a fact will rush to say no, and reasonably. They will say the history of the Left has been a history whose outstanding episodes are revolutions. The conclusions to which we come in this instance, then, are that Conservatives are not distinguished, as they tend to pretend, by political pacifism with all respect to all governments under which they might find themselves, and, more important, they are not distinguished by what *is* a fact, their want of such pacifism. It is possible to speculate that English and American Conservatism, compared to other English and American political traditions, is distinguished by having an actual capability of calling on the military – that it is the tradition, within those nations, that has a character owed to the fact that it can effectively make a certain threat, and does tacitly make it.

Putting aside the attitude of Conservatism to revolution, abroad and at home, do we make progress by considering whether Conservative governments are distinguished by a general foreign policy? This has sometimes been supposed. Conservatism has been supposed to have a distinctive inclination or commitment to imperialism, which is to say the establishment, maintenance or extension of an empire. Necessarily Conservative governments in Britain in the nineteenth century and part of the twentieth were rightly associated with the British Empire. Something of a related sort can be said of American governments, most recently in connection with South America. Disraeli, as Noel O'Sullivan reports, may perhaps be taken to have been first to attach imperialism firmly to Conservatism. 'The Tory party,' he declared in 1872, 'has three great objects ... to maintain the institutions of the country ... to uphold the Empire of England ... and to elevate the condition of the people.'[34]

In fact any attempt to attach imperialism exclusively to Conservatism must be ill-fated. If the imperialism is ordinarily understood, as above, it is impossible to deny that the Soviet Union has been engaged in it. What it is possible to say, of course, is that Conservatism has been inclined, when the inclination has been realizable, to empires of a certain character. They have been empires inspired by what we know of already, in terms of domestic policy, which is the commitment to property and markets, to capitalism. Conservatism has been committed to an international defence of business. What we have with respect to Conservative governments and foreign policy, then, is a certain distinction, but one which does not shed much new light on the nature of these governments.

It needs adding that contemporary Conservatism, above all the New Right, has not been given only to capitalist foreign policies. Such foreign policies also fall under other descriptions. They have included toleration or support for foreign governments and regimes whose remoteness from democracy has made them into pariahs. South Africa must come to mind with British Conservatism, Chile with American. These awful facts, however, do not stand alone. Other political traditions than the Conservative have found themselves in like relations to unspeakable regimes. What can fairly be said, however, is that they have not been in these relations to make money.

Let us now return to domestic policy. In our consideration of human nature, we looked at the claim that Conservatism is distinguished by believing that the low natures of men make necessary a society of order. This we understood to be a society of hierarchy, one in which grades or classes of people are ranked one above the other, with those above having what is called authority over those below, authority being legitimate or accepted power or force, and the government having supreme authority (p. 67). We concluded that Conservatism is not distinguished by support for hierarchy in this general sense. However, it was remarked in passing that an authority, particularly a government, has the possibility of becoming authoritarian or repressive. That is, it may press or exceed the powers assigned to it, perhaps by paying insufficient attention to or disregarding the rights of subjects. To come now to a further thought about Conservatism and government, is it the case that Conservative governments are distinguished by a tendency to authoritarianism?

It is not hard to marshal evidence in support of the idea from the practice of Conservative governments and the habits of Conservative writers. Burke is pretty well unable to start a sentence about the liberty of subjects without finishing it by something firmer about the limits on that liberty, and at least an implication of the need for a government to impose order, and to err on the side of more rather than less.

> Men are qualified for civil liberty in exact proportion as to their disposition to put moral chains upon their own appetites; in proportion as their love of justice is above their rapacity; in proportion as their soundness and sobriety of understanding is above their vanity and presumption; in proportion as they are more disposed to listen to the counsels of the wise and good, in preference to the flattery of knaves.[35]

It is not hard to hear in such words, and yet easier to hear in others, an inclination not only to authority but to authoritarianism. This is so despite all of Burke's defence of established legal rights of subjects, and in good part *because of* his entire disdain of other rights.

To move from the sublime to the not quite so sublime, there is Roger Scruton. He is no adversary of authority, as indeed we already know (pp. 68, 87, 125). He has very little feeling for the Neo-Liberal as distinct from the Neo-Conservative strain of the New Right, since the former prattles about freedoms. What we must hear instead is that 'The state's relation to the citizen is not, and cannot be, con-tractual ... The state has the authority, the responsibility, and the despotism of parenthood.' The state must, in particular, do its pun-ishing with a will. It is a reassurance that our preceptor holds office in Birkbeck College of the University of London, rather than in some place where greater decisions are taken. To a question about punishment which he poses, 'Are we to take our example from the cruel and emphatic law of Islam, and institute flogging and maiming as the expression of civic virtue?', he makes the reply that 'the answer cannot be abstractly determined'.[36] Still, I mean not to indicate a preference with respect to modes of punishment on his part, but an inclination to something more than authority on the part of a government. As in the case of Burke, this inclination is the more likely in company with a disinclination to civil freedoms.

There is further reason to take Conservatism as given to auth-oritarianism in government in the repeated proposition that it is for 'strong government' or a 'strong state' or 'strong leadership', and also further reason in other features of Conservatism already noticed, including its manner of distinguishing between a true natural aris-tocracy and the rest of us. That is all very well, but something stands in the way of our finding an actual *distinction* of Conservatism in its authoritarianism. That is the simple fact that other political traditions and other governments have not been without an inclination, and sometimes very greatly more than an inclination, to that same exceed-ing of authority. The overwhelming examples are of course the totalitarian states.

What cannot be concluded, therefore, is that Conservatism is uniquely identified by what is certainly true of it, a tendency to authoritarianism. It *is* possible to conclude a lesser thing. It is *more* given to authoritarianism than two other political traditions, those of democratic socialism and liberalism. It is this lesser proposition, which is in no need of defence, that presumably has been intended by the many perceivers of Conservative authoritarianism, including many Conservative perceivers. It is this proposition which has been intended by those adversaries of contemporary Conservatism who speak of its authoritarian populism.[37]

Finally, in this survey of Conservatism and government, what is to be gained by considering the protests of twentieth-century Conservatives that to think of Fascism in their connection is to give proof of gullibility or malignancy? That to suppose that Conservatism has an extreme form in Fascism is to show oneself unfit for serious conversation? That to use the term 'Fascist' in expressing apprehension about Conservative governments is to reveal neurosis? That to think of the word with respect to certain passages quoted before now in this book is silly? That to persist in such habits, in the face of the fact that Hitler's party was the 'National *Socialist* German *Workers* Party', or the fact that Fascism spoke of itself as a Third Way between capitalism and socialism, is to be under-supplied with historical knowledge?

Well, those who are accused of these shortcomings may at least make certain replies. They may make them after having been restrained, as some need to be, by the reading of a good book or two – a book or two of what can rightly be called political science – on the different parties of Hitler and Mussolini.[38]

They may remark that modern Conservatism has shared certain principal opponents or enemies with Fascism, these being communism and liberalism, and indeed that Conservatism and Fascism have shared a good deal of general demonology. As important, Conservatism is more akin to Fascism in its attitude to the preservation of property and what goes with this than any other major political tradition. If this latter proposition falls short of the too imaginative Marxist account of Fascism as a violent and dictatorial agent of bourgeois capitalism, it has the recommendation of being very arguable.

Conservatism's tendency to authoritarianism also relates it more closely to Fascism than democratic socialism and liberalism are related. The same is to be said of its reluctance about democracy, and in particular its distinct want of enthusiasm for civil liberties. There is also what it says of instinct, and occasionally of heredity and blood. To put aside all else, including race and nationalism and a good deal about the 'organic' society, which will get some attention soon, European Conservatism is connected to Fascism by an unbroken linkage of intermediate parties and movements, those labelled Conservative Right, Conservative Authoritarian, Right Radical, Authoritarian Nationalist and so on. It is to be added, on the assumption that actions speak louder than words, that remnants of Fascism, say the National Front in Britain, have never been confused as to where they might find most toleration. It was the Monday Club of Conservative members of parliament that the National Front sought to infiltrate.[39] They wisely spent no time on the Tribune Group, or any other part, faction or sect of the Labour Party. Again, it was a Conservative invitation that came near to bringing to England, not long before these words were written, the French politician known mainly for a certain looseness in his talk about Jews and gas chambers.

All of which does not take us far forward. It does not greatly matter either that Conservatives in general deny, or that their adversaries more truly assert, a certain connection between Conservatism and Fascism. Neither gives us much help in coming to a clear view of Conservatism. It is properly considered on its own, without attention to what, in certain respects but not others, may be said to be an extreme form of it. It is not totalitarian, not one-party, not what some call *activist*, not dedicated to the Führer principle. It does not believe that 'The state must regard as its highest task the preservation and intensification of the race ... the preservation of those original racial elements which bestow culture and create the beauty and dignity of a higher mankind.'[40]

Truth is not served by putting it, if with some reason, in this lurid light. Nor is it served, I fancy, to remember a certain precursor of Fascism, by supposing that Conservatives regard the state in such a way that they feel each citizen should pay his taxes to it in the spirit in which a lover gives presents to his mistress.[41] As do Conservatives who see communism in all persons who affront them, down to the vegetarian, we merely distract ourselves from our subject by looking to Fascism and the like. The most that can be said is perhaps along the following lines. If an inquirer into democratic socialism came to an idea of its nature, and then found that there was nothing like that nature in Communism or indeed Stalinism, he might rightly be inclined to continue his researches. So with Conservatism and Fascism. They have something in common, a good deal more than other political traditions and Fascism.

What remains is a summary of our sequence of findings about Conservatism and government, and a conclusion of a familiar kind.

Conservatism does not do greatly more than tolerate democracy.

It is committed to government which defends or seeks to enlarge property-freedom. Its intention is to give the largest possible power to a true natural aristocracy, understood in a certain way. Is there any identification of worth in saying that it is for government that is balanced or mixed? Perhaps so, but we have seen no clarification of what sort of balance or mix is in question. It is inclined to a foreign policy which is, in a word, capitalist. It is, in relation to certain other political traditions, authoritarian. Certainly these various inclinations and commitments are connected. Some are mainly means to the realization of others.

But what fundamentally unites these further distinctions of Conservatism? What unites them with those other distinctions found earlier in our inquiry (pp. 79, 105)? What is their foundation? Might we be driven to the answer of self-interest or selfishness? Perhaps a kind of self-interest tempered by realism or pragmatism? That would not be a happy upshot for Conservatives. Macaulay did himself no good when, if he did, he presented himself to his Maker, and on being asked to justify himself in his politics, he remarked that he always had an eye to the main chance.

Whatever is to be said of a rationale, a proposition of self-interest would not either give us what is different, a *distinction* of Conservatism. Whatever may be true of socialism and altruism, it is undeniable that very many members of socialist movements have sought to benefit themselves by their political efforts. They are not greatly less grubby in their political endeavours than shopkeepers and brokers.

The main conclusion of a familiar kind, then, is that Conservatives do not give us a rationale in what they have to say of their preferences with respect to government. We do not hear from them what can be said for less democracy than might be had, the role of a kind of aristocracy, and so on. A hopeful reader may think the answer is to be found elsewhere, in what Conservatives avow about the nature of society, a matter to which we shall turn after looking at a question left open earlier.

In our inquiry having to do with freedom, we distinguished the particular economic freedoms to which Conservatives are committed and then looked over the arguments given for them. One was that these particular freedoms have the recommendation that they secure or preserve political freedoms and civil liberties (p. 112). Considered, in this connection, and rejected, was the proposition that it is only by embracing Conservative economic freedoms that totalitarianism can be avoided. Left on one side, for later consideration, was the

related proposition that it is only by embracing Conservative economic freedoms that we preserve what was called 'a liberal-democratic
political order'.

We now have what we did not have then, a decent conception of
how Conservatives conceive of that order – a conception, first, of
what *political* freedoms they suppose we ought to have. These are
freedoms which are no more democratic than need be, are not such
as to interfere with property conceived in a certain way, leave some
place for a true natural aristocracy, and are consonant with a certain
authoritarianism. We also have a second thing, arrived at earlier, a
conception of what *civil* freedoms are favoured by Conservatives.
These are, to say the very least, limited (pp. 120 ff).

To come to the question, then, or to come to a first question, do
we need Conservative economic freedoms in order to secure or preserve just the political and civil freedoms that are favoured by Conservatives? Do we need a powerful institution of private property,
and a wide and entrenched market system, in order to preserve just
the given political and civil freedoms, and to save us from larger
ones? Well, it seems likely enough that such an institution of property
and such a market system will do a better job than less institutions
and systems. To put the point simply: given various connections
between property and business on the one hand and politics on the
other, a society where property and business are more to the fore is
more likely to be one which has only the more limited political and
civil freedoms. If property-owners and businessmen have greater
economic power than they might, we are all more likely to have only
the kind of political and civil liberty which suits them.

So far so good, but evidently all of this raises a little problem. We
now have Conservative economic freedoms recommended as more
effective means – let us leave aside complications having to do with
necessary and sufficient conditions – to a certain end. But is that end
a good or defensible one? Opponents of Conservatism do of course
maintain that it is not. Still more to the point, Conservatives do not
provide, and we have failed to discover, a foundation or rationale for
the limited political and civil freedoms supported by Conservatives
(p. 122). At the very least, then, we can now draw the conclusion
that the argument we have been considering – Conservative economic
freedoms are justified as means to Conservative political and civil
freedoms – is radically incomplete. For any means to be justified by
ends, the ends have to be justified.

There is another question. Conservatives do not effectively distinguish the given argument from another, for good reason. It is run together with something less precise: that Conservative economic freedoms are justified as means, indeed the unique means, to the end of political and civil freedoms conceived in a less doctrinaire way – in fact *greater such freedoms*. To speak only of the political freedoms in question here, they are more democratic, less deferential to property and what goes with it, not such as to serve a true natural aristocracy, and less consonant with authoritarianism. For a given system of economic freedom to serve *this* end would, to very many people, recommend the given system.

Does Conservative economic freedom serve this end? It does not, for precisely the sort of reason just noticed. A society where property and business are more to the fore, given various connections between them and politics, is precisely one which is less likely to have the greater political and civil freedoms.

So much, then, for the general claim that Conservative economic freedoms secure or preserve political and civil freedoms, whether construed as having to do with the avoidance of totalitarianism or with the alternative of 'a liberal-democratic political order'.

– 6 –
Society

... a clause in the great primaeval contract of eternal society, linking the lower with the higher natures, connecting the visible and invisible world ...

Edmund Burke

Lord Balfour, leader in the House of Commons of England's Conservative Party for twenty-one years until 1911, and the writer of a book or two, including *A Defence of Philosophic Doubt*, speaks for many in a memorable pronouncement. 'I am more or less happy when being praised; not very uncomfortable when being abused; but I have moments of uneasiness when being explained.'[1] In considering their views on society, let us save Conservative authors some moments of uneasiness, at any rate for a time, by having before us sizeable selections of their own words. Their subject, more particularly, is what is called among other things the organic society or the organic state. In allowing them their own voices, we also serve other larger ends, mentioned earlier, having to do with reassurance and the matter of Conservatism and style (p. 11).

Society is indeed a contract. Subordinate contracts for objects of mere occasional interest may be dissolved at pleasure – but the state ought not to be considered as nothing better than a partnership agreement in a trade of pepper and coffee, calico or tobacco, or some other such low concern, to be taken up for a little temporary interest, and to be dissolved by the fancy of the partners. It is to be looked on with reverence; because it is not a partnership in things subservient only to the gross animal existence of a temporary and perishable nature. It is a partnership in all science; a partnership in all art; a partnership in every virtue, and in all perfection. As the ends of such a partnership cannot be obtained in many generations, it becomes a partnership not only between those who are living, but between those who are living, those who are dead, and those who are to be born. Each contract of each particular state is but a clause in the great primaeval contract of eternal society, linking the lower with the higher natures, connecting the visible and invisible world, according to a fixed compact sanctioned by the inviolable oath which holds all physical and all moral natures, each in their appointed place.[2]

As noted earlier (p. 14) Burke here mingles several themes and intimations. What he says of a contract has little or nothing to do with an original agreement between founding fathers of a society, or tacit agreements between citizens and their rulers or states. What he says faces a little difficulty, which we need not deferentially overlook, having to do with the dead and gone and those not yet on hand. There cannot be contracts between persons never in touch with one another in order to make them. Perhaps the best that can be supposed, as we did earlier, is that we are to understand that we of this generation have received a benefaction from Society, or more particularly its past, and in virtue of this we must make a return to it, or more particularly its future. So with every other generation. This, of course, might be thought to be just a matter of fairness between generations, earlier generations being fair to later ones, rather than any agreement between them, but Burke evidently seeks to convey much more.

There is another theme or intimation in the renowned passage, to some extent presupposed by what is said of a contract, but important in itself. It is our present business, and is to the effect that a society, if it is not broken by revolution or harmed by lesser interference, is a kind of great natural growth in accordance with a kind of law of no human contrivance, a natural law. This great natural growth has fundamental to it what is somehow one with the law, a principle of inheritance. The principle has to do with a family's property and privileges, passed from father to son, but also a people's institutions, religion and government. Society transmits and preserves its holdings as it is natural that a family does.

In this choice of inheritance we have given to our frame of polity the image of a relation in blood; binding up the constitution of our country with our dearest domestic ties; adopting our fundamental laws into the bosom of our family affections;

keeping inseparable, and cherishing with the warmth of all their combined and mutually reflected charities, our state, our hearth, our sepulchres, and our altars.[3]

If we were to forget we are merely 'temporary possessors and life-renters' in an ongoing society or commonwealth, if we were to forget that we have this inheritance to transmit, and if we therefore were to waste or harm or change it, then 'the whole chain and continuity of the commonwealth would be broken. No one generation could link with the other. Men would become little better than the flies of a summer.'[4]

The nineteenth century was not short on celebration of the organic society, but let us come forward quickly to 1933 and to Mr F. J. C. Hearnshaw, whose personal political progress, as he records, began with a milder sort of socialism and came to a grand climacteric in Conservatism. It is true that he takes Conservatism to be not merely untheoretical and unintellectual but to be silent, lethargic, confused, incoherent, inarticulate and unimpressive.[5] Still, there is no doubt some promise of instruction from his *Conservatism in England: An Analytical, Historical and Political Survey*, since it has lately been republished under the auspices of the American New Right. The Conservative, according to Hearnshaw, feels that the past is in a real sense one with the present.

He has an organic or biological conception of society, as opposed to the inorganic or legal conception prevalent among the philosophical radicals. To him the great community to which he belongs – e.g. the national state – is a living entity, albeit of a psychological rather than a physical type; a spiritual organism to which every individual in the community belongs. He feels with St. Paul that we are all members of one another; all joined together in the large and enduring life of a mystical body, whose abode is a mother-country or a fatherland. Hence he is impressed by the need to preserve the integrity of this communal life, which is larger and more enduring than his own brief individual existence; he strives to safeguard the body politic from injury at the hands both of malignant enemies and injudicious friends; he struggles to maintain the communal identity amid all the changes that time inevitably brings.[6]

Clinton Rossiter can speak for American Conservatives, on the
same lines but on a somewhat more limited subject, not something
which is both society and state. No doubt he is typical of his Conservative countrymen in introducing a strong distinction between
society and state.

> Society is a living organism with roots deep in the past. The
> true community, the Conservative likes to say, is a tree, not a
> machine. It rose to its present strength and glory through cen-
> turies of growth, and men must forbear to think of it as a
> mechanical contrivance that can be dismantled and reassembled
> in one generation. Not fiat but prescription, not the open hand
> of experiment but the hidden hand of custom, is the chief creative
> force in the social process. Society is cellular. It is not an agglom-
> eration of lonely individuals, but a grand union of functional
> groups. Man is a social animal whose best interests are served
> by cooperating with other men. Indeed he has no real meaning
> except as a contributing member of his family, church, local
> community, and, at certain stages of historical development,
> occupational association. The group is important not only
> because it gives life, work, comfort, and spiritual support to the
> individual, but because it joins with thousands of other groups
> to form the one really stubborn roadblock against the march of
> the all-powerful state.[7]

Roger Scruton strikes another note or two to which we must try
to listen. As noticed earlier (p. 15) he is not content with a vision of
society and the state, which he takes to be really inseparable, as
merely organic.

> Most human activities, and most relations that are worthwhile,
> have no purpose. No purpose, that is, external to themselves.
> There is no 'end in view', and to attempt to provide one is to
> do violence to the arrangement ... Indeed, if friendship has a
> basis it is this: that a man may desire the company of someone
> for whom he has no specific purpose ... So too in politics. A
> statesman may have aims and ambitions for the society which
> he seeks to govern. But a society is more than a speechless
> organism. It has personality, and will. Its history, institutions
> and culture are the repositories of human values – in short, it
> has the character of end as well as means. A politician who

seeks to impose upon it a given set of purposes, and seeks no understanding of the reasons and values which the society proposes in return, acts in defiance of friendship.[8]

Lincoln Allison, in this instance, is more restrained. The nation, he says, develops in a slow and complex way, its institutions responding so as to fit the whole.

> The analogy of the organism has both positive and negative implications. Negatively, it stresses the complex interconnections between the parts of the organism and the consequent dangers and difficulties of radical change ... But the analogy also suggests several attractions and advantages of life in a society which is not only like an organism but respected and accepted as being so. In an organic society the individual is part of something which has a character of its own beyond the complete control of conscious plans. His incorporation into this larger entity gives his life meaning, place and purpose.[9]

Finally, Anthony Quinton. For him, the first principle of Conservatism is traditionalism, as we know (p. 2).

> The second principle is that of organicism, which takes a society to be a unitary, natural growth, an organized, living whole, not a mechanical aggregate. It is not composed of bare abstract individuals but of social beings, related to one another within a texture of inherited customs and institutions which endow them with their specific social nature. The institutions of society are thus not external, disposable devices, of interest to men only by reason of the individual purposes they serve; they are, rather, constitutive of the social identity of men.[10]

Let us struggle to separate out various currents contained in this stream of Conservative utterance about society.

The first is that *society is a thing persisting through time*. There is a tendency to take that seemingly simple proposition as carrying with it an uncertain little load of implication or suggestion, a tendency to hear the plain English word 'thing' as reverberating with additional sense. It is a 'real thing' or a 'great thing'. If we start by firmly putting aside implications and suggestions, which will be considered separately, what we have is an undeniable truth – if not one that has greatly more content than the yet plainer proposition 'there are societies'. Certainly we can single out societies, and, if we spend some time on the definition of the idea of one, we can come to an effective way of distinguishing them and therefore counting them. Perhaps we can come to judgements as to when they begin and end.

In none of this, however, is there any distinction of Conservatism, or any noticeable premise for political conclusions. No socialist fails to regard a society as a thing in the minimal sense in question. In any case, what argument could conceivably be based by a Conservative on the given truth? Society is not said to be a *kind* of thing, from which something or other might be supposed to follow.

Society is a thing which is more than the sum of all its parts – that is the second current in the organic stream. It may, of course, be one of the additions made to the item we have just noticed. The sentence has many counterparts. It is one of a number, each to the effect that something or other is more than the sum of its parts. Minds, brains, organisms of all kinds, and assorted revered institutions or entities are subjects of them. Is there any more dismal bundle of sentences, any that are more guaranteed to make the heart fall, to inspire a desire to think about something else or be fast asleep?

What seems to be the case with all such declarations is that they resolve into mere truisms of no import on the one hand, and palpable falsehoods on the other, with very little remainder of any interest.[11] One of the truisms is that a whole has properties lacked by its parts. Yes, indeed. The Thames or the Potomac is wet and does flow, and none of the molecules of which it is composed is wet or flows. To take a very different example, the Republican Party can take decisions at its conference that can be taken by no member. Is it not true of *everything* that has parts that it is more than the sum of them in this sense? Is the particular truism about society of any use to Conservatism? By itself it is of no use whatever, since it specifies no particular property of the whole of society, let alone recommends that property successfully and shows it to be owed to or perserved by Conservatism.

So too with another truism, that something has certain properties as part of a whole, or when it is part of a whole, which it would lack if it were not part of that whole. Certainly if I take my scissors apart, so that I am left with two halves and a bolt, neither half will do what it did before. It will not in a certain way cut paper. Nor will a quarterback for the Jets have the property of remaining upright long enough to throw forward passes in the absence of help from other members of the team. What we need and typically do not get, when this truism by itself is applied to society by Conservatives, is some real content and argument. What is it that I am supposed to be in virtue of being in society, and what has Conservatism got to do with it? I was, until it was privatized, a happy commuter on that gift to society, the 24 bus, but this is not what Conservatives can be taken to have in mind.

As for the falsehoods, one sample is this: that we cannot describe the behaviour of a whole by describing all the behaviour of all its parts. Certainly a regiment, mob or choir may be described as doing things, and things that would not be done but for the fact of people being together, but that is not to say that its action cannot be fully described by enumerating the actions of the individuals in it. Several other falsehoods, like this one, give evidence of the mysterious charm, felt by some, of the idea that there exists some little wonder of a fact not too distantly related to $2+2=5$, or maybe, with a following wind, 7.

If we do not try to hear a great deal in it, a great deal that can be distinguished from it, and to which we are coming, what we have in the utterance that a society is more than the sum of its parts is therefore a bit of loose talk which comes to nothing much. It is not, alas, peculiar to Conservatives.

Those Conservatives who do go in for it also go in for something else. It is an inclination in the direction of saying that society consists in more than members, classes, generations, government, law, religion, other institutions, customs and so on as ordinarily understood – the things that are the stock-in-trade of the mundane sociologist. A society, it is intimated, involves something in addition to all this. It involves that spirit which infuses state, hearth, sepulchres and altars, that which abides mystically in mother-country and father-land, that which not only speaks in its own voice but expresses its personality and will.

This is not exactly the irritating proposition at which we have just looked, that society is more than the sum of its parts. Nor is it exactly the proposition that society has, in addition to its mundane parts, a spiritual part. Rather, what we are offered is the temptation to think, if what is offered is clear enough to be a thought, that *a society is a somehow personal or spiritual entity in various ways mundane or with various mundane parts*. We are invited to contemplate, or anyway nudged in the direction of contemplating, if one is to be allowed to speak out plainly in the midst of all this decorous intoning, that a society is a person. How could it be that something *personal* in the intended way was not a *person*?

Such a view, as it gives one a mild and unpolitical satisfaction to record, has been carried to its unembarrassed climacteric not in the English language, but another. The view when declaimed as something like a literal truth is owned by Germans. It is identified with their national period of Romanticism, with what philosophers call Absolute Idealism, and above all with the ramified works of the egregious Georg Wilhelm Friedrich Hegel, 1770–1831. For him, a society is indeed a person, most superior when of Teutonic character, and somehow related to a yet more sublime character, Herr *Geist*. The latter gent is ultimate Spirit or Mind, very supranational, and also known as Freedom, Rationality and the Absolute. English and American Conservatives ask to be excused from subscribing to Hegel's declarativeness, and of course the elevation of the *volk*, the state-worship and the concentration camps to which it might be thought to have contributed something. They ask that we should consider only their lesser intimation. Let us do that.

What conclusions are thought to follow from the intimation that society is a personal entity in various ways mundane? Well, we should not be quick to announce shortcomings of our state or society, let alone set about alterations with a will, since to do so would be to do more than to concern ourselves with a mere system, contrivance, set of laws and institutions as ordinarily understood. We are to conclude of the state, says Burke, 'that no man should approach to look into its defects or corruptions but with due caution; that he should never dream of beginning its reformation by its subversion; that he should approach to the faults of the state as to the wounds of a father, with pious awe and trembling solicitude'.[12] Roger Scruton, although he may discern the state or nation to be of the other gender, gives the same advice. We are to see revolution as unthinkable: 'it is like murdering a sick mother out of impatience to snatch some rumoured infant from her womb'.[13]

No doubt an author – I here speak of myself – is under some duty to take seriously what he finds before himself when he chooses to consider a subject and invites others to spend time with him. The duty, in the case of this part of Conservatism having to do with state, society or nation as personal, is onerous. To my mind metaphysics is one thing, which continues to attract a good philosopher or two, and political metaphysics another thing. I beg to be let off lightly. The state is not personal, of the order of a person. That is one fact. Another is that we can have no relations to it of the kind we have to persons. That is impossible for anyone not touched with dementia.

What presumably is really in question is an exhortation that *we should attempt to feel and act towards our societies* as if *they were personal*, that we should in our feelings and actions enter into a kind of pretence that will be good for us, or anyway good for somebody. What is to be said of that? Let me be brief again. Such an exhortation is not exclusive to Conservatives. When they offer it, furthermore, they must be taken to have in mind a particular kind of society and state. Their words do not convey what this is. They are not at all inclined to urge pious awe and trembling solicitude on the members of all societies and the subjects of all states. With respect to some sick mothers, they have not been reluctant to have some rumoured infants snatched from their wombs. Mother Russia comes to mind.

We can get back into a better temper, and come to something that must seem more promising, in the proposition that *a society is a thing which has grown rather than been constructed*. It is, whether or not it is a primaeval contract or whatever, more like a tree than a clock. Or, as members of the New Right would no doubt have preferred to say, more like a tree than a cash-dispensing machine. That is, it is not the case that a society can properly be regarded as having been devised and constructed by some limited group of workmen, constructed according to some antecedent plan or blueprint. That proposition is none the worse for falling short of the idea that society is *alive*, that it has a life distinct from the lives of its members – which idea may be left behind in the care of Anthony Quinton, who, as a glance back (p. 152) will show, is somewhat less fastidious in this matter than others.

All of the passages given above might be thought, perhaps a bit carelessly, to contain this proposition that a society is not an artifact, or anyway not an artifact of an ordinary kind. Is the proposition of use in identifying Conservatism? Let us in charity say that it is not – that not all or even too many Conservatives believe it, and that others than Conservatives do believe it. That is fortunate for the Conservative tradition since, if the proposition is taken in the intended sense, it is false. If it is closer to the facts to say of many societies, including the British and American, that they have developed and not been constructed, it is certainly closer to the facts to say that Soviet society has indeed been constructed. It was done by Lenin, Stalin *et al*.

What then of what must really be in question, the idea that

Conservatism is distinguished by the different declaration that *societies ought to be allowed to develop,* that *they ought not to be constructed*? This is the best thing we have happened on so far. Still, it is of no great use, indeed no use at all, in identifying Conservatism. The reason for this is like others we have encountered before, first of all in connection with change and reform. It is very clear that Conservatism opposes some possible unconstructed societies, supports some possible constructed societies. In fact it opposes some actual unconstructed societies and supports some actual constructed ones. It is arguable that in the course of imperialism it has tried to manufacture some societies to its taste, and had pretty good success. American Conservatism has done this in South America.

The fundamental fact of the matter is that Conservatism is in favour of unconstructed societies that have a certain character or certain features, societies possessing Conservative property-freedom and lacking a certain social and civil freedom. It is also for such constructed societies. As it happens, many unconstructed societies have the approved features, and a number of constructed ones, above all Lenin's, have lacked them. That does not affect the plain truth that we get no mark of Conservatism in any amount of metaphor and simile, however breathed into and over, to the effect that it is only in favour of societies left to grow.

There is a closely related theme having to do with trees and cash-dispensing machines. It has to do with the fact that serious alteration of the first destroys them, and such alteration of the second does not in the same way destroy them. That is, to separate the roots from the tree destroys it – there is no ordinary possibility of reassembling the tree. Nor can we put a limb back on. To separate parts of the machine does not in this sense destroy it – there *is* precisely the possibility of reassembling it. The theme in question is this: *societies which are tree-like must not be subjected to serious alteration, since this destroys them.*

Let us suppose that what it is for a society to be tree-like, in literal terms, is for it to be such that certain changes to it will end it. What there is thereafter will never be the same as before. Perhaps we can conceive in greater detail of such societies, and specify the fatal changes. Let us suppose, further, what is uncertain, that there *are* such societies.

Are Conservatives, whatever they say, committed to or inclined to the proposition that all such societies must be protected from serious alteration and thus destruction? Very certainly they are not, for reasons we know, and noticed a moment ago, having to do with their passion for a *kind* of society. Further, there would be a kind of irrationality in any such position, since it is not far from the absurd proposition that radical change, *any* radical change in *any* circumstance, must be for the worse. Perfectly clearly, there are conceivable societies that ought, if they existed, to be destroyed. Indeed, there are *actual* societies that ought to be destroyed – ought to be subjected, if they can be, to the serious alteration which will guarantee that what comes after will never be the same as before. South Africa was such a society. There I speak for myself, but it must be as true of Conservatives that they are in favour of certain destructions. There is no great need for illustration, let alone petty illustration, but Margaret Thatcher provides one. She did for a time reiterate the intention to make it impossible that a society should ever return to the degree of fairness which was true of it before her election. There was to be no more socialism.

We have by no means come to the end of currents that can be distinguished in the stream of Conservative rhetoric about the organic society. Indeed we have not come to the end of the currents visible in the passages quoted earlier. One is the idea noticed at the beginning of our inquiry, to the effect that *an individual's identity or nature depends on society* (pp. 12 ff). Anthony Quinton appears to take this as of great importance to the Conservative principle of organicism. It is of no greater value here in clarifying Conservatism than it was in the context of talk about change and reform.

As for Burke, part of what he says (p. 184) might be brought into the clarity of literalness by supposing that he is singing the praises of, among other things, a society that is *natural in the sense of being informed by a certain system of inheritance*. What is to be said here, in part, is that commitment to a certain property-system does indeed distinguish Conservatism, as we know. We get no further distinction in Burke's verbiage. To recommend that property-system as natural is to make as little contribution as do those others who have recourse to talk of what is natural with respect to their various subject-matters. What is natural, to be brief, is what actually happens, from which it does not follow that it ought to, or else it is what ought to happen, which is what was to be proved. Certainly we do not get the *rationale* of Conservatism here, nor anywhere else in what is said of the organic society.

It is perhaps worth adding that there are more ways than one in which we can have generations linked together and thus save ourselves from being little better than the flies of a summer. We might have a society not so given over to the low concerns of deals in pepper, coffee, callico or tobacco, and the bequeathing of the proceeds to offspring, and a continuous chain of governments to go with it. We might have generations – there have been, are, and will be such societies – linked by something at least as impressive, an ideal or struggle or culture, and not to be confused with some large phantom called Society and born of dismal rhetoric.

Burke also touches on what is separable from the notion of the state or society as a personal entity in various ways mundane. That is the different notion of *a society as ordained by God*, and not itself to be confused with Him. In the quoted passage, no doubt in order to raise the tone, Burke chooses to refer only to *the invisible world*. Elsewhere he is more plain-spoken: 'God willed the state.'[14] We had better not interfere with it then. F. J. C. Hearnshaw is as explicit and in his book speaks of society not only as existing by the will of God but continually directed and guided by Him.[15] American Conservatives of the Fundamentalist persuasion outdo Hearnshaw easily. No doubt Senator Goldwater had their support when he said that 'the laws of God, and of nature, have no dateline. The principles on which the Conservative political position is based have been established by a process that has nothing to do with the social, economic and political landscape that changes from decade to decade and century to century.'[16]

We can content ourselves here with the thought that Anthony Quinton has a decent success in his endeavour to distinguish a non-religious from a religious tradition in Conservative thought and feeling. It is not essential to any Conservatism that it have dealings with the invisible world and our Creator, or subscribe to the truths which have no dateline.

Roger Scruton is engaged in flights rather more Hegelian than most Conservatives of the English language (p. 151). If we put these aside, there remains the recommendation that *it is an end in itself, a thing of not merely instrumental value, that a citizen be on friendly terms with his state*. These terms, otherwise described, are terms of patriotic subordination. The citizen accepts his obligation to be ruled by his large friend. The citizen is not over-impressed, either, by the way in which he himself and his fellow citizens vote (pp. 125, 142). This stuff is not common among Conservatives, and understandably disquieting to some of them. It cannot be that the Conservative tradition is to be identified with the proposition that citizens are to be on such terms of friendship with *any* state.

Still other organic thoughts are to the effect that a society supports a member as a living body supports a part, that as members of a society we do or should co-operate with one another, that societies stand in other analogies to families than we have noticed, that there is no real class conflict, that we ought to have some society of harmony without class conflict, that our membership of a society gives meaning to our lives, that we can feel some identification with the pasts of our societies. There is also the thought that each nation is a distinctive organism, with its own peculiar institutions, and the notably unpersuasive contention of a relativistic kind that the Conservative is committed to his own society but has no conception, no theory at all, of how societies in general ought to be (p. 39).

Most of this, as it stands, is not peculiar to Conservatism, as a moment's investigation of various other ideologies will establish. It conceals rather than reveals certain commitments of Conservatism. None of it has to detain us. There remain some Conservative themes about society that can be looked at by themselves – admittedly it is possible to put them in such a way that they become characteristic parts of the orotundity about organicism, but there is no need to do that.

The first theme, plainly put, is that Conservatives support the traditional society, or, better, what is traditional in a society. This generality is perhaps separable from the more metaphysical idea lately looked at, that societies ought to be allowed to develop and ought not to be constructed. However, the generality *cannot* be separated from, and indeed is a fundamental part of, the yet more accommodating proposition that we began by considering, that Conservatism is against change (p. 1). As will be expected, there is an inescapable objection to attempting to identify Conservatism by way of the generality. Conservatism does not have allegiance to all traditional societies, or to all that is traditional in a society.

Shall we then ask if there are *particular* traditions in society that do have the support only of Conservatives or more support from Conservatives than from other political traditions? Well, we know the answer is yes. Conservatism supports certain economic traditions having to do with private property, certain traditions of opposition to social and civil freedoms, and certain traditions of government. What can more usefully be asked, rather, is whether there are other particular traditions, of a social character, which are uniquely supported or more strongly supported by Conservatives. The Conservative, as Hearnshaw tells us, takes it as one of his soundest maxims that 'unless it is necessary to change, it is necessary not to change'. In particular he stands for the necessity of 'the universal and permanent things of life; for the ancient traditions of the race; for the fundamental laws of his people'.[17]

It comes to mind to wonder if Conservatism is distinguished by its feelings for or commitment to what can be called the dominant racial and cultural group within a society, or perhaps several dominant racial and cultural groups. Such a group will be large, and one which is central to the history and in some sense the origins of the society, perhaps a group whose history can be said, without too much damage to the truth, to be *the* history of the society. It will also be the group, if there is but one dominant group, whose own language is the official language of the society, and whose culture is most pervasive and is in some sense accredited. It owns the public holidays and has the streets named after its departed generals and great and good personages. Such a group, finally, will at least be perceived as of a distinct race.

It comes to mind to wonder, more especially, if Conservatism is to be identified with particular attitudes to others than the dominant racial and cultural group or groups within a society, a want of sympathy for them, or prejudices against them.[18] For example, is Conservatism more anti-semitic than other political traditions?

Burke, in forecasting the doom to fall on France as a result of its revolution, insists that the result will not be an equal society. 'Believe me, Sir, those who attempt to level, never equalize.' There will be a new nobility. He is consistent with one of his habits in what he says of that new class. 'The next generation of the nobility will resemble the artificers and clowns, and money-jobbers, usurers, and Jews, who will be always their fellows, sometimes their masters.'[19] Conor Cruise O'Brien appends a footnote to this passage, a footnote in which he says the best he can for Burke as anti-semite.

In his writings on the Revolution Burke's frequent references to Jews are almost invariably slighting or hostile, but he distinguishes between classes of Jews: 'We have in London very respectable persons of the Jewish nation, whom we will keep, but we have of the same tribe others of a very different description – housebreakers and receivers of stolen goods, and forgers of paper currency, more than we can conveniently hang.'

Perhaps that distinguishes Burke from those who say, when they are under a little suspicion, that some of their best friends are Jews, but it is not what you might call an entire exculpation.

To come up to date quickly, and to put aside German and French Conservatism, and Fascism, and Fascist remnants in Britain, there has been a noticeable ambiguity in some writing of the New Right. Scruton again:

> ... while it is a long-standing principle of British law that the fomentation of hatred (and hence of racial hatred) is a serious criminal offence, it is not clear that illiberal sentiments have to be forms of hatred, nor that they should be treated in the high-handed way that is calculated to make them become so. On the contrary, they are sentiments which seem to arise inevitably from social consciousness: they involve natural prejudice, and a desire for the company of one's own kind. That is hardly sufficient ground to condemn them as 'racist', or to invoke against them those frivolous fulminations which have been aptly described as 'death camp chic'.[20]

I take it that the persons who engage in the chic in question are those whom other Conservatives describe as merely fashionable liberals – persons sometimes identified as inclined to the modishness of Hampstead, a salubrious part of London once thought to be enlightened in politics. In speaking of racial exclusiveness and indeed racism, they may connect it in a way with Dachau and Buchenwald. That they speak truth is not to be allowed to excuse them. Whatever they are charged with, I would rather be of their number than to have been able to use the odious description with which the passage ends. There are things about which it is not near to decent to be obscure.

There is less obscurity about the existence of Conservative attitudes in America and Britain to people of other than white skins. American Conservatives have been as faithful as history has allowed to their ancestors in the American South, the Old South, those defenders of slavery. Their accommodation to racial tolerance has been like their accommodation to democracy, which is to say unwilling. The British Empire, which is not unreasonably regarded as a work of Conservatism, is not memorable for its colour-blindness. It is not memorable, more importantly, for any success in perceiving the humanity and culture of those who were subjected to colonialism.

The New Right's contribution to this history of colour prejudice has been significant. To speak again of Britain, it has not been just the National Front, when taking time off from its thuggery, who have perceived that good sense requires that blacks be sent back where they came from. John Casey, who sits well forward in a circle of culture-thinkers in the University of Cambridge, comes to much the same conclusion, couching it in a usage of greater dignity. If we are to deal with the problem of preserving our traditions, then 'the only radical policy that would stand a chance of success is repatriation ... The alternative ... would be retrospectively to alter the legal status of the coloured immigrant community, so that its members become guest-workers ...'[21]

There is also Anthony Flew, a philosopher, once the tribune of the atheists and now giving rather more time to other causes. Our endeavour must be to offer non-white immigrants two alternatives, the first of which is spoken of as the object of the exercise and might be thought to pose them some difficulties. '... the object of the exercise ... is ... so to assimilate our immigrants that they become English or Scots or Welsh who just happen to have skins of a minority colour ... Those who want to remain Bangladeshi ought to be planning ... to be returning to Bangladesh.'[22]

There is, too, Enoch Powell, MP, who once offered, with what is sometimes called his characteristic integrity, to serve as 'Minister of Repatriation'. His earlier announcements on race had sometimes been exemplary, if not such as to make for trustworthy prediction. 'I have set and always will set my face like flint against making any difference between one citizen of this country and another on grounds of his origin.'[23] That announcement in 1964 was followed, four years later, when he was offering his services as Minister for Repatriation, by speeches of a certain character. In one, he conveyed that unfortunately he had no right to refrain from stirring up a little racial hatred.[24] This was accomplished by retailing a story to the effect that an elderly English lady, an old-age pensioner, after refusing to rent rooms to coloured immigrants, had excreta put through her letter-box and was followed in the street by chanting piccaninnies. Powell went on to discharge his responsibility further by considering the prospect of further coloured immigration and the possible result. 'Like the Roman, I seem to see "the river Tiber foaming with much blood".'

The tone of this, whose truth was never established, was reported to have been too much for his leader, Edward Heath, to his credit, and Powell lost his position in the Shadow Cabinet of the Conservative Party. That is one point. Another and a larger point is that the speeches in question were made by an acute and successful politician, a former Minister of Health, and he judged them to be speeches that had a chance of advancing his ambitions within the Conservative Party, in particular his ambition to lead it. They were speeches owed in part to a judgement of the susceptibilities and principles of Conservatives.

We have some relevant evidence, then, and there is more to be had, but *are* Conservatives in general, as against the general run of supporters of other political traditions, more for a dominant racial and cultural group or groups, in the ways of feeling in question, and more against what we can call minority groups? An answer must be qualified by remembering that not all Conservatives are within dominant groups in the given sense, and not all members of such groups are Conservatives. Further, there is the qualification that Conservatives are not against all those in minority groups, and certainly are against some members of dominant groups. They may have good words to say for minority entrepreneurs, as entrepreneurs, or those individuals who know their station and its duties. They are not keen on, say, persons of good family who have abandoned state, hearth, sepulchres and altars for socialism or some other heresy. In saying they are not keen, I mean, of course that they have attitudes to them over and above political disagreement.

Still, if we limit ourselves to the United States and Britain, and like places, it is undeniable that the written traditions of Conservatism in question are more given to denigration and rejection of minorities than the like traditions of their opponents. There is no Jew-baiting or anything relevantly like it in the work of John Stuart Mill or the democratic socialist Richard Tawney. It is a sad fact that Marx, although Jewish, is justly described as an anti-semite.[25] That does not much affect the general fact that the written traditions of the Left have been greatly more free of prejudice than the Conservative.

There is a lesser and qualified truth, but a truth, about American and British traditions of Conservatism taken as including not only writing but also practice. The truth about practice must accommodate the fact of Disraeli, known to some Conservatives as their Hebrew Conjurer, and the inclusion of Jews in governments of the New Right, and the existence of immigration restrictions having to do with race in the policies of non-Conservative governments. But it can indeed accommodate these things. Given the fact that very many members of dominant racial and cultural groups are likely to have long been beneficiaries and upholders of Conservative property-freedom, and therefore are in any case more to the taste of Conservatives, and that Conservatives take themselves with some reason to have arranged the way of life into which minority groups do not choose to fit, this conclusion as to practice as against theory can hardly be contentious.

If we widen our horizons and take in, say, the Communist societies, matters are complicated by national habits of other than a political kind, and also considerations within international relations, but there are related truths. It requires a certain vulnerability to propaganda of several sorts to suppose that contemporary Marxism and contemporary Communism are anti-semitic movements. Whatever the failings of Soviet governments at certain times, Marxism and Communism are by comparison free of that grim taint. They are free of racial prejudice generally.

These propositions about Conservatism both in theory and practice, having to do with dominant groups, are more useful in distinguishing it than anything about the organic society. They are important, despite the fact that they must be used with some caution. One reason for caution has to do with the qualifications about group membership noticed above. A second reason is that support for dominant groups within such societies as the American and British is not always easy to separate from support for an economic system – Conservative property-freedom and what is connected with it. A third reason, consistent with what was said of the toleration of minorities in Marxist and indeed all ideologies of the Left, is that there are disagreeable group-feelings not only among Conservatives but elsewhere in human life.

We do here add something of significance to the characterization of Conservatism. We add something, certainly, that puts in question its humanity in a particular way, and is hardly touched by what Conservatives have long been inclined to say about *noblesse oblige*, their concern for and obligations to the lower orders. We add something which is not to be confused with the fact that Conservatives, like others, disagree with their political opponents, and may do so passionately. It is one thing to disagree politically or morally, indeed to be condescending about arguments, and another to stigmatize, to engage in kinds of condescension to groups and classes, to fail to accord respect to those who are different. If it were possible, in considering the range of cultural traditions, to see some as richer or higher, they would none the less remain inferior if informed by certain kinds of vicious feeling. T. S. Eliot is not made decent in his prejudice by the worth of his poetry.[26]

A word or two needs to be said about Conservative attitudes not to a dominant racial and cultural group, or to racial and cultural minorities, but to what Burke seems to have had roughly in mind, or to have anticipated, in speaking of a swinish multitude.[27] This, under the name given to it by many later Conservatives and others in the nineteenth century, is *the mass*, and is taken to owe much of its nature to the Industrial Revolution. It contains many members of a society's dominant racial and cultural group, but certainly not all. It may also contain members of the minority groups we have had in mind, or some of them.

It is to be defined, in so far as it can be, partly in terms of its particular culture, its culture in a narrow sense. Englishmen and -women are of one general or common culture, a culture in the sense in which we have lately been using the term, mainly in virtue of a shared language and a shared national history. They are of various different cultures in the narrow sense mainly in virtue of different educations and other opportunities. It is cultures in the narrow sense that are often associated with social class or occupation, and may be described as working-class, bourgeois, low-brow, high, scientific, suburban, Californian and so on.

Burke's swinish multitude casts learning into the mire, and treads it under its hoofs. Thomas Carlyle about a century later, as already noticed, characterizes more or less the same large aggregate of persons as capable of no more than being drilled into rudimentary order by their superiors (p. 47). Carlyle takes them to raise a pressing problem of closer definition. 'Who is slave, and eternally appointed to be governed ... is a matter we must try to settle once and for all.'[28]

George Santayana, a philosopher who spent some decades at Harvard University before retreating to Europe, had a certain amount to say in 1922 of the condition of the mass. Hopelessly out of the running in the race for wealth, it drifts into squalor, crawls into whatever tenement is cheapest, seeks the society in which least effort is demanded, drifts into some syndicated servitude or some great migration, and may end up

under the shadow of railway bridges, breweries, and gas-works, where the blear lights of a public-house peer through the rain at every corner, and offer ... the one remaining joy in life; for joy is not to be mentioned in the same breath as the female prowling by the door, hardly less befuddled and bedraggled than the lurching idlers whom she endeavours to entice ...[29]

Robert Nisbet casts some further and less dramatic light. 'I use "masses" in the sense in which we find it in the writings of Ortega y Gasset and Hannah Arendt, among many others: an aggregate discernible less by numbers than its lack of internal social structure, integrating tradition, and shared moral values.'[30]

It would be consonant with what was noticed earlier, Conservatism's disinclination to democracy and to social freedoms, and its inclination to a true natural aristocracy and authoritarianism, to suppose that it is also distinguished by something between condescension and revulsion with respect to what we may persist in calling the mass. Still, there are reasons not to struggle to establish such a feeling as a defining feature of Conservatism. If Conservatives often enough appear to be in the grips of a particularly virulent antipathy to the mass, they are not alone in having such unhappy feelings about it, or above appealing to its prejudices.

There are liberals, certainly, who are not charmed by past or present vulgarity. Mill, in his attachment to the higher rather than the lower pleasures, provides enough of an example.[31] There are also revolutionaries – perhaps they are the typical revolutionaries – whose arguments for revolution contain no such thing as serious celebration of the working class, but rather an argument which begins from precisely a conviction of its present degradation. Its awfulness, not its nobility, is what would make action necessary if there were a chance of success. I cannot say myself, despite having no affection for the stuff of Burke, Carlyle, Santayana and friends, that I am any enthusiast for the culture of the people.

No doubt the attitudes to that culture discernible in the tradition of Conservatism owe something to both guilt and apprehension. As for the guilt, there can be no question but that Conservatism, in virtue of features we know it to have, has made a signal contribution to the creation and entrenchment of the culture it abhors. One of these features, which will not be overlooked by any recent observer of England, is its commitment to a certain market-freedom (cf p. 94). As for apprehension, apprehension of possible political changes which would not be profitable or agreeable, it is likely to give a certain cast to feelings about the mass, those who would benefit from such changes. Given these particular and unique sources, it is no doubt also true that Conservative attitudes to the multitude could be differentiated from other wants of enthusiasm. But that endeavour can be left to others.

Let us leave too the endeavour of coming to a firm judgement on at least two other matters, the attachment of Conservatism to institutions of religion, notably an established church for a society, and to a certain morality.

The Church of England may once have been, but certainly is no longer, the Tory Party at prayer. There are not enough persons at prayer to make the idea compelling. To touch on a related consideration, Burke was determined and confident that religion would continue to play its immemorial role of long-term reassurance.

> The body of the people must not find the principles of natural subordination by art rooted out of their minds. They must respect that property of which they cannot partake. They must labour to obtain what by labour can be obtained; and when they find, as they commonly do, the success disproportioned to the endeavour, they must be taught their consolation in the final proportions of eternal justice.[32]

The successors of Burke are not so confident that religion's offer of the consolation of immortality is placating, and have less attachment to those whose business it is to offer it. Also, their attachment is strained by dissident bishops and socialist priests.

As for morality, or morality having to do with private life, Conservatism has always had a good deal to say of it. The New Right, in one of its regiments, zealously sought to reform, among others, those women among us who are not absolutely committed to the idea that all conceptions ought to be followed by births. Not all Conservatives share this moral zeal.

No doubt there are qualified truths to be arrived at in these two neighbourhoods, institutions of religion and customary morality. The same is the case, incidentally, if the thing can be incidental, with respect to feminism. Patrick Jenkin, MP, not too long before his services as Secretary of State for Social Services came to an end, spoke for many of his party. 'Quite frankly, I don't think that mothers have the same right to work as fathers do. If the Good Lord had intended us to have equal rights to go out to work, he wouldn't have created man and woman. These are biological facts.'[33] Let us save our energies for what is greatly more fundamental to Conservatism; its thoughts and feelings having to do with equality generally.

Equality

As the Dodo said in *Alice in Wonderland*, '*Everybody* has won, and *all* must have prizes.'

Milton Friedman

John Adams reported in one of his letters in 1814 that he had seen fifty infants in one room of the Hospital of Foundlings in Paris and that they were all different. He went on to declare that what other Americans had to say about equality was as gross a fraud as ever was practised by such un-American persons as monks, Druids, Brahmins, priests of the immortal Lama, and, worse than all of them, the self-styled philosophers of the French Revolution.[1] To Burke, what was put about by those philosophers on the subject of equality, and by their English sympathizers, was no better. It was 'that monstrous fiction, which, by inspiring false ideas and vain expectations into men destined to travel in the obscure walk of laborious life, serves only to aggravate and embitter that real inequality, which it never can remove ...'[2]

Burke had been inoculated against the monstrous fiction of our common equality, of course, by his formative experience of encountering the true and wonderful superiority of some of us, in the person of Marie Antoinette before she came to the throne of France, and before the Revolution overturned it.

It is now sixteen or seventeen years since I saw the queen of France, then the dauphiness, at Versailles; and surely never lighted on this orb, which she hardly seemed to touch, a more delightful vision. I saw her just above the horizon, decorating and cheering the elevated sphere she just began to move in – glittering like the morning-star, full of life, and splendour, and joy. Oh! What a revolution! and what an heart must I have, to contemplate without emotion that elevation and that fall![3]

There has not been much change nor much lull in Conservative denunciations of egalitarianism in a wide sense, or, what comes to the same thing, the politics of the Left. Egalitarianism in this sense consists in a number of political traditions opposed to Conservatism and having to do with equality, notably democratic socialism and what in the United States was called liberalism before the name was claimed by the New Right.

Peregrine Worsthorne in one of his pieces lets us know, in the words of its heading, *How Egalitarianism Breeds Robbery and Yobbery*, the latter being a form of loutishness peculiar to the British Isles in the time of Thatcher governments.[4] David Cooper begins his book by recalling that just as Tom Wolfe, on whom we are to depend for a judgement of abstract painting, was given the revelation at a particular moment that there is nothing to it, so he himself, while ploughing through yet another egalitarian tract, experienced a similar moment of perception about doctrines of equality. There is nothing in them. They lack, among other things, any real unity.[5]

William Letwin, bringing the resources of the Dismal Science to bear on his endeavour, finds that egalitarians of all shades are pursuing a fetish and will-o'-the-wisp, are deluded by loose thinking and utopian fantasies, and that their convictions suffer from internal contradictions and rest on no coherent intellectual foundation. There is no determinate ideal of equality.[6] Keith Joseph and his collaborator Jonathan Sumption discover in their contribution to restrained political philosophy that egalitarianism consists in muddled thinking, logical incoherence, semantic chicanery, screens of verbiage, emotional arguments, confusions that a few moments of honest reflection can save us from, and misconceptions of facts. The last-mentioned misconceptions prevent egalitarians from seeing, for example, that the entrepreneurial manufacturer of electric cocktail shakers may have spent many penniless years seeking a market for his goods before being rewarded by prosperity.[7]

To revert, as Burke would have us, to our betters, there is also His Royal Highness the Duke of Edinburgh, whose book of speeches Mr Worsthorne had in mind when he wrote in another column that the idea of equality had become so broadly comical a notion as now to be open even to royal jocularity, jocularity by a royal house which takes care not to offend. In his *Men, Machines and Sacred Cows*, in between thoughts on fuel technology and on being a vice-chancellor in Wales, and not far from the truth that horses are horses, the Duke provides a reflection on helicopters. Are they socially unjust because only a few people own one? Since there is not an equality of helicopters, are they all to be put down? His Royal Highness evidently feels he has not come to the end of his flying time.[8]

This tutorial refrain on the part of Conservatives will come as no surprise, given what we have learned already of their politics: its opposition to social and civil freedoms, its commitment to private property and to incentives, its coolness about democracy and resistance to more of it, its condescension to the swinish multitude and awareness of a natural aristocracy, its inclination to racism and the like. (Those facts about Conservatism far outweigh what we also noticed, that it has sometimes prided itself on a fact of legal equality having to do with property-freedom.) Still, the general refrain against equality is distinct from all of that. To see what use it is to us in characterizing Conservatism, and what justice there is in it, we need to do one thing at a time. We need to look at each of a rather large number of propositions about equality, or families of propositions. Most of them are assigned by Conservatives to their various opponents within the Left. They themselves take different views of them.

The first has to do with what can be called *natural equality*, and is much belaboured by Conservatives. It, unlike most of the other propositions in question, is a factual proposition, something true or false in the plain sense, and hence not recommendatory or evaluative.

What John Adams declared to be so false was 'that all men are born with equal powers and faculties, to equal influence in society, to equal property and advantages through life'.[9] His countryman, James Fenimore Cooper, carried forward the same cause of enlightenment some years later. 'Men are not born equals, physically, since one has a good constitution, another a bad; one is handsome, another ugly; one white, another black.'[10]

Anthony Flew reminds us, similarly, that Abraham Lincoln was right in his comment on the Declaration of Independence. 'The authors of that notable instrument,' said Lincoln, 'did not intend to declare all men equal in all respects. They did not mean to say that all men were equal in colour, size, intellect, moral development, or social capacity.' Anthony Flew also feels called upon to remind us that Thomas Jefferson had the suspicion that the blacks are inferior to the whites in the endowments both of body and mind. Indeed he voiced other opinions about them, which our author in his delicacy is reluctant to repeat, but to which he can bring himself to allude.[11] William Letwin seeks to instruct us by denying that we are all genetically equal, and by letting us know that genetic differences give rise to this or that eye colour, more acute hearing, and such oddities as vestigial fingers.[12] Keith Joseph points out that in fact we have different wants, and that 'it should not be necessary to devote much space to making the point that mankind is not, in fact, as homogenous as the egalitarian must perforce assume'.[13]

It is plain indeed that it is not just one proposition of natural equality that Conservatives assign to the Left but many, an awful bundle. One that is implied, and may have had some small effect on innocent readers, would require for its truth that we have been living a dream. It is that each of us really is the same, down to the colour of our identical non-vestigial fingers. Another is that we are equal in fundamental respects, perhaps what can be called powers and faculties. A third is that we have the same wants, not generally speaking but nearly at the level of wants as specific as those for electric cocktail shakers. A fourth is to the effect that there are no significant racial differences between us.

Four questions arise about this collection. The first is whether the propositions are true. The answer, at any rate if we take a little care in their formulation, particularly the last, is that they are false. The second question is whether they are in fact asserted by the opponents of Conservatives. The short answer is that they are not. (A longer answer would take into account another of Anthony Flew's useful reminders, that the US Department of Labor said in 1965 that blacks are potentially as intelligent as whites.[14] Jefferson, we are to understand, knew better.) The third question, more interesting, is whether *other* propositions about equality, recommendatory ones, do in fact depend on or presuppose any of the various absurdities. Are egalitarians in fact committed to some of this nonsense? We shall keep that question in mind in what follows. The fourth question, in fact separable from the third, is why Conservatives have been so persistent in assigning propositions of natural equality to their opponents. We shall come to an answer to that.

A second sort of proposition about equality has to do with what can be called, for want of a better name, *spiritual equality*. Here again we have a factual claim, something true or false in the ordinary sense – or anyway an approximation to such a thing. In one form, perhaps the oldest, it is to the effect that we are equal in the sight of God. In Russell Kirk's brief summation, we will be equal when we turn up for the Last Judgement.[15] Is it this fact, perhaps, that is implied in the Declaration of Independence when it is asserted that we are all 'created equal'? In another form, owed to the philosophy of Immanuel Kant, the proposition is to the effect that each of us is an end-in-itself, something that has value for itself and not as a means to anything else. In yet another form the proposition is plainer, and to the effect that each of us is alike in having autonomy, which is to say a unique capability of deciding things for ourselves, including right and wrong. This is not far from the assertion of Free Will.

Conservatives assign such a conviction to their opponents, but are quick to point out that it does not distinguish them. Conservatives themselves, they declare, do not disdain the conviction, but share it. (Burke, by the way, avows something related, which is 'the true moral equality' of mankind, consisting in the fact that we can all be happy in following virtue in whatever condition of life we find ourselves, however disagreeable.[16]) Conservatives are not much less quick to point out, and with good reason, that what follows from such a conviction is not too troublesome to them.

One thing that follows from it, and indeed is not wholly distinguishable from it, is the recommendation of *equal respect*: each of us is to be accorded an equal respect. In Kant's version, which is fundamental to his moral philosophy, and has the name of the Categorical Imperative, it is this: 'Act in such a way that you always treat humanity, whether in your own person or the person of any other, never simply as a means, but always at the same time as an end.' Not a great deal of sense has ever been made of that except perhaps by transforming it into something mundane, perhaps that no one's interests should be left out of consideration in deciding on a course of action. No one should be forgotten about, whether or not one concludes that anything should actually be done to their benefit (cf p. 85).

It may be supposed, differently, that what follows from our spiritual equality is a principle of *equal political rights*. That is, each of us ought to have certain political rights. These may be summed up as the right to have a government to which one consents, the right to minimally democratic government. Perhaps Colonel Rainborough asserted no more than this in the Putney Debates after the English Civil War.

Really I think that the poorest he that is in England hath a life to live as the greatest he; and therefore truly, Sir, I think it is clear, that every man that is to live under a government ought first by his own consent to put himself under that government;

and I do believe that the poorest man in England is not at all bound to that government that he hath not had a voice to put himself under.[17]

If Conservatives do not have the splendid Colonel Rainborough among their favourite people, they are, as remarked, willing at least to tolerate the recommendation of equal political rights as conceived and also the recommendation of equal respect – at any rate equal respect when also minimally conceived. More to the point, they can insist with some reason that in Britain, America and like places, we have at least for the most part acted on these recommendations. Here, they say, is no cause for dispute. Egalitarianism is in this respect morally truistic. They add, further, that in none of this is there a principle which could justify anything in sight of the depradations of the socialist state. Here there is no fundamental principle of equality, with such a thing taken to be a principle which would sanction robbing the rich to give to the poor.

Various questions arise, including the question of to what extent egalitarians of the several kinds do depend on spiritual equality and whether they assert, about respect and democracy, only what is said to follow from it. But let us press on, and look to a proposition which is in one respect similar. It is the principle of *formal equality*. It is owed to Aristotle, and is that we are to treat like cases alike, and different cases differently. Or, as comes to much the same thing, we are to treat cases differently only if we are able to cite a relevant difference between them. The principle might, at first sight, seem to be something useful to various adversaries of Conservatism. This is so since it might be thought to have the upshot, say, that equally hungry people are to have equal amounts of food, and unequally hungry people to have unequal amounts.

As Conservatives have been fond of pointing out, however, the principle by itself has no such unique outcome.[18] We can abide by it as readily by treating alike those who are hungry to whatever extent *and* can pay for food, and treating differently those who are hungry and cannot pay. Indeed, South Africans can abide by it by treating blacks one way, the way they do, and whites in another way, the way they do. All depends on how cases or people are compared, or what is taken to be relevant in considering them. The principle says nothing at all about that. As has often been remarked, the principle reduces to no more than an injunction to be consistent, to follow some rule or other, however dismal. Here there is no foundation for any politics in particular. Nor, by the way, has anything different been supposed by any egalitarian who has come to my notice. Conservatives are inclined to pay a little attention to R. H. Tawney's book *Equality*, indeed to accord it a kind of respect. So far as I can recall, Formal Equality does not get into it. Aristotle appears only with respect to his well-known views on the fittingness of the institution of slavery.

Is there hope for the Left in *equality before the law*? This is not a matter of the Last Judgement but, so to speak, the lower courts. If any egalitarian thought so, he is disabused of the idea by a line of Conservatives from Burke onwards. He is rightly disabused unless he or she is under the misapprehension that the equality in question consists in an equal freedom to use and be defended by the law, a freedom in the sense settled earlier (p. 84). Equality before the law, as Conservatives and indeed the usual run of lawyers have it, consists only in every citizen being subject to law, none having special privileges or disabilities in terms of what the law says, all being able to have a fair trial – where none of that involves a reassurance for someone who cannot raise the legal fees or, say, has been engaged in a miners' strike which a government has enthused its judges to punish.

It is the Conservatives, rather, who can be most enthusiastic about their support of equality before the law, as traditionally understood, and fit it effectively into their politics. You may wonder, of course, if equality before the law might be construed differently, so as to be something that might enter uniquely into a politics different from Conservatism. Indeed it might – as equal respect might – but let us leave that aside for a time. Our present concern is the outlook of Conservatives with respect to equality, and it behoves us for a while to stick to their terms.

What of *equality of opportunity*? What is said here, first, is that there is a plain kind of it that is defensible. This kind of equality of opportunity arose out of the French Revolution, and is the only mitigation of that disaster. What is in question was conveyed by the demand for '*la carrière ouverte aux talents*', which is to say open competition for certain careers, with the results of the competition being determined not by rank, money or family connections but by talent or ability shown in a common entrance examination. This, say Conservatives, with whatever degree of good faith is consistent with their traditional commitment to an old boy network, and a true natural aristocracy, is all right by us. This is not something owned by our opponents. In this instance too egalitarianism as something both sane and distinctive evaporates.

However, say Conservatives, our opponents now go further, for two reasons. First, they have discovered a flat contradiction in their doctrines. Plain equality of opportunity does not contribute to a larger and vaguer thing they also want, so far unmentioned. It does not contribute to what can be called *an equal society*, but to its opposite. For a start, it contributes to greatly unequal material rewards, attached to the higher careers. As Keith Joseph reminds us, all Englishmen in the early years of this century had an equal opportunity of founding Morris Motors, but only one of them did, and he became very rich.

Second, there is the question of who gets the greater material rewards, the members of what social or economic class. Our opponents explain this, say Conservatives, by the proposition that some of the persons taking the common examinations can still be said to have unequal and better opportunities. They are better prepared for the exams, by having come from better schools or from homes with books in them. What we now need, they say, is equal opportunity where that is not only the common exams but equal preparation for taking them, equally good backgrounds. This *fair equality of opportunity*, they suppose, is right in itself and also *will* issue in or contribute to an equal society.

Conservatives have much to say against fair equality of opportunity. One thing is that a good background isn't really needed for success. After all, as Keith Joseph informs us, the founder of Morris Motors was of humble origins, little education, no inherited wealth, and began life as a bicycle repairer. It is no surprise to our informant, we may assume, that he didn't do quite as well as John D. Rockefeller, since, as we are also informed, *he* was brought up by a quack medicine salesman and a mother who used regularly to tie him to a post and beat him.[19]

That is not all. If we were really to secure equal backgrounds for all those entering the common examinations, we should have to follow Plato's mad dream and abolish the family. We should have to have, as William Letwin sees, infant-farms. That is not all either. There is a yet madder dream to which thinking about equal backgrounds leads.

Is it not the case that some of the candidates from the local infant-farm would do better than others in the exams? Some would have greater powers of concentration. They, surely, could thereby be said to have a greater opportunity of success. Something would have to be done about this, to secure equal powers of concentration. We would need to secure *real equality of opportunity*. The least that Conservatives have to say against this proposal is that egalitarians have now collapsed the distinction with which they began, and on which all this reflection depends if it is to be sensible. That is the distinction between opportunity on the one hand and talent or ability on the other. What we have is a mess, says David Cooper, and a perversion of that original good thought about opportunity at the time of the French Revolution.[20]

Nor are we near to finished with the disgraces of the Left. Another of them, according to Conservatives, is that it involves the injunction to treat everyone alike – *equality of treatment*. But that, as Lincoln Allison is not alone in supposing, would issue in our dimwittedly providing the same amount and kind of food for all, irrespective of age, size, nature of work, appetite, vegetarianism and so on. He might have added, with the Duke of Edinburgh in mind, that equality of treatment commits us to helicopters for everybody, or at any rate equal flight time. Further, if we try to find something more sensible for the egalitarian to say about treatment, we come up with too many possibilities: allocating food according to work, and so on. There is no particular policy that can be called the egalitarian approach. Conservatives have in fact spent too much time arguing against egalitarianism, and not quite enough to see what is true, that there is nothing much to argue against.[21]

William Letwin sees what he takes to be yet more fundamental difficulties with equality of treatment, and in particular the utopian recommendation of *equal pay*. Is the latter the recommendation of the same rate of pay per hour of work? If so, and if workers happen to work different numbers of hours per week, some will be paid more than others per week. Is the idea, maybe, that everyone should get the same annual pay? If so, and if they work different numbers of weeks per year, as may happen for one reason or another, they will again be getting unequal weekly pay. We have it, in short, that any equality of pay for a particular period of time involves inequality of pay for another period of time. To set out to produce equality is necessarily to produce inequality as well. Egalitarianism is no less than internally incoherent.[22]

We have so far looked at natural equality, spiritual equality, equal respect of a kind, equal political rights of a kind, formal equality, equality before the law, equal opportunity, fair equality of opportunity, real equality of opportunity, equal treatment – of which more will be said – and equal pay. In none of these, it seems, whatever else is to be said of them, have we found a *fundamental* principle or set of principles of equality, a foundation for the politics of the Left. That would be something that is distinctive and defensible, and takes first importance – it underlies all other egalitarian principles, rules and maxims, which are brought into conformity with it. It may well entail the rejection of one or more of them. Is such a thing to be found in a large and impressive book which has a very great deal to say of equality, in a number of ways, John Rawls's *A Theory of Justice*?

It advocates some principles of justice, ranked in a certain way, and also an argument for those principles of justice as ranked. The argument has to do with an imaginary social contract, one which is made by contractors who are ignorant of their personal advantages, and we may excuse ourselves from considering it.[23] It has been belaboured by some Conservatives, and something will be said of the belabouring later (p. 219). The principles, by one method of counting them, are three in number. They can be considered independently of the argument for them.

The first is the Principle of Liberty, that in our societies each of us is to have as much liberty as is consistent with each other member having as much. There is to be an equality of liberty at the highest possible level. The second principle is that there is to be a kind of equality of opportunity to get into any positions of favourable socio-economic inequality in our societies. The third is the Principle of Socio-Economic Differences. It is to the effect that we can have, and indeed we must have, only exactly as much socio-economic inequality as has a certain recommendation. It must, on one reading of the principle, make the worst-off members of the society better-off than they would be without that degree of inequality. As for the ranking, the first principle takes precedence over the second, and the second takes precedence over the third. A society should aim first at realizing the first principle, and preserve it rather than the others in any case of conflict – it cannot be that any departure from greatest equal liberty is justified by a gain either in opportunity or in connection with socio-economic advantages. So with the second principle in relation to the third.

Do we here have a unifying set of principles for egalitarianism? Do we here have the means of bringing order into the egalitarian muddle? Conservatives have not been much alarmed at the threat, for what seems to me good reason, better reason than they themselves have supplied in any clear way.

What are the liberties or rights of which the first principle speaks? It is curious, and can be a source of reassurance in itself, that Rawls does not use many of his 607 pages in specifying them. In fact he does not use one. What we are told is not much more than this:

> The basic liberties of citizens are, roughly speaking, political liberty (the right to vote and be eligible for public office) together with freedom of speech and assembly; liberty of conscience and freedom of thought; freedom of the person along with the right to hold (personal) property; and freedom from arbitrary arrest and seizure as defined by the concept of the rule of law.[24]

No doubt it can be assumed, from the rest of *A Theory of Justice*, that Rawls is not himself inclined to that particular right to hold personal property that enters into Conservative property-freedom. Still, what he says leaves it open to others to interpret 'the right to hold (personal) property' as they like, and he does not declare himself against Conservative property-freedom or argue against it. Something the same is true, to mention something else of importance, of the mentioned political liberty. It is left open to interpretation. It must also be reassuring to Conservatives that what we are to have in each case is only maximum equal *liberties or rights*, which is not to say freedoms in the sense settled earlier in our inquiry (p. 84). Conservatives have long allowed that we ought to be equal in those, which does not come near to committing them to the proposition that we ought to be *equally able*, say, to acquire private property.

That is not the only ground for reassurance. A second one is that if the kind of equality of opportunity favoured by Conservatives is a more minimal one than is favoured by Rawls, his is not out of sight. The third and main ground has to do with the Principle of Socio-Economic Differences. What it says, to repeat, is that we are permitted and obliged to have any inequalities of wealth, power and standing that improve the lot of the worst-off: the worst-off are made better-off than they would be without them. The fact of the matter is that until more is said we have no idea of what society we get from the operation of this principle.

Imagine a society where socio-economic goods are shared in perfect equality, and it is also true that allowing some members to become rich, powerful and respected, relatively speaking, would result (a) in others being worse-off in absolute terms than they were before, or (b) would leave them exactly as they were before in absolute terms. The Difference Principle certainly has it that the society is to persist in its perfect egalitarianism if (a) is true. Depending on a common reading of the principle, it has the same consequence if (b) is true – we are not to allow some members to become better-off even if no members become worse-off.

On the other hand, imagine a society where there are such socio-economic differences as have not so far been dreamed of in the philosophy of the New Right. The distance between rich and poor is greater than the distance between the estate of a prince or the ranch of an oil billionaire and the cardboard box of someone whom inheritance and the market have not favoured. Imagine that it is also true of this society that any reduction of the well-being of those on the top of the pile would in some degree worsen or would not improve the lot of those on the bottom. The Difference Principle certainly has it that the society is to persist in its perfect inegalitarianism on the first assumption and perhaps on the second.

A Theory of Justice does not give attention to the essential and battered question of whether our actual societies are like the first or the second of these two imagined ones, or like others in between. It does not open the question of whether incentives in terms of income and wealth are necessary, or to what extent they are necessary, if the worst-off are to be better-off than they would be without them. As a consequence, to come to the conclusion of these reflections, it is entirely open to Conservatives to embrace this fundamental part of the given theory of justice, then to argue that great incentives *are* necessary, and thus emerge with a justification of society as it is. It is open to Conservatives to conclude, yet again, that egalitarianism in so far as it advocates something sensible, advocates no more than they do. What the egalitarianism of Rawls comes to, when the argument about incentives is added to it, is something about which we can all fall into contented agreement.

There is something more distinctive, another idea or sort of idea on which the Left is said to attempt to rely. It was in view earlier when 'the equal society' was mentioned (p. 176). It was in view too when we earlier touched on social and civil freedoms (p. 119). It calls for more attention than anything considered so far, as do the many objections made to it. It is sometimes called equality of results or outcome, sometimes equality of condition or circumstances. Let us settle on *equality of results*.

Keith Joseph uses the term and speaks of 'what the great Victorian jurisprudent Dicey pithily describes as "the equalization of advantages among individuals possessed of unequal means for their attainment" '. It is what is sought, we are told, by those who wish to organize societies so as to make all men equal, and perhaps part of what was in the mind of the alarming priest John Ball in the Peasants' Revolt of 1381. 'Things never shall go well in England,' he said, 'until all things are in common and all of us are of one condition.' It is the principle, I take it, which brings to the mind of several of our Conservatives a recollection of Procrustes – 'a celebrated Greek highwayman who used to tie travellers to a bed, lopping off their legs if they were too long for the bed and stretching their spines if they were too short for it'.[25] Procrustes now, of course, is the welfare state, also known as the ever-expanding state machine, the central enforcer of equality of outcome, and so on.

For Milton Friedman, apparently not too mindful of the history of the twentieth century, let alone the Peasants' Revolt, equality of results is something that has emerged in the United States in recent decades.

> In some intellectual circles the desirability of equality of outcome has become an article of religious faith: everyone should finish the race at the same time. As the Dodo said in *Alice in Wonderland*, '*Everybody* has won, and *all* must have prizes.' ... 'Fair shares for all' is the modern slogan that has replaced Karl Marx's 'To each according to his needs, from each according to his ability.'[26]

William Letwin is distracted by his obligation to deal with the confusions of egalitarians, and so cannot spend much time on bringing equality of results into clear view. He has it in mind, perhaps, when he concerns himself with the bare injunction 'All persons should be equal', and speaks of the idea that people should be equal in respect of certain general and vital goods. These include income, wealth, esteem, political power, legal rights and education.[27]

Conservatives, in attending to equality of results, generally have Tawney's *Equality* in mind. He speaks of 'equality ... of circumstances, institutions and manner of life', and equality of 'social and economic environment'. To seek this equality is to allow that individuals may differ profoundly in capacity and character, but to maintain that 'they are equally entitled as human beings to consideration and respect, and that the well-being of a society is likely to be increased if it so plans its organization that, whether their powers are great or small, all its members may be equally enabled to make the best of such powers as they possess'. The idea is that it is regrettable 'that different sections of a community should be distinguished from each other by sharp differences of economic status, environment, education, culture and habit of life'. The idea, again, is that

> it is the mark of a civilized society to aim at eliminating such inequalities as have their source not in individual differences, but in its own organization, and that individual differences, which are a source of social energy, are more likely to ripen and find expression if social inequalities are, as far as practicable, diminished.[28]

It is noticeable that what is called equality of results is not wholly distinct from equality of treatment (p. 177), at any rate if we think of equality of treatment in something other than the idiotically specific way proposed by some Conservatives. We can take it, that is, as having to do with treatment or provision more *generally* conceived – education rather than this or that specific sort of education, travel rather than rides in helicopters, and so on. The close relation between equality of results and equality of treatment is reflected in what Conservatives say of it. Procrustes, if he can be thought about in terms of results, certainly goes in for treatment.

What can be argued to distinguish equality of results and equality of treatment is that the aim of treatment does indeed concern only *activity* with respect to people, what is done to or for them: giving them food, giving them pay, providing the means to travel. This treatment or provision is itself to be equal, whatever is the case with the upshot of the treatment or provision. The aim of equality of results can rather be taken to be about, fundamentally, the upshot of treatment or provision, which treatment or provision *may* be other than equal. What we are to be equal in is satisfaction of hunger, or what comes of our weekly pay, or comes of such aids as old-age pensions. One thing that brings equality of results and equality of treatment into connection, despite what has just been said, is that it is very often an ideal policy, and yet more often the only practicable or realistic policy, to pursue the end of equality of results by the means of equalities of treatment.

It is to be allowed, perhaps, that Tawney did not succeed in giving fully effective and economical expression to his recommendation of equality of results. Let us take it to be this:

> A society should seek to secure, as far as is practicable, lives of equal satisfaction for all its members. It should do this by in general seeking to secure, as far as practicable, equality of income and wealth, equality of respect (where that is other than what was noticed earlier, the mere recognition of the relevance of all persons), equal political and legal freedoms, the full development of the different potentials of individuals by means of education and in work, equality in housing and environment, equal medical care and provision for old age.

That is not so clear and determinate a recommendation as we might like, but it will do for our present purposes – which are to look at Conservative objections to equality of results, of which there is no shortage. Almost all Conservatives, certainly, take what we have as sufficiently clear and determinate so as to be open to conclusive refutation. They do not put it aside as unclear, but as wrong.

The first of ten objections – here it will be worthwhile being thorough – has to do with the actual facts of inequality in our societies and hence the appositeness or urgency of the recommendation. George Saintsbury, who is introduced to us by Russell Kirk as, among other things, a genial essayist, could bluffly inform Englishmen of the lower orders, about 1922, that they had no great need to think about inequality. 'The goods you have are real, and the ills, in all probability and experience, to a large extent imaginary – certainly bearable in that they have been borne.'[29] Keith Joseph, on a page where he accepts the need for a welfare floor or minimum standard of living, so that the poor do not sink into a condition in which they would prefer well-fed slavery to indigent freedom, also has something to say about the facts or extent of poverty.

> A family is poor if it cannot afford to eat. It is not poor if it cannot afford endless smokes and it does not become poor by the mere fact that other people can afford them. A person who enjoys a standard of living equal to that of a mediaeval baron cannot be described as poor for the sole reason that he has chanced to be born into a society where the great majority can live like mediaeval kings.

By any absolute standard there is very little poverty in Britain today.[30]

Those words were written for a book that was published in 1979, the first year of Thatcher governments. They would not, I fancy, have been written a decade later, after the immiseration of a part of the British people by those governments, with the writer of the words to the fore in them. But that is not the main point, which has as much to do with the genial essayist.

Nor is the main point one that might be attempted by the miserably impoverished, that the tradition of Conservatism is not unique, but has liars in it. They would be the counterparts of those of their opponents who assert that there is no way whatever in which socialist governments restrict freedom or engage in coercion. The lie on the part of these contemplated Conservatives, to put it one clear way, would be this proposition: the inequality which exists in Britain or America is such that if people generally had a real awareness of its reality, they would not take it to be sufficient to make the recommendation of equality of results arguable or worth consideration – that is, the facts of inequality are such that people if well-informed would not feel any need to go on to consider what else can be said against the recommendation of equality of results, since they would take its presupposition about significant factual inequality to be a fiction.

It is not of much importance whether either our genial essayist or our politician is a liar by this test, or whether such a proposition is their main concern. The main point is that their words, when taken to suggest the given proposition, as they can be, are not worthy of consideration. They are not made so, certainly, by any additional content having to do with absolute and relative deprivation or the fact that mediaeval barons lacked vacuum cleaners or anything else. Nor would we do justice to the large tradition of Conservatism by assigning the offensively false proposition to it.

There is not much more need to linger over a second kind of objection, if that is what it is, to equality of results. This consists in *ad hominem* retorts of two kinds, the first kind directed to proponents of this equality who are themselves decently well-off. We shall believe them to be honest enthusiasts, says Burke, and not as we now think them, cheats and deceivers, when we see them throwing their own goods into common.[31] Paul Elmer More, he who wished Rockefeller not to be mealy-mouthed about shooting strikers, knows that if you

hear a man talking overmuch of egalitarianism, you can be pretty
sure he will be slippery or dishonourable in his personal transactions;
Anthony Flew reminds us that Bernard Shaw, although in favour of
equal incomes, remained representative of his prosperous co-believers
in not surrendering the part of his own income that was above
average; Milton Friedman points out that while equality of outcome
has become almost an article of religious faith among intellectuals,
from whom he evidently distinguishes himself, they do not go off to
live in a commune or a kibbutz.[32]

The *ad hominem* objections of the second kind are directed to those
who would themselves benefit from a society's securing something
like equality of results. They, in their present unfortunate state, are
charged with the sin of envy. The support for equality of results by
these possible beneficiaries is the product of their resentment of those
who are better-off. Keith Joseph, it is true, has a word to say for
envy, or for the possibility that it can be aroused or increased in
people. 'Envy is capable of serving the valuable function of making
the rich moderate their habits for fear of arousing it. It is because of
the existence of envy that one does not drive Rolls-Royces through
the slums of Naples ...'[33] Most of his fellow-Conservatives, while no
doubt as prudent, are more given to pointing to envy as a means of
discrediting the idea of equality under consideration. Elsewhere in
his reflections, our politician perhaps moves towards joining them,
announcing as he does that equality of results has something to do
with naked class interests.[34]

We shall eventually come round to the general subject of naked
class interests. For the moment, not greatly more is required with
respect to the *ad hominem* retorts than the reminder that it is widely
accepted that the worth of a recommendation or principle is not a
function of the personal morality, whatever that may be, of its
proponents or its beneficiaries. Also, there is the consideration that
a well-heeled proponent of equality of results, while advocating
that unachieved state of things, can in the meantime properly be
restrained in disposing of his income by certain comparisons –
between himself and his family on the one hand, and, on the other
hand, *others* than the worst-off. His sons and daughters and their
aspirations can be regarded in terms of more comparisons than one.
Proponents of equality of results need not be saints, and certainly
cannot be called to that condition by Burke and his epigoni.

To reflect for a moment on the envy of the poor, the extent and
gravity of their sin is unclear. I take it that the lawful owner of a Rolls-

Royce is not to be much abused for envying the now advantaged state of the Neapolitan who stole it from him. What he mainly feels, he will say, is something different from envy, which is not merely righteous but rightful indignation. And, if he also owns up to envy, he is unlikely to be so paralysed with guilt as to come back from his holiday a broken man. He will in fact not take his envy as greatly culpable.

So – not all resentment having to do with the advantages of another person is to be much condemned. In particular, if it is the case that we ought to achieve equality of results, and hence that our present unequal distributions are wrong, and, furthermore, that the wealth of some enters into the explanation of the poverty of others, then the feelings to which the poor are subject are partly in the category of rightful indignation, and, for the rest, the envy is human enough. Even if it is supposed there is a connection between principles and certain feelings of those who hold them, Conservatives cannot effectively proceed from the charge of envy to the refutation of the principle of equality of results. They must rather proceed in a way which is not easy, and not of the greatest use to them, from a refutation of the principle to the slight addendum of a charge of culpable envy.

A third sort of response to equality of results is that a society which achieved it would not be natural, as egalitarians are supposed to believe, but unnatural. Alas there have been egalitarians given to such stuff, in some cases conjoining it with a certain optimism. Matthew Arnold of the Victorian Age was one of these: 'A system founded on inequality is against nature, and, in the long run, breaks down.'[35] No doubt he has some twentieth-century successors who also have recourse to the ineffective notion of the natural. Let us leave them to contend in some safe place with those of their Conservative opponents who are also attracted to the notion.

There are a good many of the latter, as we already know. They are, differently described, advocates of the organic society, or certain of the societies named as organic. They advocate certain of the societies that have grown rather than been constructed, certain of the societies which are tree-like and which alteration will destroy, and also the society of inheritance (pp. 152–60). Advocacy of any of them is what might be called naturalistic opposition to the principle of equality of results. Let us not go back to all that. To recall the essential fact about attempts to defend a thing as natural, it appears that the defence reduces to claiming that the thing exists or will persist if not interfered with, from which nothing follows as to whether it ought to exist or persist, or the defence is already the judgement that the thing ought to exist or persist, which is the conclusion for which support is supposed to be being provided. Resort to the natural is the resort of a true believer who finds himself short of an actual argument.

A fourth objection to equality of results is the regular one that a society will in fact never achieve it. We earlier noticed in another connection (p. 161) Burke's dictum about what egalitarians, when they get into power, do with it.

> Believe me, Sir, those who attempt to level, never equalize. In all societies, consisting of various descriptions of citizens, some description must be uppermost. The levellers therefore only change and pervert the natural order of things; they load the edifice of a society, by setting up in the air what the solidity of the structure requires to be on the ground.[36]

To take a later example, from 1948, there is Bernard Braine's prescience in *Tory Democracy*. 'Within a very short space of time this new equality will have vanished into the mist. Some men will be rich, some will be poor. Some will be masters, some will be servants. A few will lead, the rest will follow.'[37]

A part of a reply to this sort of thing is that to achieve equality of results would not in fact be to achieve anarchism, where that is an absence of government. Nor would that be the aim. As Conservatives are all too ready to insist, as we shall see soon, equality of results could only be achieved by government, and hence through the inequality of power that all government involves, including fully democratic government. That inequality, however, is consistent with various fundamental equalities on the part of the governed and to some large extent the governors. The fact of government, too, whatever bureaucracy it involves, is consistent with an absence of such ascendant classes as now exist in our societies. As for Bernard Braine's certainty that there will always be the rich, it must come to mind that there do now exist societies, whatever else is to be said for or against them, which plainly are without a class of the rich as we know them. I trust that he can be brought to tolerate what has hitherto been thought to be a pretty firm proposition, that what is actual is possible.

To bring together two more small but persistent objections to the recommendation of equality of results, a fifth and sixth, Conservatives manage to suppose that the recommendation rests on the factual premise that we are all equal, and that acting on the recommendation would produce a terrible uniformity. The first idea, that the recommendation rests on one of the bundle of propositions about natural equality (p. 171), should not survive reading Tawney's sentences about our differences in capacity and character, our greater and smaller powers (p. 183). Whatever the recommendation rests on – and there is more to be said of this – it does not rest on some kind of blindness as to the actual differences between us.

Nor, in any fatal sense, would equality of results issue in uniformity. It is not, if English retains its sense, the proposal that *everyone should be made the same*. It is better described as the proposal that we should be equal in the worth of things rather than the things themselves, that we should have lives of equal value rather than the same lives. Having said that, it remains true that the proposal of equality of results is indeed the proposal of *equality* of income and wealth and so on, as far as is practicable. In another sense, then, it *is* the proposal that we have certain uniformities. To object to it as such, evidently, is to be engaged in this ungripping line of argument: the proposal of certain equalities or uniformities is mistaken because it proposes certain equalities or uniformities. Is there something else in the objection of uniformity? Is there something, incidentally, which takes into account the very real uniformities in our existing societies of inequality? Perhaps there is, but not enough to detain us.

We come now to what is a seventh and the most used set of Conservative objections to equality of results or the equal society. They will need little illustration. They are to the effect that equality of results is inconsistent with *freedom or liberty*, that we cannot have both, that such equality reduces, threatens or destroys freedom or liberty. We need to pay them somewhat less attention because we have in fact encountered them already, in other settings, differently expressed.

(A) One liberty-objection is that equality of results carries the risk of or issues in totalitarianism. We in fact encountered and took a view of something close to this objection in considering the argument, in our inquiry into Conservatism and freedom, that to abandon Conservative property-freedom and market-freedom is to run the risk of totalitarianism or be fated to succumb to it (pp. 112f). This latter claim as to the risk or result of not having Conservative economic freedoms is close to the objection that equality of results runs the risk of totalitarianism. This becomes clear as soon as it is supposed that giving up the Conservative economic freedoms is on the way to embracing the principle of equality of results. If that supposition is not quite true, it is certainly true that many of the serious adversaries of Conservatism, in opposing Conservative economic freedoms, do indeed propose and attempt to replace them with an equal society or something like it.

We concluded that giving up Conservative economic freedoms very definitely has not been shown to issue in totalitarianism. We can conclude now, by the same or similar arguments, that embracing equality of results would not necessarily issue in totalitarianism. The latter conclusion might be modified by our making further distinctions, but not upset. If the argument for the earlier conclusion was sound, as certainly it seemed to be, something like it is as effective here.

(B) We also considered, some way back, the closely related matter of whether Conservative economic freedoms can be recommended as securing or preserving what was called 'a liberal-democratic political order' (pp. 146–7). We drew two conclusions. The first was that Conservative economic freedoms do indeed serve as more effective means to the end of such a political order when it is defined as consisting in just those limited political and civil freedoms proposed by Conservatives, but that restricting such freedoms to those particular ones needs justifying. The second conclusion was that Conservative economic freedoms do not serve the end of 'a liberal-democratic political order' when that is taken to be a matter of greater and more widely supported political and civil freedoms.

We can as readily draw certain conclusions about a second liberty-objection to equality of results, that it conflicts with what can be called, 'a liberal-democratic political order'. We can readily allow, first, that the equal society or equality of results is *not* an effective means to, or does not contribute to, just the limited political and civil freedoms allowed or proposed by Conservatives. We can as readily argue, second, that the equal society or equality of results *can be* the effective means to or *can* contribute to greater political and civil freedoms. The short story, then, is that equality of results does not issue in what very many people do not want, and it may issue in what they do want. Equality of results does not lack but rather may have precisely the recommendation which Conservatives imply that it lacks.

(C) There is a third thing that equality of results may be said to have as a consequence, something that perhaps can be regarded as in between totalitarianism and just the sort of infringement we have

had in mind of political and civil freedoms. This too is at least close to
something noticed earlier (pp. 137 f). We noticed that Conservatives
are in fact not wholly opposed to revolution, but only to a kind of it.
They are well capable of contemplating revolution to overthrow
governments to which they are radically opposed, including governments of their own nations, notably governments which are excess-
ively democratic or have no reverence for private property. Burke
could contemplate a different sort of Cromwell, and Macaulay a
despotism that would save civilization. We may add Lord Salisbury,
who in 1883 had a fear, in particular, of the growing strength of the
trade unions. If England were to succumb to them, he wrote, 'we
would welcome the military despotism that should relieve us'.[38]

As will be clear enough, this third thing to be said of seeking
equality of results is that it will issue not in the totalitarianism of the
Left or any totalitarianism, but in an undemocratic regime of the
Right, most probably a military regime. Conservatives, partly because
of their determination to present themselves as good constitutionalists,
are unlikely actually to specify as a third liberty-objection to equality
of results that they themselves, or those who share their commitments,
and in fact are distinguished from them only by their uniforms, would
resist its achievement by resort to force and military government.
What they are reluctant to announce, however, is something which
they are capable of leaving in the air, indeed putting into the air.

It is evidently more of a threat than an objection of principle.
It is not, at least in the ordinary sense, a moral objection to equality
of results, but a grim prediction that the thing will be resisted by
force. The prediction, no doubt, has for good reason done more to
restrain ambitious socialist governments than any argument they
have had to meet. Our present concern *is* argument of principle.
What is to be said, then, is that no argument of principle against
equality of results is provided by saying that if a democratic argument
is lost, the loser will in the end reply with tanks.

(D) To turn instead to what can be regarded as an argument of
principle, it is provided for us by Robert Nozick, and beloved by
those who swear by him, or did for a time.[39] It stands in some relation,
which we need not look into, to the second liberty-objection to
equality of results. The argument is directed against more things
than equality of results, but certainly against that.

Contemplate the equal society, a society that has in fact achieved
equality of results. The distribution of goods, and the upshot of that
distribution, is just what is called for by the idea of equal results. The

pattern is in accord with that idea. For one thing, there is the required distribution of income and wealth. In the society there exists a basketball player, one Wilt Chamberlain. He is, as Professor Nozick explains, a great gate attraction, and makes a certain contract with his team. The result is that people cheerfully buy their ordinary tickets to games and also drop a separate twenty-five cents into a special box with his name on it. Wilt Chamberlain winds up, in one season, with $250,000, far greater than the average income. It gives him, too, far greater wealth than is had by others in what was the equal society. We are not to forget, and Professor Nozick is in no danger of letting us forget, about the fans, that 'Each of these persons *chose* to give twenty-five cents of their money to Chamberlain. They could have spent it on going to the movies, or on candy bars, or on copies of *Dissent* magazine, or of *Monthly Review*. But they all ... converged on giving it to Wilt Chamberlain in exchange for watching him play basketball.'

Nozick implies a good deal about all of this, and introduces some talk of justice that is likely to confuse matters. But his main purpose is clear enough. It is to assert that if the equal society or any like society is to be maintained, this must be done by infringing freedom or liberty. The fans must be stopped from making Wilt rich. To preserve the pattern of distribution in the equal society the liberty of both the fans and Wilt must be violated. 'Liberty,' we are to see, 'upsets patterns.' No such principle as that of equal results 'can be continuously realized without continuous interference in people's lives'.

Shall we join the thinkers of the New Right and some other suggestible persons in their awe of this argument? We need not rush.

We have a tolerable idea of what, in general, a freedom is. It is, in one manner of speaking, perhaps the most ordinary, *being able to act on a desire*. To have a freedom with respect to something is to have a certain power to do it or to get it (pp. 76, 84). There are, as we saw, and will see again, other ideas of freedom, but none that could alter our present line of reflection. It could be pursued exactly as well, although perhaps not as neatly, in terms of those other ideas and various supplements. To come to a first point, then, are all freedoms in the given sense powers that ought to be possessed, abilities that persons rightly possess? Very evidently not. I should not have, and my society does what it can to prevent my having, the power to harm others in certain ways. It strives to limit or indeed to destroy the freedom of the rapist, the car thief and, perhaps, the fraudulent broker.

Would the equal society, if by law it stopped the fans making Wilt rich, because of apprehensions about further developments, be affecting their freedom and his? Indeed it would. There is not the slightest doubt about that. But would it be wrong to do so? Would it be wrong to take steps, such as the one in question, to preserve itself as an equal society, one where private wealth does not result in closed wards in public hospitals? Would a democratic majority who voted for preserving what are of course the *freedoms* of that society be acting wrongfully? That is the only question of interest, of any interest whatever. In the political folk-tale we have before us, it is of course assumed that it would be wrong to infringe a freedom which would issue in the destruction of an equality or of certain freedoms, but *no reason at all* is given for that assumption. What we have is not an argument of any significance against equality of results, but rather a certain amount of persiflage.

There is the same conclusion if we turn our attention to the idea of liberty. What is a liberty? Well, it is at least natural to say that the fraudulent broker may unfortunately have been free to defraud the widows, but that he had no liberty to do so. A liberty, in this common way of speaking, is a freedom to which one is entitled, or better, a defensible or justified freedom. Would the equal society, if it ruled against Wilt's box for the twenty-five-cent pieces, be infringing his liberties and those of his admirers? Nozick says yes. Others say no. The trouble is that our professor, who is conducting this seminar, only *says* so, and does not explain in his folk-tale what entitles him to his usage.

Elsewhere in his book he is attracted to reflections on the subject of *rights*, which subject we have already noticed (p. 107). Such reflections lead to the idea that what the equal society must do, in order to maintain itself, is to violate the non-legal rights of the persons in question. But to say someone's non-legal rights to do something have been violated, if we leave out a certain amount of ancient or sacred obscurity, is to say something of this sort: as follows from some moral principle of worth, he ought to be able to do the thing. There is no avoiding the question of what the principle is, and of what is to be said for it. There is no argument on hand in the absence of answers.

What we have so far with respect to equality of results in connection with liberty, putting aside the military threat, is that this equality cannot be said to issue in totaliarianism, *does* contribute to our having political and civil freedoms which have a wide appeal, and is not to be put aside by way of the folk-tale. It is possible, on the basis of these and others of our reflections, to come to several summaries. Both of them demonstrate the inanity of supposing that there is a simple opposition between equality and freedom, and, perhaps more important, that either side in the dispute has the possibility of simply claiming that it is more virtuous with respect to freedom.

On the one hand, it would be absurd to say that equality of results would not conflict with or destroy certain freedoms. It is inescapable that any such programme or policy, like any legislation, will not only give powers to people but also reduce or take away powers from people, sometimes the same people (cf p. 83). A society which secured equality of income and wealth would in so doing go against Conservative property-freedom and very likely conservative market-freedom. Similar concessions, if that is what they are, need to be made with respect to every element in the conception of equality of results – with respect to education, for example (p. 183). Further, in so far as the point is a separate one, and as was granted in what was said of the 'liberal-democratic political order', equality of results would have an adverse effect on precisely those constrained political and civil freedoms which Conservatives allow. It would replace them or tend to replace them. *On the other hand*, to come to have an equal society would patently be to come to *have* certain freedoms. Nothing is clearer. It would be to come to have a property-freedom of a certain kind. Similar and more important propositions are indubitably true with respect to every element in the conception of equality of results. The equal society would give us freedom from kinds of disdain, freedom to work, and so on. Further, to revert to 'the liberal-democratic political order', in so far as the point is a separate one, equality of results would secure or contribute to political and civil freedoms greater than those supported by Conservatives.

So much for one summary. A second one makes use of our earlier categories of freedoms (p. 119).

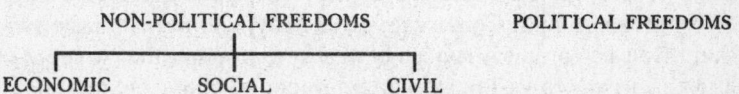

Equality of results, as we have conceived it, is itself nothing other than a matter of certain freedoms of all these kinds. It would secure certain freedoms in each category. With respect to economic freedoms, to give an example, it would no doubt allow for certain goods to be distributed by a market, not so many as Conservatives would like. With respect to social freedoms, it would secure freedom to have a job, and, with respect to civil freedoms, perhaps a considerable freedom of information. With respect to political freedoms it would secure greater democracy.

It is exactly as true, if we are charitable in connection with what is sufficient to count as a social freedom, that Conservatism can be said to secure freedoms of all the kinds. It provides for an extended market. A welfare-floor can be regarded, charitably, as a beginning on or a form of social freedom. Conservatism obviously secures lesser civil and political freedoms than would exist in a society of equality of results.

The fundamental questions, of course, are what in fact unites each of these two arrays of freedoms, the Left or egalitarian array and the Conservative array, and what can be said for and against each. An effective answer to the first or analytical question in each pair is essential to an effective answer to the second or evaluative question. An effective summation of what unites the Conservative array would be what we have been pursuing for some time, a rationale of Conservatism. Something will be said below of the rationale of the freedoms involved in equality of results – or, at least, something will be said of what Conservatives claim it to be (pp. 202 f).

Before leaving what we have been calling liberty-objections to the equal society, there is need for a little more repetition, of another sort. Believe me, there is need. Equality of results, it was said a moment ago, would involve freedom to work. Conservatives, whom we know pride themselves on not being quick to learn, will be prone to a certain reply. It is a denial that what is in question is properly called a freedom. So too with other elements of equality of results.

What indubitably is in question, as all must agree, since it is part of the definition of equality of results, is the securing of *a state of affairs where everyone, with some obvious exceptions, is in fact able to act on a desire, the desire to have a job.* Conservatives, as I say, will persist in the view that this is not properly spoken of as a freedom, and that to speak of it in this way is to seek to gain an improper advantage in argument. Indeed it is to be dishonest, to go in for the sort of thing to be expected of persons who are slippery or dishonourable in their personal trans-actions. That it is dishonest is said by Keith Joseph, in his role as moralist and linguist, at the end of the section in his book called 'Property is not Unfreedom'.[40] In a proper and honest way of speaking, we are to understand, freedom to work is no more than something like this: *a state of affairs consisting in the absence of legal barriers to getting a job, or the absence of coercion in this regard, or the absence of coercion by other specifiable individuals.* Hence, what our egalitarians are demanding, with respect to jobs, and what we are contemplating, is *more* than a freedom (cf pp. 84 f).

How tedious it all is. Suppose we take up the preferred usage. What we now say is that equality of results would secure (a) freedom to work, and (b) whatever else is needed in order to get a job. We call the latter thing something or other – power, means, real opportunity or whatever. We follow the same sort of distinction with every other item of equality of results – say in connection with housing and medical care. We then do the same with each item in the array of Conservative recommendations. *Nothing whatever* is affected with respect to the answers to the fundamental questions except their expression. They become: What unites the egalitarian array of freedoms and also powers or whatever, and what can be said for and against it? and What unites the Conservative array of freedoms and also powers or whatever, and what can be said against it? We will proceed in the simpler way in due course, but not just now.

We now leave behind liberty-objections to equality of results, or what can be called equal freedoms, and not too soon. We turn to an eighth kind of objection which often seems to be offered to all of the recommendation of equality of results, but, at least in the first instance, pertains only to part of it. The whole of the recommendation, to recall, is that so far as is practicable all members of a society should have equally satisfactory lives secured for the most part through equalities in income, wealth, respect, political and legal freedoms, housing, environment, medical care and provision for old age, and the full development of the different potentials of individuals by means of education and work (p. 183).

The objections to which we turn, at least in the first instance, are that to enforce equalities of income and wealth will somehow do more harm than good with respect to income and wealth. This has to do with the claim that such equalities deprive us of incentive. *Not* enforcing such equalities, and therefore allowing incentive, will somehow improve matters in terms of income and wealth. The objections, further, since typically they are offered as objections to the entire recommendation of equality of results, are presumably also to the effect that not enforcing equalities of income and wealth will somehow improve matters in terms of the other elements of the recommendation. There will be benefit, for example, in terms of respect and self-development.

We have already spent time with this kind of argument, having to do with incentive. We first considered whether it could be other than a piece of *theory*, as Conservatives wish it to be, and concluded it could not. That left open the possibility that it is a true piece of theory (pp. 29 f). Subsequently we looked at Conservative incentive arguments as based on a premise about human nature, and in particular our low or self-concerned natures (pp. 63 ff, 69 ff). Here we did not find what end-result it is that a system of incentives is supposed to have, whether described as 'economic well-being' or in some related way. A description of the end-result in terms of such economic totals as Gross National Product, it was remarked, is consistent with various distributions of goods. So too the description of it as a situation where everybody is better off. Finally we looked at incentive arguments as defences of Conservative property-freedom and market-freedom (pp. 100 ff). Our difficulty about the proposed end-result persisted, and was not resolved by considering the Hidden-Hand Vindication of Conservative economic freedoms, itself a form of incentive argument. Shall we do better now?

Keith Joseph declares on one page that the opulence of one's own way of life, in contrast to the drabness and squalor of others' lives, arouses one's feelings of guilt, but that to think that the opulence of the rich has anything to do with poverty is in fact to be emotional and subjective rather than logical and objective. On the next page, however, it comes over him that there is, on the contrary, a very good connection, one which is certainly to his taste.

> The relief of poverty has not in the past been thought to require an equal society and it is difficult to find any necessary connection between them today. On the contrary, everything in the experience of this country since the last war has combined to demonstrate that you cannot make the poor richer by making the rich poorer. You can only make the poor richer by making everyone richer including the rich.[41]

Harold Macmillan, for a time leader of the Conservative Party in Britain, was not of the New Right, and is to his credit not so definite. '... it is only by giving their heads to the strong and to the able that we shall ever have the means to provide real protection for the weak and for the old.'[42] Friedrich Hayek strikes a related if less concerned note.

> If today in the United States or Western Europe the relatively poor can have a car or a refrigerator, an airplane trip or a radio, at the cost of a reasonable part of their income, this was made possible because in the past others with larger incomes were able to spend on what was then a luxury. The path of advance is greatly eased by the fact that it has been trodden before. It is because scouts have found the goal that the road can be built for the less lucky or less energetic ... Even the poorest today owe their relative material well-being to the results of past inequality.[43]

William Letwin is keen to prove there is but a grain of truth in the Argument of Diminishing Marginal Utility. That is the argument for the view that the goal of the Utilitarians, sometimes called the Greatest Happiness of the Greatest Number, and less misleadingly called the Greatest Total Satisfaction, is served by an equal distribution of goods. According to the argument, if we have three similar persons on hand, and three English breakfasts, each of the persons will get less satisfaction from a second breakfast than a first, and still less from a third than a second – therefore, to secure the Greatest Total Satisfaction, we must see that each person gets one breakfast. For various reasons, according to Letwin, it doesn't work that way with incomes. In fact, to secure a more equal distribution of incomes would depress the absolute level of everyone's income, including the incomes of the badly-off.[44]

Milton Friedman, his fellow economist, is a little more cautious in his conclusion. The Conservative alternative to equality of results 'enables almost everyone, from top to bottom, to enjoy a fuller and richer life'.[45] Not everyone, but almost everyone. He also informs us why attempting to implement equality of results will not work, as it did not in Britain after the Second World War.

> The drive for equality failed for a ... fundamental reason. It went against one of the most basic instincts of all human beings. In the words of Adam Smith, 'the uniform, constant and uninterrupted effort of every man to better his conditions' – and, one may add, the condition of his children and his children's

children. When the law interferes with people's pursuit of their
own values, they will try to find a way round. They will evade
the law, they will break the law, or they will leave the country
... When the law contradicts what most people regard as moral
and proper, they will break the law – whether the law is enacted
in the name of a noble ideal such as equality or in the naked
interest of one group at the expense of another.[46]

Anthony Flew does not try to tell us why equality of results has
not been achieved, but does have feelings that it should not. There
is, he says, a strong case for concluding that

> if what you want is indeed to improve the absolute rather than
> the relative condition of the less and the least advantaged,
> then you should go for overall growth, rather than for those
> confiscatory taxes on the more advantaged which give so much
> satisfaction to procrusteans. Even if it is not strictly true – to
> borrow words used by President Kennedy in recommending
> across-the-board cuts in income taxes – that 'a rising tide lifts
> all boats', still it does make larger resources available for a
> possible transfer, whether voluntary or compulsory.[47]

Various related questions are raised by all of this, and they must
have brief answers. The answers taken together give an evaluation
of the given sort of Conservative objection to the equal society. They
also provide a response to the idea that we have come upon the
rationale of Conservatism in what is offered as an alternative to the
equal society, which is said to be one in which everyone is better-off.

(1) *Are incentives of greater income and wealth the only incentives, as
Conservatives in general seem to suppose?* Clearly they are not (pp. 73 f).
As against these extrinsic incentives, there are intrinsic incentives,
which are of at least as great importance to very many people in
many occupations and professions in our societies as they are. They
would be of greater effect in an equal society. They would compensate
greatly for the lack of greater economic incentives, whatever is said
in advance by those who are wedded to the results of extrinsic
incentives.

(2) *Would the equal society involve* no *incentives of greater income and
wealth?* That is not written into the recommendation, which specifies
that we are, *so far as is practicable*, to have equal income and wealth.
As for the question of how much greater a possible income must be

in order to serve as an incentive, we have no argument at all for what is assumed by Conservatives, that it must be large. It is worth adding that they commonly say that it is not the money that matters, but what it signifies, which is recognition or achievement. But it is wonderfully plain that a society might be of such a nature or such attitudes as to effectively confer recognition by only slightly greater incomes. If I alone among my peers was known to have a *higher* salary, or for that matter some significant speckled beads, that would do nicely for my morale.

(3) *Would those of us who have refrigerators and cars lack them, as Hayek declares, if our societies had in the past achieved equality of results?* To say the least, that is unproved, as are like propositions about the future. That our societies were not in the given way equal, and that we have the refrigerators and cars, is one thing. That if our societies had been different in the given way, we would not have them – that is another thing. But suppose, even, that it *is* true that avoiding equality of results has given us the items in question. The proposition is consistent with something else, that avoiding equality of results has also given us ongoing extreme poverty and of course ongoing immense inequality of fundamental kinds. The historical proposition is also consistent, by the way, with a car now being of nothing like the value of the car in which Hayek's scout made his forward progress.[48]

(4) *As the rich got richer, in the Britain of the New Right, did the poor get less poor?* No tolerable definitions of either group have the slightest chance of making the answer yes. As the rich got richer after 1979, the poor got poorer. Indeed, living in the time in question, with the facts impossible to overlook or manipulate, no Conservative said otherwise when in danger of hearing replies. Nor was this historical episode unique.

(5) *Is it established as a general truth that making the rich more rich makes the poor less poor?* Given only the history of Britain during the period of the New Right, no such generalization is conceivable. It is no surprise, and no doubt to their credit, that Milton Friedman cannot bring himself to say that further enriching the rich makes *all* groups better off, and that Anthony Flew falls notably short of saying the thing. Harold Macmillan too was honest.

(6) *Relatedly, does making the rich less rich make the poor poorer?* Given only another recent period of history, the history of Britain after World War Two up to 1979 and the rise of Conservative governments of the New Right, no such generalization is conceivable. This period

was one of which it was true that wealth was somewhat affected, and poverty was greatly and honourably reduced.

(7) *More precisely, is it established that it is only by having the incentives which go with Conservative economic freedoms – by having a society as remote as that from the equal society – that we can have the possibility of alleviating the condition of the badly-off?* It is notable that not even Conservatives can be found who specify or state plainly the extreme inequalities that are or would be involved in the fully-realized Conservative society, and argue that *those* equalities are or would be necessary to alleviating the condition of the badly-off.

(8) *Do Conservatives in fact believe, let alone prove or establish, a view of human nature from which it follows that the incentives which go with Conservative economic freedoms are required if there is to be economic progress?* It is more than difficult to suppose so (p. 65). It is one thing to argue, as Milton Friedman does, that Conservatives break the law in order to defend what they have, and quite another to take their behaviour as the inevitable result of an unchangeable human nature. They may be resolute, and not so much given to law and order in this instance as in others, but they are no more the creatures of a curious biological fate here than elsewhere in their lives. If they took themselves to be so, they would be deprived of other arguments of which they are fond, and indeed, as we shall come to see, of what some of them suggest is their rationale.

(9) *Suppose the argument about Diminishing Marginal Utility fails – does that show that the equalities of treatment called for by the principle of equality of results or the equal society will not achieve their goal?* Certainly not, since the egalitarian goal never was the Utilitarian one of the largest possible total of satisfaction. It has long been clear to all but a sorry rump of Utilitarians, and one or two others, perhaps including William Letwin, that the Greatest Total Satisfaction is not identical with justice, and more particularly with equality of results. Many of those who support the latter ideal do so precisely because it does not have the traditional fatal weakness of Utilitarianism, which is unfairness. There is no reason to confuse egalitarianism or the Left with Utilitarianism.

(10) *If we accepted, as our Conservative spokesmen imply, that the goal of their own politics may be the one which equality of results is supposed not to achieve – everybody being better-off – would that give us a rationale underlying Conservatism?* It would not. One reason is that there are many conceivable moves from our present distribution of incomes and wealth that would make everybody better off. Suppose we now have five

occupational classes of greatly different incomes, with the top class getting ten times the income of the bottom. One move that would make everybody better-off would be to increase the income of the top class very little indeed, and the incomes of the other classes more, and differently in each case, with the income of the bottom class lifted dramatically – the upshot being an approximation to equal incomes among the classes. It does not need saying that no Conservative, living or dead, would support that. It is inescapable, then, that the rationale of Conservatism is not given by talk of making everybody better-off (cf p. 70). To put much the same point differently, any Conservative who does want everyone better-off also wants, consistently with that, to have us very unequally better-off. What is it that justifies that?

It is of interest in itself that when Conservatives are not faced with talk of equality, not on guard, they tend to specify their own end-result as other than everybody better off. When they are not concerned with an egalitarian challenge, their end-result is spoken of, mainly, in terms of individuals having the rewards of their labour or of the risks they take with their money. Things are only different when the moral challenge of egalitarianism needs to be met. Here is a related question of interest. If God, weary of our confusions about human nature, opened the heavens and dispensed the truth that greater income and wealth do *not* serve as incentives, would Conservatives be a whit less resolute in justification and defence of what they have? We have no need of another divine dispensation for the answer.

(11) *Do Conservatives, in their commitment to incentives taken by itself, somehow reveal a rationale?* Well, for a start, are Conservatives devoted to the same sort of incentives for the badly-off as for the well-off? Consistency requires of them some movement in this direction, and such movement sometimes suits them. But, as the excellently egalitarian John Baker points out, there is a large division in their feelings.[49] If a production manager would get only £5,000 more per annum if promoted to managing director, and someone has the idea that that is not an incentive for him, the Conservative conclusion is likely to be that managing directors should be paid more. If an unemployed labourer would get only £10 more a week if he gave up living on the dole or welfare and got a job, and that is not an incentive to him, then what is given to the unemployed should be lowered. In short, one sort of incentive is created by raising the higher of two incomes, and another by lowering the lower. What principle gives

the answer that the first sort is right for production managers and the second for unemployed labourers? Answer comes there none.

(12) *Would a commitment to having everyone somehow better-off accord with commitments we know Conservatives actually to have?* Some of the latter commitments are to a true natural aristocracy, less democracy, an extreme institution of property, economic freedoms as against social and civil freedoms, authoritarianism, a lesser standing for minorities, an amount of racial condescension, the rewarding of those superior persons who can respond to incentives. None of these could be said to issue from a *communal* impulse. None could be said to reflect a concern with the brotherhood of man, leave alone the sisterhood of women. It would be bizarre if, in the middle of this collection of sentiments, there was to be found a generalized beneficence of any great significance.

We leave behind the objection having to do with everyone's being better-off under a Conservative dispensation, and turn to the ninth and tenth objections to equality of results. The ninth has to do with justice, in two ways. Conservatives protest, first, that egalitarians and in particular those of them who propose equality of results are guilty of something or other in speaking of equality as *justice*.

> ... to those who are in any way in the business of enforcing equality of outcome, it is extremely important to be able to see themselves, and be seen by others, as engaged in the hot pursuit of justice. For it is only and precisely in this perspective that their activities are legitimated, both in their own eyes, and in those of the rest of the world.[50]

Thus Anthony Flew, who goes on to argue that the activities of the persons in question are not legitimated. If we take him to be insisting merely that any egalitarian who claims that 'justice' means 'equality', or that equality is the only thing that can be called justice, he is on to a good thing. No doubt there have been such misguided persons, as indeed there are very many Conservatives who have identified justice with the property-freedom they favour.

The other Conservative line of thought having to do with justice may be thought to be more consequential. It is to the effect that something called justice is what Conservatives propose or defend, and it is the ground of their opposition to equality of results. What is this justice, and also, to ask the inevitable question, do we find in it the rationale of Conservatism?

David Cooper, like some others, depends for his answer on Robert Nozick.

> The justice or otherwise of a distribution has to do with how the distribution came about ... Suppose a number of pioneers hack out equally valuable chunks of property from previously unowned, virgin territory; and suppose that two of them die, leaving their property to another of the pioneers, under no duress and without violating any claim anyone else might have had to their land. The lucky pioneer will now have three times as much property as any other; but there can be no injustice in this.[51]

What that comes to, in the way it must be understood, is that justice consists in something close to Conservative property-freedom. The just society is the one which has been and is governed by that particular ideal. Whether or not the society governed by the ideal is called the just society is of little importance. One of two important things is whether we here have an objection to equality of results, the equal society. Do we? It must seem not. We are already too aware that what Conservatives oppose to the equal society is, at bottom, one of Conservative property-freedom. What we are supposed to be getting is a reason why the latter society is preferable to the former. There is no reason given at all, certainly, by declaring that the latter society is one of freedom (p. 98) or dubbing it the just society. Nor, to remember, were we successful in our attempt to find a justifying basis in Conservatism for the kind of society in question (pp. 105, 123). In the objection from justice to the equal society, the objection as just understood, we evidently do not come to have a justifying basis or rationale of Conservatism.

Other Conservatives have something else in mind in maintaining that they are for the just as against the equal society. Milton Friedman, in place of equality, would have *equity*, which thing he does not trouble to explain.[52] Since he could not usefully have in mind just one of the legal notions of equity, he leaves us in the dark. If we turn to the dictionary, and find that equity in an ordinary sense consists in fairness, or resource to principles of justice, we shall get no more light from his reflections.

Anthony Flew for his part is inclined to take justice to consist in what is suggested by a fine old legal maxim: '*Honeste vivere, neminem laedere, suum cuique tribuere*, that is, To live honourably, to harm no one, to allow to each other their due. ... this lawyers' tag contains as good a definition as we are likely to get.'[53]

The resolute John Lucas, to remember the titles of his articles, was *Against Equality* in 1965 and *Against Equality Again* in 1977. Furthermore, there is his book, *On Justice*. Still, he is not the greatest help either. If Friedman says too little, Lucas says rather too much. Justice, in accordance with the ancient idea, is everyone's having his due. But that is a matter, as it turns out, of quite a lot: at least rights, desert, guilt, retribution, agreements made, entitlement, status, rank, need and reasonableness. Justice is not doing people down. Justice is somehow being concerned with the underdog but not forgetting what is named the plight of the overdog. We must not avoid the truth that justice is complex. 'Instead of seeing justice as a simple static assignment of benefits, responsibilities and burdens, we should see it as a dynamic equilibrium under tension, wanting to treat the individual as tenderly as possible, yet being prepared, for sufficiently compelling reasons, to take a tough line.' If we go for tidiness in our conception of justice, indeed, we reveal a tendency to a totalitarian view of society.[54]

Both Lucas and Flew, in one respect, are aimed in the direction of what can be contemplated as the rationale of Conservatism. They do not do anything like *expound* it. We shall return to them (p. 219) but what we can conclude at the moment is that they do not provide us with a clarified objection to equality of results, or, what would come to much the same thing, the rationale for which we have been looking.

The tenth and final objection made by Conservatives to the equal society does not have to do with justice – at any rate, we need not drag it in. It is to my mind, as may come as a surprise, a telling objection. It can be laid out briefly. The equal society, to recall once more our conception of it, seeks as far as is practicable to secure lives of equal satisfaction for all its members, mostly by securing equalities in income, wealth and so on. The objection, plainly put, is this: What is good about exactly *equality*, about individuals *being related in a certain way to one another*? No doubt it is a good thing that I get enough to eat, and a drink before dinner, but what is the recommendation of my being equal or roughly equal to others in that respect – or in any other respect, however generally described? This is the question raised by what is unique and fundamental to the conception of the equal society. The conception, if we do not confuse it with anything else, and in particular with what might be called humanitarianism, is precisely about no more than one possible *relationship* as against others.

David Cooper says that egalitarians suppose it to be self-evident that we should be equal. It is not self-evident to him. Why should it be thought that a reason for my having something is the amount that someone else has? Does not the reason have to do with *me*? My being hungry is a reason for having something, but is there a discernible reason in my being as hungry as you? Why should my relative position with respect to someone else matter, as distinct from my absolute position – as distinct, that is, from whether my needs are satisfied and so on? Why should I receive more because others receive more, or less because they receive less? What matters is what I have got, or have not got. One Mr Astbury, a striking lorry-driver, seems to have said, 'If lorry-drivers are unable to afford food to eat, why should anyone else?' He had a right to nourishment, David Cooper might allow, but that has nothing to do with the state of the stomachs of others.[55]

Keith Joseph, at long last, can also be reported as being in sight of something that does need attention by the Left. 'What is it about the mathematical process of dividing a thousand apples by a hundred persons which confers a special legitimacy on the possession by a particular individual of ten as opposed to some other number of apples?'[56] Anthony Flew is of the same puzzlement. Equality of results treats 'mere relativities' as goods in themselves, but why should it be supposed that they are?[57]

The objection may be a bit elusive. It becomes clearer when what seem to be several consequences of equality of results are considered. Suppose, with William Letwin, that we have a choice between two states of affairs in a society.[58] One involves all members having equally satisfying lives. We could say of them, if we were able to quantify satisfaction in terms of new and useful units rightly called Benthams, that in this state of affairs each of them would get a balance of 5,000 Benthams over the course of his or her life. The other state of affairs is one in which some members get 5,000 Benthams and some 10,000. (Those that get 5,000, by the way, may get that number partly as a result of being made a bit unhappy by their awareness of the better condition of the others. None the less, everything taken into account, they *do* get 5,000.) Equality of results, which has to do only with securing an *equality* of satisfaction, commits us to the first state of affairs. In the second, however, some people are better-off and no one is worse-off. Surely it is the better state of affairs.

A second and related consequence of equality of results has to do with waste. Suppose that one class in a society of two classes is flourishing for the reason that it possesses certain goods, certain means to satisfaction. It is not easy to think of such goods which could not be transferred to members of the other class, thereby improving their lives, but suppose that there are some. (There is the unwinning idea that the goods might be books.) Then, in order to secure equal satisfaction between the two classes, the goods in question must be subtracted from the flourishing class and put to no use at all. As some Conservatives will say, the equality-commissars must destroy the goods for fear that the once-flourishing class will regain them and destroy the new equality.

The whole objection, including the two consequences just noticed, may be named the objection of *mere relativities*. It is that the principle of equality of results is intolerable because it recommends or defends mere relativities, whose recommendation is at least obscure, and which can involve consequences which all of us, if we see the matter clearly, will take to be irrational or worse.

Will my non-Conservative readers reply that the objection somehow misconceives the principle of equality of results? Will they say there is more to equality of results than 'mere relativities'? Will they say they had something else in mind in the course of contemplating all the previous Conservative objections to equality of results, and in taking those objections to be weak ones? They will indeed, but for what reason? Is it not the case that the principle is indeed about securing a certain relationship between people?

What is there in it, to come to a third and yet more annoying consequence, to enable its proponents to avoid the charge that they are committed to having everyone equally satisfied – in possession of the same number of Benthams, maybe very few – when there is the happy alternative of having *everyone* better-off, if unequally so? What is there in the principle of equality of results to stop us from making a worst-off class of persons yet worse-off if this secures that all classes are in equal if terrible circumstances?

It is sad to have to allow that whatever the intentions and feelings of Tawney and those who think and feel like him, what they *propound* is open to the understanding which faces the objection of mere relativities. Indeed it is difficult to avoid the feeling that this vulnerable understanding of the principle of equality of results has been part of *their* understanding and of their inclination. We shall return to the matter of equality, but let us end this inquiry into it with some conclusions.

One is that we have a further large distinction of Conservatism. It is the ideology which is most firmly opposed to the principle we have latterly been considering and also to certain other propositions about equality, including the related proposition of equal treatment, and those about fair and real equality of opportunity. Further, it is the ideology most committed to yet other propositions of equality, including a limited kind of equality of opportunity, and limited kinds of equality of respect and equality before the law.

A second conclusion is that those attitudes having to do with equality do not reveal to us a rationale of Conservatism. Those who speak against equality do not state their own fundamental position, and it cannot easily be inferred from what they do say. It cannot by any means be read off what is said of justice or against mere relativities. It is no help to be told, as we are by some Conservatives, that if they are against equality, this does not mean that they regard inequality as an end-in-itself.

A third conclusion is that we cannot be said to have found a fundamental principle of the Left, something that is both arguable and gives unity to it. Such a thing is necessary to any final judgement on Conservatism. Conservatives, as we have seen, speak much nonsense about equality. They have had right on their side, however, in declaring that at least an arguable understanding of the principle of equality of results, the only real candidate for a fundamental principle that has been much in evidence in the history of egalitarianism, appears in the end to be a disaster, at any rate when understood in an arguable way. It might be added that if Conservatives do allow it to be clear and refutable (p. 183), it is not what you might call an exemplar of lucidity. Let us leave the matter for a time.

– 8 –
Conclusion

It is a great and dangerous error to suppose that all people are equally entitled to liberty. It is a reward to be earned, not a blessing to be gratuitously lavished on all alike ...

John C. Calhoun

We now have a characterization of Conservatism but we have not got what it surely has, an underlying rationale. We now have a complete, analytical and instructive characterization, as comparing it with some other accounts of Conservatism emboldens me to say, but we have not got its rationale. We have listened to exponents of Conservatism throughout its history and in a recent period of aggressiveness. But we have not been given for it, as it is piquant to note, just the very thing Conservatives take to be disgracefully and fatally missing from the politics of the Left. We have not been supplied with a fundamental principle to explain it or give it unity, and by which it can be judged. We do not have a general answer as to how goods are to be distributed in a society.

Surely there must be such a thing if it is true that Conservative thoughts, policies, practices and governments are recognizable by friend and foe, as in general they are. They are readily recognizable, surely, by being in accord with some fundamental idea had by Conservatives of how things are to be, an idea of what goal is to be served by a society's laws and institutions. Could it possibly be that the identification of Conservatism is owed *only* to the sizeable collection of distinctions we have brought together? Could it be that we have to make our way through a mixed list of marks of identity in order to recognize a new policy or practice as Conservative? That is very unlikely for several reasons, but we can leave unargued this matter of policy-identification, as it might be called. There are two other reasons of yet greater force for supposing that there does exist a rationale of Conservatism.

One reason is that we rightly expect that there must be some *best summation* of Conservatism's commitments, a summation not too extended or variegated, not too remote from what was earlier called a *maxim*. That there is some summation which is the best one is a necessary truth. That this summation is not only brief but also enlightening is not too far from a necessary truth.

The other reason has to do with the fact that we have recurrently failed to find what is supposed to justify or explain this or that particular commitment – say to this sort of government rather than that, or this freedom rather than that. It would be remarkable, indeed stunning, if the justification or explanation in each case was different, peculiar to that commitment. It would be stunning if each of the distinctions of Conservatism was a value-on-its-own, had its very own peculiar recommendation having nothing to do with the recommendations of other distinctions. There is something on which they all rest. Conservatism is not exactly a ragbag, and nor is it near to being a ragbag.

Let us look back over our inquiry. We did not get the rationale of Conservatives from their opening declaration that they are against change, partly for the reason that they are not against all change but only some of it, which sort goes undefined. Nor did we get it from their more reflective declaration that they are in favour of reform as against change, which distinction is left obscure. Partly for the reason that many of them engage in theorizing and ideology, and also for the larger reason that they cannot avoid theory, we did not get their rationale either from their description of themselves as being against theory, ideology and the like, and given instead to some other mode of understanding and decision-making. Nor did we acquire their fundamental commitment, needless to say, from what we ourselves contemplated initially as a *distinction* of Conservatism, that (1) it is *covert* about that fundamental commitment, that it keeps it to itself.

To leave change and theory, and come on to human nature, it was difficult to allow that Conservatives actually possess what they have often claimed to possess, an importantly different or importantly lower estimate of all our characters. We did find distinctions in a consequence Conservatism purports to draw from its supposedly distinctive view, having to do with an incentive system. Conservatism (2) is opposed to what it calls something like social compulsion and is better called *social persuasion*, and (3) is disinclined to *social altruism*. But if we found these distinctions we did not find any rationale. Nor did we find it in the various uncertain or ambiguous descriptions given of the goal or end supposed to be served by an incentive system.

The same was true of the distinction which is (4) the particular claim as to a greater need for *external incentives*. So too with (5) a particular tendency to act on our common assumption about our natures, the assumption of *Free Will*, first of all in connection with punishment but also in connection with those of us who get and those of us who fail to get economic rewards.

It was hopeless to suppose that Conservatism could be encapsulated as the politics of freedom. That is no more than the weak stuff of weak politicians. It *is* a large truth that (6) Conservatism is indelibly distinguished by its commitment to what is closely related to its favoured incentive system, *a large property-freedom and market-freedom*, and to certain arguments for them. Here too, however, it fails to provide us with its underlying principle. So too in the case of (7) its resulting and important want of enthusiasm, to call it no more than that, for *social and civil freedoms*.

Let us pause a moment. The matter of a rationale is not entirely simple, not something about which there can be no difference of opinion at all. Might it be reasonable to say that we *do* have the rationale of Conservatism in what we have just recalled, its elevation of the economic freedoms over social and civil freedoms? Might we embrace the proposition that Conservatism is the politics whose fundamental principle is that its chosen economic freedoms ought to be pursued or defended at the expense of social and civil freedoms? No doubt this preference casts some light on our subject, but only in the way that light is cast by what we have been calling distinctions. The preference rears up a large question.

Why are the given economic freedoms to be favoured over the social and civil freedoms? It is undeniable that they are all freedoms, or, if a certain benighted recalcitrance about usage persists, it is undeniable that each of them is a freedom and a power. *What is the difference between them?* What is properly called a rationale would seek to justify or explain the Conservative distinction between freedoms or freedoms and powers.

Did some member of the New Right, having been subjected to a little moral philosophy while not running for office in the Conservative Students Association, perceive that the difference between Conservative freedoms and other freedoms is just that the first are good and the second bad? Did he announce, that is, that Conservative freedoms are not to be defended by any argument that they serve some end which is not served by the other freedoms? That Conservative freedoms are intrinsically good or goods-in-themselves? This reply, if in a sense possible, is about as underwhelming as any arbitrary dubbing of something not hitherto taken as self-recommending as a good-in-itself. We would do no justice to Conservatism by identifying it with this stratagem of last resort.

We would open it to the easy retort from the Left, precisely as persuasive or unpersuasive, that the social and civil freedoms are goods-in-themselves. We would assign to Conservatism something that carries no conviction. To say the least, we would assign to it something that would raise the suspicion that something else substantial lay behind what would seem as close to subterfuge as stratagem. Further, it *is* the habit of Conservatives to speak as if their chosen freedoms have some unrevealed great and good effect – much the same great and good effect as is secured by a particular incentive system.

Our inquiry into government gave us more marks of Conservatism. (8) It is not by first intention *democratic*. (9) It inclines to a *true natural aristocracy*.(10) It is given to a *foreign policy* in line with its preferred economic freedoms. (11) It is, by one comparison, *authoritarian*. None of that, for the same sort of reason as with the several freedoms, provides us with a rationale. These various items, like all of our distinctions, will on further reflection fall together in leading us to contemplate a possible rationale, but they do not come stamped with one, and Conservatives, if they see it, make no significant effort to produce it. As for their declarations in favour of the organic society, we do better justice to their tradition to pay them no great attention. There is more that is unique to Conservatism in connection with (12) its attitudes to *dominant and also to minority racial and cultural groups* in societies, and perhaps (13) in its feelings about *the mass and its culture*. But no light shed of the kind we need.

Finally, to revert to our struggle just ended, having to do with equality, there is commonly no help in the declaration of Conservatives that they are against equality – no more help than in the declaration that they are for freedom. We do have another clutch of distinctions, but no rationale, in (14) their preoccupation with the falsehood of propositions of *natural equality*, their acceptance of only (15) *limited equality of respect*, (16) *limited political rights*, (17) *limited equality before the law* and (18) *limited equality of opportunity*. There is a more fundamental distinction, related to and at least as fundamental as the one having to do with Conservative economic-freedoms. It is (19) the opposition to *equality of results*. Again, however, any root or ground of the opposition is almost always left unmentioned, always left inexplicit. Nor is anything explicit said in the refrain about incentives and some general upshot of them, economic well-being or whatever, when that refrain is heard in the context of the subject of equality.

Three other matters need a bit of attention before we press on towards enlightenment. One is the thought that we might get what we have been looking for by amalgamating the three principles of Conservatism proposed by Anthony Quinton and considered separately at different points in our inquiry. They are said to derive from what we have not been enthusiastic about, the idea that Conservatism has a distinctive view of all our natures as imperfect. The first principle is that of traditionalism, having to do with attachment to familiar institutions and hostility to revolutionary or like change. The second principle is that of organicism with respect to societies, to the effect that a society is a natural whole which gives its members their identities. The third is political scepticism, to the effect that we must not turn to theory and speculation but rely on accumulated experience (pp. 2, 152, 25).

It will be very clear, given what has been said already about change, the organic society, and theory, that there is no overlap between these ruminations and our own on the distinctions of Conservatism. It is arguable that the three principles, if we stick just to them rather than what might be read into them, could in fact be realized in a society without private property as we know it. Anthony Quinton's account of his politics, to my mind, does not do much to disturb his own or the aplomb of his comrades, and it does not give us what we want. Perhaps his account is more arguable when taken as having to do not only with the tradition of Conservatism we have been considering (p. 3) but also something that preceded it. It is not much help with our subject. He does, however, have another less official perception, to which we shall come.

To turn to the second matter, it is the thought that we might succeed in our quest by bringing together the rather more sprightly considerations of Robert Nozick, which have also been treated one at a time. Some of these have to do with the recommendation that we have no more than the minimal state, which will not go in for much of the forced labour that is called taxation, but will do a good job at preventing theft and enforcing contracts. Others of his considerations attempt to provide a justification for Conservative private-property, along the lines of John Locke, having to do with labour-mixing and what are called voluntary transfers. There is a kind of summary of this in his maxim.

> From each according to what he chooses to do, to each according
> to what he makes for himself (perhaps with the contracted aid
> of others) and what others choose to do for him and choose to
> give him of what they've been given previously (under this
> maxim) and haven't yet expended or transferred.[1]

To these various items are added the cautionary tale of Wilt
Chamberlain and a certain amount of talk of rights.

Nozick, to my mind, gets further forward with distinguishing
Conservatism than does Quinton in his three principles. He is concerned with what is uppermost in the politics of his comrades. His
bundle of propositions, however, for reasons now known, does not
deliver us the goods: a rationale. The bundle is centrally concerned
with what can be brought into far clearer view, Conservative economic freedoms and Conservative attitudes to social and perhaps civil
freedoms, and several arguments for them. He does not tell us their
ground or basis. His maxim lacks definiteness of precisely the kind
needed. It evidently has to do with the given freedoms, but it is yet
less enlightening than declarations about them and the arguments
for and against them of which we know. It tells us that certain
freedoms are to exist, but gives no foundation for them.

The third thing to be remarked on before we proceed has to do
with the definition of the tradition of Conservatism and the question
of who counts as a Conservative. We began by taking Conservatism
to be the tradition of belief, feeling, legislation and action starting
with Burke and exemplified by the Conservative Party in Britain and
part of the Republican Party in the United States. What we can now
say, more satisfactorily, is that it is the political tradition which
possesses the nineteen distinctions just enumerated – a different style
of description would of course produce a different number. More
might be said, chinked, in connection with the general and troublesome subject of definitions and certain philosophical problems, but
I desist.

As for the question of who counts as a Conservative, the rough
answer must be that it is anyone who has or reflects a *considerable*
number of the distinctions of the tradition, including in the number
the distinction having to do with private property. Certainly there
can be room for dispute here, as with all similar questions of membership of a tradition or the like, but let us pass it by. As will be

assumed, all the personnel who have been mentioned, different from one another as they may be, seem to me to pass the test. None is very close to failing it.

To come closer to the light, consider first the distinction of Conservatism that can reasonably be seen as most important to it, and to have most consequences or repercussions elsewhere in it. This is its defence of a certain property-freedom and market-freedom. Conservative property-freedom, to recall, is in several ways extensive and gives an advantage in a society to entrepreneurial and efficiently acquisitive individuals, and also to those who already own property and those whom they benefit, above all their children. What, at bottom, might be the recommendation of this particular freedom?

I suspect the idea that is likely to come first to the mind of what philosophers are sometimes inclined to call a naive subject, in this case someone who has not spent too much time in the company of Conservative ideologues, is that a society which accords individuals such a freedom is one which *really allows individuals to get what they deserve, their rewards*. Individuals get the private property they deserve because of their personal characteristics or strengths, and because of what they do. Their characteristics include diligence, say, or inventiveness. What they do, for a start, is to work hard. To have the property they deserve, further, is for them to have a full right to dispose of it as they choose. Their desert is both that they possess it and also that they be able to give it or sell it to others.

If we turn to arguments we considered for this Conservative property-freedom, perhaps the most traditional and persuasive is the one first given by John Locke in the seventeenth century and, as just noticed, refurbished by Robert Nozick in our own. It is, in brief, that property is rightly held by those who laboured on what was unowned and those who were sold or given it by others who laboured on it or were sold or given it.

Much labour has been mixed with this idea, but, as was remarked when we considered it, nothing is more natural than to say it has to do with desert – whatever Nozick may wish to say to the contrary, for reasons which we shall see. I come to deserve to own what I have laboured on in certain circumstances, and what I deserve includes the right to sell or give it to another. Nothing about intrinsically-good freedoms, or rights, or my having a title deed to my own body, is so natural an understanding of the argument. Nothing else, furthermore, suits all of Locke's words better, as Alan Ryan and Lawrence Becker come close to suggesting in their admirably apolitical books on property,[2] and nothing suits better what is conveyed by Conservatives in general who retail the argument.

Consider now the different thing that has recently been offered as the principal argument for Conservative private property, the argument having to do with incentive. We looked at it first in connection with the subject of theory, then with human nature, freedom and equality. *Why* are Conservatives so given to the demand for external incentives, in particular larger salaries and profits, and why do they diminish internal incentive, which could be more effective than it is? Why are they opposed to social persuasion, which at bottom is some means, not necessarily at all draconian, of bringing it about that individuals contribute to their societies for lesser rewards or for something other than economic rewards? Why are Conservatives so unenthusiastic about social altruism? In each of these connections, it appears that Conservatives look on larger salaries and profits not merely as means to a certain social end, called general prosperity or economic well-being or the like. They do not look on them primarily as incentives. Each of the four attitudes is surely motivated at least in part by a demand for *rewards* for the individuals in question. That they may be incentives is another and quite different matter.

The incentive argument, then, like the argument owed to Locke, seems to rest to some large extent for Conservatives on the idea, whatever it comes to, that individuals have deserts. This thought about Conservatives gets a kind of support from the fact of another of their distinctions. It is that they are more attached than others to a certain presupposition of supposing that an individual deserves something for a certain action or activity or endeavour. The presupposition, of much feeling about desert, is that the individual was free in a strong sense in the action, activity or endeavour. He was not fated to engage in it, but rather might have done otherwise, given things as they were. He had Free Will. Quite as much to the point, *other* individuals also had this possibility, and did not use it. They could have got up earlier, and didn't. The distinction of Conservatives that they are more inclined to act on our common assumption of Free Will, or of the falsehood of determinism, accords very well with the thought that they are basically or ultimately concerned with desert.

There is another important word to say about the incentive argument, but consider now the fundamental opposition of Conservatives to social freedoms, those most closely associated with such twentieth-century advances as the Welfare State and the War on Want. What explains the opposition? Well, such freedoms are most often regarded in terms of *need* as against desert. Such freedoms can be said to be capabilities of satisfying need, and are not commonly said to be means of securing deserts. They are commonly said to ignore desert. As for civic freedoms, they include a number which have served the end of the struggle for social freedoms. One is freedom of association and organization, essential to the endeavours of trade unions. The New Right in Britain, in savaging that freedom, can be supposed to have been moved by an idea of desert.

What might explain a related and clear distinction of Conservatism, its opposition to equality of results or the equal society? Several Conservatives, after belabouring this ideal, caution us that their opposition to equality should not lead us to suppose they take inequality to be good-in-itself or an end. As we know, they are in general not enlightening about what *does* lead them to their opposition. A commitment to desert would. Or, to speak more carefully, they could be led to this opposition to equality by being committed to our having unequal wealth and the like as our proper deserts for certain personal attributes or activities. The same sort of speculation is in place with their favouring of a certain limited equality of opportunity – one in which certain obstacles to competition are removed but individuals are left to their own resources and not much helped to become effective competitors.

To persist with the distinctions having to do with equality, why do Conservatives put so much effort into denying what no sane egalitarian has ever asserted, the false bundle of propositions about natural equality? Why, although they may read him, are they in this connection so remarkably oblivious to Tawney? The idea comes to mind that a commitment to desert would explain it. Such a commitment has point only if we are *not* all equal in all respects or fundamental respects. Whatever use the assertion or denial of natural equality is to egalitarians, its denial will be insisted upon by anyone inclined to have our societies run on some idea of desert. It comes to mind to speculate, also, that Conservatives, themselves overcome by some idea of desert, are moved to suppose that egalitarians too, at least in some part of themselves, are similarly captured. What better policy, then, for dealing with the Left, than the steadfast insistence that we are not all equal in our capabilities?

As for equality of respect, a fuller kind of it than is favoured by Conservatives would make less difference between people, provide a lesser ground for rewards and distinctions. There is at least the possibility of related comments on limited political rights and limited rights before the law. To say only one thing, greater political and legal rights would detract from the worth of the rewards, in terms of property, called for by Conservatism in its central commitment. One's large bank balance, however many dollars it has in it, is not so satisfactory if it does not secure better lawyers than others get, or, perhaps more to the point, secure lawyers when others lack them.

But let me not press on indefatigably with this refrain. The possibility of continuing it will be evident enough from just a reminder of most of our remaining distinctions of Conservatism: inclinations to less democracy rather than more, to a true natural aristocracy, to authoritarianism and to certain social prejudices. Let me say only that these distinctions can be described in terms of the ideas that some deserve more of a say than others, some deserve to be able to keep others firmly in line and some deserve a kind of social ascendancy – just as the others deserve less of a say, and to be kept firmly in line and to know their places.

There is one last and unavoidable thought, which takes us back, as promised, to the Conservative incentive argument for the private property they defend. Our earlier inquiries into that argument left us without anything like a satisfactory account of what is supposed really to recommend the upshot of the given incentive system. What is the state of affairs, certainly a state of affairs which centrally involves Conservative private property, which results from and recommends the incentive system? It is no good, as we saw, to go on about economic well-being, or everyone's being better-off, or the like. We now may seem to have an answer to our question, the only answer consonant with the speculations to which we have been drawn. It is, inevitably, that the state of affairs is the one in which people get what they deserve. It is the state of affairs such that individuals, taking into account certain of their attributes and activities, get the rewards of those attributes and activities.

What we have, in sum, is the speculation that Conservatism is founded on a recognizably moral principle, what we can call a principle of desert. Although Conservative thinkers are for the most part unsystematic, and are not given to setting down and clarifying a rationale of their politics, and although they may have reason not to go on too much about desert, it would be unsettling if they had nothing to say of the speculation. It is therefore reassuring to be able to recall, first, that a very great deal of what Conservatives say, above

all about incentive, carries strong implications as to desert. The
regular use of the word *reward*, although its meaning is not constant,
is but one clear example. Second, a goodly number of Conservatives,
if they do not clarify it or actually develop an argument having to
do with desert, do speak explicitly of it. If they leave it to us to reflect
on the thing and make some judgement of it, they do themselves
produce it.

John C. Calhoun, perhaps the best of spokesmen for American
Conservatism of the Southern variety at the time of the Civil War,
spoke more plainly than many of his successors, perhaps all of them.

> It is a great and dangerous error to suppose that all people are
> equally entitled to liberty. It is a reward to be earned, not a
> blessing to be gratuitously lavished on all alike – a reward
> reserved for the intelligent, the patriotic, the virtuous and
> deserving – and not a boon to be bestowed on a people too
> ignorant, degraded and vicious to be capable either of appreci-
> ating or of enjoying it.[3]

Burke is more typical of Conservatives in eschewing such declarations but in seeming to imbue most of what he says of traditional
rights to property, rank and power with the suggestion that they are
well deserved by their possessors. He suggests or implies, yet more
strongly, that the goods in question would *not* be deserved by those
who might get their hands on them by way of a revolution.

> The occupation of an hair-dresser, or of a working tallow-
> chandler, cannot be a matter of honour to any person – to say
> nothing of a number of other more servile employments. Such
> descriptions of men ought not to suffer oppression from the
> state; but the state suffers oppression, if such as they, either
> individually or collectively, are permitted to rule.[4]

It would perhaps be rash to reduce the passage to the proposition
that some do and some do not deserve to rule. It would be as mistaken
to deny that the passage carries a certain suggestion. It is that a better
class of persons has a natural right on account of their excellences to
the offices of the state, that others do not, and, perhaps, that a nation's
deserts are served by having the better class of persons in charge. If
God willed the state, as indeed Burke wrote that he did,[5] it is difficult
to suppose that he did not will an entity which would reflect our

various degrees of righteousness, virtue, merit and contribution. Marie Antoinette, as morning star among us, was indeed deprived of her rightful rewards.

Let us leap past, among other things, a nineteenth-century view that 'the poor are poor because they are vicious',[6] and come on to Harold Macmillan, leader of the British Conservative Party for a time, who had no such venom in him. Still, he found against equality on three grounds, of which the first is our present concern. It is stated, more explicitly than Burke stated it, in this passage:

Human beings, widely various in their capacity, character, talent and ambition, tend to differentiate at all times and in all places. To deny them the right to differ, to enforce economic and social uniformity upon them, is to throttle one of the most powerful and creative of human appetites ... It is wrong morally; because to deny the bold, the strong, the prudent and the clever the rewards and privileges of exercising their qualities is to enthrone in society the worst and basest of human attributes: envy, jealousy and spite.[7]

Anthony Quinton, not entirely at one with his own three principles, discerns an alteration which took place in Conservatism in the early part of the twentieth century, away from faith in the superiority of ancestral wisdom. With respect to the British Conservative Party, at any rate, the governing aim

has been to maintain a social order in which excellence, both of capacity and of will, is at once rewarded and through its rewards, enabled to develop and become effective. Its conception of justice relies on a criterion of desert or merit, not of equality or need. The ancient constitutional pieties are invoked only for ritual purposes.[8]

Neither Quinton nor Macmillan, if they are explicit enough, take time to reflect on the idea to which they have recourse. They neither expound nor examine it. The same is true of the combative Anthony Flew, who complains against the Left that it ignores our deserts, and who has the distinction among recent Conservatives of at least implying that Conservatism is at bottom a commitment to two things, desert and entitlement.[9] That is, Conservatism is at least by implication the politics of justice, and justice is everyone's having his due, which consists in everyone's having his deserts and entitlements.

John Lucas, whom I take with slightly less confidence to speak for Conservatives, also moves in this direction. He too damns egalitarianism for not paying attention to desert, which he takes to have to do just with the deeds a man has done. If his account of justice, as we have noticed, is a rich one, he gives a priority to desert.

> ... although there are other bases than desert for determining how people ought to be treated, desert is pre-eminent. People ought to be done by according to how they deserve, and how they deserve depends on how they have done, which in turn presupposes responsibility and freedom.

> Being an agent, I am what I do, and therefore am, as of now unalterably, what I have done. The things I have done constitute the most uncontestable, although not the only, premisses for any argument about what should happen to me. Hence the fundamental significance of desert.[10]

He adds, after the second passage, that *exclusive* pre-eminence is not had by desert in his sense. 'Merit could also claim to be equally constitutive of what a man is, and so equally incontestable as a basis for argument.' What Lucas calls merit, however, is one part of what we ourselves have had in mind in speaking of desert. That is, his merit consists in personal qualities or characteristics of an individual, as against what he or she does.

What we have come to is the speculation that Conservatism has as its rationale a principle of desert, which speculation arises naturally from a consideration of the distinctions of Conservatism, and gets further support from both the implications and also the declarations of its advocates. The idea is also inevitable for another reason, the very strongest: there appears to be no other principle of a moral or like character that is a possibility. Certainly, for reasons with which we are all too familiar, no declaration about freedom can serve.

Do we then have the conclusion for which we have been waiting? Is this the blissful dawn? It would be more than premature to think so.

What is the principle of desert? It is easy enough to say that it is the principle that *each individual is to get what he or she deserves on account of personal qualities or his or her actions and activities*. That is suggested by the fact noticed several times, that we take people to deserve things on account of (i) their intentions, virtues, character, persistence, wickedness, intelligence, looks and the like, and also (ii) their deeds, endeavours, contributions, offences, heroic acts, examination answers, life-long struggles and the like. What they deserve are promotions, bonuses, directorships, bishoprics, medals, perhaps inheritances, prizes in beauty contests, degrees, long sentences in prison, perhaps death and so on.

However *natural* it is to say that Conservatism is founded on this principle of desert, as we are calling it, there are three obstacles in the way of saying a word more.

The first and simplest obstacle has to do with the fact that claims of desert can be made with respect to *a very great deal indeed*. It can be said, even, as we are reminded by the author of a book on the subject, that Cleveland is an interesting city and therefore deserves better publicity.[11] No doubt that makes the point in a way which will not accord perfectly with the memories of all tourists, but make it it does. The first difficulty is that the opponents of Conservatism can readily assert, if they are so inclined, of the different institutions and policies which *they* favour, that these are in accordance with the principle.

We all of us deserve, they may say, on account of our humanity or our struggles, to have societies which do better by all individuals than societies which are or would be shaped by Conservative property-freedom. Or, those of us who are least-equipped to play good roles in an entrepreneurial society do nevertheless deserve, on account of doing as well as we can, decent lives. We do not deserve poverty. All bright children have a moral claim to good schools. Miners deserve to keep their jobs. Unmarried mothers, given their struggles, deserve effective help. Security in old age is due to those who have worked all their lives.

That, mainly about social freedom, is but a beginning. It can be said that we all deserve decent shares of the nation's wealth, that we deserve to have things which through no fault of our own we cannot buy. We deserve, given the possibilities of our human decency, the chance of responding to social persuasion, the chance of being governed by an altruism, our better selves. We deserve to live in such a way as to be able to value the intrinsic worth of our jobs.

We deserve, having paid what taxes we are able to pay, the impartial protection of the police. They should not be made careless by our skin colours or our accents. We deserve, on account of our rational natures, such as they are, to be given the knowledge secured by another civil freedom, knowledge which will enable us to judge the worth of the claims of politicians about protecting our environments and the purity, if any, of the drinking water. We deserve to be told, as it comes to mind to add, the rationale of Conservatism.

For the same sort of reason, our capability of rational judgement, or just the reason of self-interest, we deserve to have more democracy, not the democracy which is hobbled or half-blinded by a political press. We deserve, on account of that spiritual equality in which Conservatives also purport to believe, a government neither authoritarian nor over-filled with those who take themselves, even if they have reason to do so, to be our betters. We deserve, because of the intelligence of some of us, real equality of opportunity, and not some simulacrum that better suits the well-off fathers of dolts than the clever children of others.

Will Anthony Flew, ruffled by this line of thought, now alight elsewhere, on something other than the general principle of desert we have been using? Very well, let us join him. It is possible, of course, to devise a different principle of desert, one which specifies a particular mixed set of personal attributes and activities that are to be rewarded. The Conservative system of private property, to remember, favours what were called persons of the entrepreneurial and efficiently acquisitive sort. Let us have them and also some others, perhaps those who are by nature bishops, or by nature repose beneath the shadow of the British oak, in a specifiable category of persons. The rationale of Conservatism, we can now say, is the principle of desert that *each individual of the category in question – each individual possessing features in the given set – is to have proper deserts.*

Tempted as I am to chink importunately, let it be said only that the adversaries of Conservatism can as happily devise a principle of desert to their different liking. Here, needless to say, what will be called for is the suitable reward of socialist and like virtues, of a full day's work, a good record in not crossing picket lines, of having no susceptibility to wisdom without reflection and above it, and so on.

Should we be reluctant to draw the conclusion which appears before us, that Conservatism can lay no more claim to a rationale of desert than opposing political traditions? Perhaps we *should* be reluctant. It was remarked earlier that social freedoms are most often spoken of as enabling individuals to satisfy needs rather than procure deserts. It is arguable, with some hope of success, that Conservatism as an ideology is *more* amenable to description in terms of desert than the ideologies opposed to it. It is arguable that it has *better* claim to talk of desert, whatever that talk is worth.

To make that concession, however, is not to make another. If there were nothing else to be said of desert, which there certainly is, the situation of Conservatives could not be a contented one. They could, at best, defend themselves as a party *more* capable of calling upon claims of desert to justify themselves. That leaves open the possibility, or rather, leaves untouched the fact, that their adversaries need not depend *only* on desert in order to justify their different ways. They, unlike Conservatives, have another moral string to their bow, as we shall see.

That is the first of three obstacles in the way of the enterprise of regarding Conservatism as the politics of desert. The second is yet greater.

Do all who possess private property to the Conservative extent deserve it? If we were to put more serious effort into defining what Conservatives can speak of with good heart as the class of the deserving – those who are deserving according to their chosen principle – we would come quickly to the conclusion that by no means all of the beneficiaries of a Conservative system of private property are in that class of the deserving. There is nothing about *inheriting* property that makes one, say, an entrepreneurial and efficiently acquisitive person in the relevant sense. It does not much matter that it can be said to be the desert of the father, having struggled successfully with the electric cocktail shakers, to leave his profits to whom he chooses. That will not convert his languorous daughter into a member of the class of the deserving. It will not convert her, even, into what is different, someone who has responded to incentive in anything like the required sense. Nor is there any known connection between being an heiress and exercising one's Free Will to good effect.

Some way back it was indeed said that it is natural to suppose that what recommends Conservative property-freedom is that it really allows individuals to get what they deserve. That is true. It *is* natural, and the fact has very much to do with the inclination of many Conservatives to talk of their politics in terms of desert. What is also true is that only a permanently naive subject can persist in thinking that anything more than a considerable fraction of the results of a Conservative property system could be justified by desert.

The same sort of thing is therefore to be said in connection with closely related matters. The general state of affairs to which an incentive system tends, the goal of economic well-being or whatever, cannot in fact be conceived satisfactorily by Conservatives in terms of desert. This is not just a matter of inheritance. Consider the wealth of fortunate individuals got by way of this or that revolutionary product that makes it into all the supermarkets. Not all of these fortunate persons have struggled overmuch, or at all. There are windfalls. There is wealth owed to no noticeable mixture of labour.

There is the same kind of conclusion with certain other distinctions of Conservatism which, for the naive subject, are satisfactorily bound up with desert. The true natural aristocracy serves as one example. This body of worthies cannot be understood in a way that satisfies the instincts and traditions of Conservatives, including family commitments, and also is such that the worthies are in any half-defensible class of the deserving. So too with the matter of condescension to certain minorities. Unless the definition of the class of the deserving is made ludicrous, in part by being made racist, it cannot be that it will accord with the given condescension.

That I need not persist in elaborating this clear and intractable difficulty is indicated by the fact that whatever is true of the generality of Conservatives, we have Conservative thinkers on hand who take it to be insuperable. Keith Joseph is sometimes one of these. He and his collaborator, it is true, bring to their perception of the difficulty no little talent for inconsistency and also a certain idiosyncrasy, some of it inherited from Friedrich Hayek. Some of the idiosyncrasy is what appears to be a conviction about assessable merit. 'There is no such thing as assessable merit. The Snark will always turn out to be a Boojum in the end.'[12] One might have supposed that the merits and demerits of heroes, Olympic high jumpers, managing directors, thugs, rapists and crooked brokers were noticeable, but no matter. Our authors are helped towards their conviction by the idea, idiosyncratic in itself, that all desert is 'moral' desert. Let us leave all that.

Robert Nozick, also of the New Right, is another who sees that a principle of desert will not really give him the society he wants. It will not give him, for a start, Conservative property-freedom. What he supplies in place of desert as a rationale of Conservatism, as we know, is what is summarized in his unserviceable maxim (p. 213). We are to have certain freedoms whose fundamental recommendation we do not know, and for that unknown reason be deprived of others.

Anthony Flew does not join him in abandoning a principle of desert, but deals with our difficulty by adding to the principle. We are to understand, as remarked several times already, that the rationale of Conservatism has to do with two things, deserts and entitlements. Are the latter, as might be expected, the particular rights which are accorded to us in a Conservative dispensation? Are they certain property-rights, rights to engage in a certain kind of market, and the various other rights which can be enumerated by making our way through the list of distinctions of Conservatism? Do they include, that is, a right having to do with large external incentives, rights having to do with an absence of social persuasion, truncated social and civil rights? Flew is more active in laying out what he takes to be the egalitarian and other sins of the Left than in making clear his righteous alternative. That, however, makes no great problem for us.

Either the rationale he offers is in part desert and in part a matter of exactly Conservative rights or freedoms, or it is in part desert and in part a matter of some near-Conservative rights or freedoms. So, Flew's rationale is in one part desert. We might suppose, if it were not the case that socialists and like persons can also lay claim to desert, that this would enable him to explain some part of what is possessed by persons in a Conservative or like society. What of the second part of the rationale? Our inquiry has long since settled that it is no good, if one is engaged in giving the foundation of one's politics, simply to cry freedom, or to cry rights either. There are lots of both freedoms and rights, and one's choice needs explaining or justifying. To speak in his way, there are lots of possible entitlements, and one's choice of them needs explaining and justifying. Flew's rationale in this part is a bare declaration in favour of his favoured items. In this part it is no rationale at all, but a question in need of an answer.

So far we have assumed that there *is* something that can be called a general principle of desert, or there *are* a few such things. We have assumed there does exist a kind of general proposition that might be thought, at least for an innocent moment, to explain or defend all of what Conservatives want to defend. That is to say no more than that *we have assumed that such a general proposition can be made tolerably clear*. Our conclusions so far, resting on that charitable assumption, are that such a principle is not near to being the private property of Conservatives, but can about as readily be used against them, and that it will in any case not come near to explaining or defending all that they want.

Is there in fact such a principle? Can such a thing be produced? Is it possible to clarify to some decent extent a principle which at least *prima facie* gives an explanation or defence of Conservatism?

It *is* possible, we know, to form sentences that sound promising or reassuring. *Everything ought to get what they deserve for their personal qualities and activities of entrepreneurial and certain other kinds.* But what does that sort of thing come to? The idea is that there is a general sort of argument available to us. Its premise is of the form *Person A deserves Y for being or having done X*, and its conclusion is of the form *A ought to get Y.* But how are we to understand the premise? Are we to take it, very naturally, as saying at least in part that *A* ought to get *Y*? If we do, our desert argument seems to collapse into uselessness – into saying that something ought to happen because it ought to happen. Should we give up this idea as to what a general principle of desert would look like? But what is the alternative?

Well, we might try the principle that everybody ought to get *the means* to what they deserve for certain personal qualities and activities. The idea here is that there is a general argument of another sort. Its premise is again of the form A *deserves* Y *for being or having done* X, but its conclusion is of the form A *ought to get the means to* Y. As for *Y*, it might be some sort of fulfilment or happiness, and the means to it a certain salary. Here we can be said to escape the embarrassment that the premise already says that *A* ought to have what the conclusion says he ought to have. The conclusion says that he ought to have the means to *Y*, not *Y* itself. Whatever is to be thought of this artful strategy, we are left with the fundamental question of what is to be meant by saying that one thing is deserved for another thing. Do we know?

Our talk of desert is pervasive, and takes endless forms. For the most part we eschew the somehow tainted noun itself, for whatever reason, but we are forever saying, in one way or another, that someone deserves to have something or to do or be able to do something, since he or she has this or that recommendation or short-coming consisting in a characteristic or the fact of having done something. To say that all of this is without meaning or sense would indeed be to be a bit crazed, a kind of Canute. But allowing it makes sense does not begin to deal with our problem of whether it contains *a useful general proposition or argument*.

It is no surprise that we have ways of talking which reflect the large fact that we take what people are and do as somehow supplying reasons for what we or others should do, but the ways of talking and the large fact by no means guarantee or even make likely that we have a fundamental principle. To put the question again in the clearest way, do we have a premise for a general argument to the effect that people ought to have certain things, a premise to the effect that one thing is deserved for another thing?

Punishment, where talk of desert is institutionalized, might be expected to have got the answer into view and in good shape. As it turns out, however, the philosophers, theorists and official suppliers of punishment have done nothing that is of use to the Conservative in pursuit of a general rationale. They have not made useful sense of saying that *A* deserves *Y* for *X*.

To my mind the best that can be done with punishment is to understand the premise and hence the whole argument in this way: Since *Y*, a penalty, satisfies a grievance of persons affected by the offence *X*, it is right that *A* gets *Y*. A grievance in the intended sense is a desire for the distress of somebody else. That is an appallingly weak reason for punishment, given what can be said against it, but that is not our present concern. What is relevant is that this sort of thing does not apply *at all* to what Conservatives are as much concerned with – an individual's getting, on account of his persistence or the like, the reward of private property or the like. It is inconceivable that my having some private property is to be justified or defended by the fact that my persistence gives rise to grievance or even wholly different desires on the part of other people, desires whose satisfaction requires that I have the property.

The fact that there are wholly different and conflicting attempts to make sense of a premise about desert in connection with punishment cannot be reassuring to a Conservative who looks in this direction to find an acceptable general principle or argument. There is no agreement. The diligent Conservative must turn to another book for most of the attempts.[13] Furthermore, none of them helps.

One is the supposition that *Person A deserves* Y *for having done* X means, in effect, that we have rules or laws connecting *Y* and *X* – connecting a particular penalty with a particular offence. Some of us may indeed mean that, or partly mean that, in talking of offenders deserving particular penalties. But we get nothing that can rightly be called a rationale of punishment from these habits, let alone a rationale of Conservatism. This is so since what we have in mind raises, and does not answer, the question of why we have the given rules or laws.

It is sometimes supposed, differently and a bit more usefully, that *Person A deserves* Y *for* X conveys that *A* has acquired a benefit or laid down a burden of self-restraint in doing *X*, and that his getting *Y* will even things out – return things to the state of affairs they

were in before he did X. But this understanding must be to the effect
that an offence is against some principle of fairness, a departure from
a fair state of affairs, and that imposing a penalty is a kind of
reassertion of that principle and state of affairs. What is the principle?
We need it in order to have any hope of getting to a rationale of
Conservatism in terms of desert. The terrible fact, from a Conservative point of view, is that we seem to be invited in the direction
of some *egalitarian* principle. Let us forget about punishment in particular and reflect on our general talk of desert and our resulting
actions.

One idea that suggests itself is that in certain circumstances our
giving someone what he deserves can be rightly described as our
telling the truth that he has a certain merit. Not giving him what he
deserves would be to withhold this information. So is desert just about
truth? One of the difficulties with taking something of this sort as a
general principle of desert is that if we were consistent, we could tell
the truth by sending to privatized penitentiaries all and only those
persons with a certain merit, say that of making money. That would
be a very effective communication. If we want to tell the truth by
the different means of somehow *rewarding* money-makers, as by God
Conservatives do, we need a reason entirely different from that of
truth-telling.

Often we have in mind, when we say in one way or another that
someone deserves something disagreeable, that he knew that that
outcome of his action was possible, likely or certain. He knew what
he was doing, and went ahead. George Sher, on whose philosophical
book about desert I am depending a bit, reports a letter to the editor
of the *Free Press* in Vermont, which said that with all the warm
weather, any fisherman crazy enough to drive his truck out on the
lake ice deserved to have the truck go under.[14]

There is no hope whatever of a general principle here. To glance
back for a moment at punishment, it isn't true that all offenders who
are said to deserve penalties do in fact take their penalties to be likely
or even possible. Some are rightly confident they will get away with
their offences. More importantly, not all entrepreneurs believe that
they will be rewarded by success. Furthermore, it is far from clear
what principle is involved in all this. Certainly we don't suppose that
people should get *all* the things they expect. Conservatives are the
first to say so.

To come on to a third idea, we make use of the rule in certain
contexts that people should be *compensated* for losses and damages that

were not their doing. Employees get compensation for injuries at work, and patients for misfortunes in hospitals. Can we find something useful here? It seems that we cannot. The idea simply does not apply to hard work, say, which is wholly voluntary, wholly the doing of the agent. Also, if compensation were the rule with respect to the rewarding of hard work, two people who achieved the same thing – say the same sales record – would get different rewards if one had to put in more effort. In any case, there is the question of what state of affairs it is that we get back to by way of compensation. What explains or justifies it?

Here and elsewhere, as in other instances, talk of desert presupposes some idea or principle that has nothing to do with desert. The force of the argument for compensation derives from some idea or principle as to a fair or defensible distribution of things. No question arises of compensating someone for a loss if that loss *gave rise to* a satisfactorily fair state of affairs. There is also another presupposition of importance. Desert as we know is a matter of characteristics or actions of individuals – good or bad characteristics and actions. It thus rests on judgements as to the worth of such characteristics and actions. These judgements, if we were to arrive at a general principle of desert, would need to be brought into clarity. They would have to take into account, for a start, that not all work can be admired. There is work that ought not to be done.

A fourth idea that can be found in our talk and action having to do with desert is that the general principle we are looking for is just something like this: What people are and do is to count in connection with what they get and what is done to them. That is true with respect to a lot of things people are and do, if certainly not all. But this *very* general principle tells us nothing at all useful. It is in fact perfectly consistent with acting on the principle of equality of results. If I do that, I do indeed pay attention to what people are and do. I take into account that their nature is that they have needs, and that they work and vote in certain ways. I do not have to take such facts as bases for desert-claims in order to take them into account.

There is a coda – two more things that need to be noticed before we draw the conclusion towards which we now really are headed. They can be regarded either as obstacles to our ever coming to find a satisfactory general principle of desert for Conservatism, or, on the assumption that we can find one, objections to it.

What makes the difference between you and me, it can be said, in so far as my getting the better salary is concerned, or the gold medal or the country house, has to do with my characteristics. It has to do with them alone, or with them as the explanation of what I am able to do. In the second case, they are necessary conditions of what I do. But, if I may somehow be said to deserve the house because of my characteristics or the activities which flow from them, I cannot be said to deserve my characteristics. If I can be supposed to deserve certain of my characteristics, because I have struggled to develop them, I cannot be supposed to deserve the more fundamental charatteristics which made it possible to succeed in the struggle. But surely, then, I cannot be said to deserve the house either? John Rawls depends on this kind of argument. It leads him to abandon thought of desert and to embrace his principles of justice instead. Replies have been made to it, but it remains very troublesome indeed.

Finally, the problem of freedom and responsibility, or, as it is as rightly called, the problem of determinism. All desert-claims having to do with actions of persons presuppose that the persons acted freely, that they can be held responsible or can claim responsibility for what they did. Some of these desert-claims can be taken to rest just on the presupposition that the agent was *voluntary* in his or her action. Others rest on the presupposition that the agent was not only voluntary in action but that it was the result of his Free Will (pp. 77 ff). Claims of this latter sort, then, rest on the proposition that determinism is false. Is it?

That it is false will take some proving. Some of us have spent some time proving that it is true.[15] Let us invite Conservatives to contemplate the matter. If they are to persist in various kinds of talk of desert, they will need to do some reading or else not be paid attention by such serious persons as the readers of this book. If they will be content with only a little attention, they will need to deal with all our ordinary deterministic convictions that fall short of coming together into a grand theory. I fancy that none of us believes that *no* constraining causes operate in the lives of different individuals in our societies. Who but a lunatic talking to a lamp post can suppose that we are equally free to get into good schools, become generals, buy effective health insurance? But then how can those of us who have no chance of doing these things be said to deserve our different lives? How can we deserve what we had no real chance, in fact no chance at all, of avoiding?

We have been entertaining the speculation, which began by seeming promising, that the rationale of Conservatism is a principle of desert. What is to be said about the speculation is that it comes to nothing. To speak plainly, it is false.

It is not that a half-decent principle can be produced, and thus the objections to Conservatism must be the earlier ones, that non-Conservatives can also rely on talk of desert if they choose, and that the principle does not cover more than a fraction of what Conservatives want to defend. *No* principle has been produced, and we can be confident that none can be. There comes a time, whatever remote possibilities remain, when the failure to find something amounts to the proof that it is not there to be found.[16]

There exists but one recent book on desert, that of George Sher, who is a moral philosopher with no noticeable political axe to grind and who is friendly to talk of desert. It is one principal conclusion of the book that there is no generic principle of desert, no single general principle or value. There is nothing to which Conservatives can have recourse. There are some of what Sher calls *local* principles, of which one is the idea mentioned above about punishment, having to do with a fair distribution of benefits and burdens. But that is the best that can be said, and no help to Conservatives who wish to explain themselves to us.

The conclusion we have drawn that Conservatism does not rest on and cannot be judged by a principle of desert is not our final one. Conservatism does have a rationale, a different one, and it can be judged by it. In order to come to the rationale and the judgement, since the judgement is importantly a matter of comparison, we need to return to what was called the politics of the Left or egalitarianism, and to some unfinished business.

We took it, after putting aside many other objections to the politics of the Left, that what has been close to its standard expression *is* open to a serious and seemingly fatal objection. That is the objection that this politics, taken as resting on the principle of equality of results, is committed to *mere relativities*. It is concerned with no more than getting people into certain relative positions, positions of equality. Thus it is committed to having everyone equally well-off when the alternative is having some people still well-off to that extent and others better-off. It is committed, worse, to having everyone equally badly-off when the alternative is having everybody better-off although unequally so. It has to be added that the principle of equal results (p. 183) is not so clear and determinate as it might be.

There is a better expression of the various political traditions of the Left, notably democratic socialism and a traditional liberalism.

This takes them to be based not on the principle of equality of results but on something related to it but significantly different. This can be dignified with the name of the *Principle of Equality*. Fundamentally this principle has to do not with treatment, with what is done to and for people, but with satisfaction. It fundamentally although not exclusively has to do, that is, with a result of treatment, what can also be named well-being, or the quality of people's lives, or freedom, or happiness. The latter term can be misleading, certainly so when happiness is somehow conceived as being a different and allegedly higher or more inner thing than the satisfaction of desires.

The Principle of Equality is directed, more particularly, to the satisfaction of fundamental categories of human desires. It has to do with the satisfaction of those categories of desire which were set out, when we were considering human nature, as giving us a general conception of that nature (p. 60). They are, you might say, the desires which define human nature.

We all want, first, the material means to subsistence, a satisfactory length of life for ourselves and for others who are close to us. We desire, that is, lifetimes of something like seventy years rather than thirty-five or forty. We want, second, material goods in addition to those which will merely keep us alive for such a time. These will include things of importance: tolerable homes and environments for a start, and many such lesser items as means of travel. They are not properly described as luxuries. Although all the categories of desire can rightly be described as desires for freedoms, the third category is the one most naturally described as having in it desires for certain freedoms and powers. Some fundamental ones are political, others have to do with independence in one's work and other such smaller contexts of life. We want, fourth, respect and self-respect, which we cannot have if we are, say, the victims of class-condescension or racism. We want, fifth, the satisfactions of personal and wider human relationships. Some of these have to do with the family, others with membership of larger groups and a society. Last, we desire the goods of culture. Here we want, among other things, not ignorance or incompetence but the satisfactions of education.

No doubt there are other possible ways of sorting out our fundamental desires, but this will do. The Principle of Equality is concerned with extents to which these fundamental desires are satisfied. It has to do with different extents of well-being, this being nothing other than the mentioned satisfaction. It is a recommendation with respect to the distribution of this satisfaction or well-being.

Its formulation depends on first deciding on a definition of the badly-off, a class of persons who are badly-off. There is room for different decisions here, and somewhat different decisions are in fact made by different traditions within the leftward part of the political spectrum. Certainly there is no *fact of the matter* which by itself determines who is to count as badly-off, and no surprise or embarrassment in that. The answer to the question 'Who is to decide who is badly-off?' is, of course, 'Anyone proposing to make and use distinctions between different conditions of life.'

Here is one central definition of the badly-off: (i) those who fail to satisfy even the first or subsistence desire, and hence are frustrated in desires of the other categories as well; (ii) those who seriously lack further material goods; (iii) those who are unsatisfied in terms of freedom and power; (iv) those who are unsatisfied in terms of respect and self-respect; and (v) those who are minimally satisfied in all categories but the first.

The Principle of Equality is roughly to the effect that we should give a priority to policies which will make well-off those who are badly-off – policies which will remove individuals from the class of the badly-off – and that we should seek to act on these policies by having certain practices of equality.

The first policy is in part that of helping the badly-off without thereby affecting at all the well-off, the remainder of the population. Here no goods, which is to say no means to satisfaction, are transferred from the well-off to the badly-off. Rather, new means are brought into existence. *If* this endeavour by itself could be successful, that would be the end of the matter. No question of transfers of goods between the two classes would arise. And, if there remained inequalities within the now universal class of the well-off, the Principle of Equality would have nothing to say of this state of affairs.

In its other part the first policy is that of transferring goods from the well-off, but goods whose loss would not significantly affect their well-being. It is arguable, to say the least, that there do exist such goods, means to well-being which their possessors do not trouble to use. Again, if these transfers could be successful in achieving the goal of the principle, that would be the end of the matter.

The second policy is that of reducing the number of the badly-off by transferring goods to them from the well-off, with the known effect that this *will* reduce the well-being of the well-off. Given our earlier scepticism of Conservative claims as to an incentive system, we can take this as a real and large possibility, in no way an ill-fated enterprise. That is, we *can* reduce the number of the badly-off in this

way. This policy may be regarded, in fact, by proponents of the
Principle of Equality, as their most important.

The third policy is a partner to the second, and not much less
important. It has to do with what can be granted, that the goal of
the principle may be served by having *a kind* of incentive system,
perhaps as well described as a compensation system. It will involve
certain favourable inequalities, of limited extent. The policy presupposes that what individuals require, by way of any such inequalities, is certainly no matter of human nature, no matter of iron law.
It is properly described, rather, as a matter of their attitudes. If
present attitudes have been passed on from generation to generation,
they are none the less open to change. To revert to terms used earlier,
they have to do with social altruism or rather the lack of it, and of
what mainly gives rise to this state of affairs, an absence of social
persuasion. The third policy, then, will reduce very greatly the
inequalities of incentive or compensation which are expected or
demanded by individuals if they are to forward the end of a society.
These inequalities are to be reduced, of course, just in order to leave
greater resources for the relief of the badly-off.

As remarked, the Principle of Equality is also to the effect that the
three policies are to be forwarded by certain practices of equality.

The most important political one is *one person one vote,* or rather, a
practice which goes further than that in securing effective democracy.
It will certainly involve fair restraints on the financing of particular
political parties and on their influence over the press and broadcasting. Also, there is the practice of equal provision of many material
goods and of many opportunities. If we are not in fact perfectly equal,
in any of the ways suggested by what was called the principle of
natural equality (p. 171), we are sufficiently alike so as to make equal
provision, for the most part, an economical and rational practice.
That we are alike is the fact of our shared fundamental desires.
Still, if these two practices of equality are of the greatest importance,
they are not the only practices allowed by the principle. If we are
alike, we are also different. It is not always true, evidently, that an
equal provision of a good will serve the end of the principle. The sick
need what the well do not.

The Principle of Equality can now be more explicitly stated.

The goal or end of a society must be to make well-off those who
are badly-off, by the policy of increasing the means to well-being
and of transferring unused means from the well-off, the policy

of transferring means which will affect their well-being, and the
policy of reducing inequalities having to do with incentive or
compensation, these three policies to be advanced in good part
by practices of equality.

This is not vulnerable at all to the objection having to do with
mere relativities. What it recommends is not the goal of people being
related in a certain way to one another, being equal. The goal is to
get people out of the condition of being badly-off. It is the goal of
ending frustration or distress. Certainly, if it is achieved, there will
be a large side-effect – all people being equal in the sense of being
other than badly-off. But nothing but woeful or wilful confusion can
give anyone the idea that the goal is itself a relational one. The same
is to be said in connection with the mentioned practices of equality.
They are greatly important means, but not the end.[17] If I am convinced that more democracy is the way to a society in which people
do not have to sleep in the streets, and want such a society above all,
it is absurd to suppose that in this respect I have democracy as an
end-in-itself.

It is as clear that the principle does not entail that we should
have everyone only equally well-off if the alternative were everyone
unequally better-off. Nor does it entail the worse upshot that we
should have everyone equally badly-off if the alternative were everyone being unequally well-off. This is the case if we understand these
several terms, 'badly-off' and so on, in the way we have defined
them, and also if they are used in related ways. Using the terms in
the defined way, the fact of the matter is that the principle does not
speak of the situation, not yet nearly in sight, where there might be
a choice between everybody's being equally well-off and everyone
still better-off but unequally so. The spirit of the principle is very
definitely for the second option. Nor does the principle have the
consequence that we should drag down the well-off if that had no
good effect, but rather made all of us equally badly-off. On the
contrary, the principle prohibits this. The second policy requires that
transfers from the well-off *decrease* the numbers of the badly-off.

The formulation we have of the Principle of Equality is not the
only one, and not identical with a formulation that has seen the light
of day in the past. We need not suppose we have its eternal and
canonical form – or a form as agreeable to all other supporters of it
as it is to those of philosophical habits. Economists, no doubt, would
couch it differently, and political theorists differently again.[18] If the

subject of the inquiry we are now ending were the Left rather than the Right, the principle would get a lot more attention. We would look into various questions raised by it and various recommendations of it, and relate it to the various generalities about equality looked at earlier.

We would also consider its great capability of withstanding objections – such as the objection about liberty – which are also withstood by the principle of equality of results. We might spend a moment or two on an issue that is less than paralysingly crucial, its name. It can be grumbled, of course, as it has been, that since the aim of the principle is not a mere equality, but the alleviation of distress, it should be called something else. There are good reasons for its name, but, if you want, call it something else. Call it, for example, because of what it can certainly be said to concern, the Principle of Freedom. For something about all of that, and for the earlier formulation, interested parties must turn elsewhere.[19]

Given that our concern is what it is, there are only two essential propositions to be noted. They will bring us to our conclusion about Conservatism.

The first, assumed already, is that the Principle of Equality is an adequate summation of what we have been calling the politics of the Left. Conceivably it is among the best of such summations. It, unlike the principle of equality of results, can properly be spoken of as giving the rationale of the Left. There can be no doubt about that. Whether or not some egalitarians have been inclined to describe themselves in the way of Tawney, in terms of the principle of equal results, it is nonsense to suppose that the actual political traditions in question have pursued mere relativities. It is nonsense, for various reasons, to suppose that they have pursued any sort of equality over any sort of inequality.

They have not, in connection with education, had a goal which might in conceivable circumstances have been achieved by destroying all possibilities of education, say by burning down all the schools, thereby producing an equality. They have not had a goal which in conceivable circumstances might have been achieved by reducing all education to some rudimentary level of instruction, thereby again producing an equality. Consider something yet more fundamental. It is the truth that in Britain the life-expectancy of the fifth social class as officially defined is strikingly smaller than that of the first social class.[20] The Left has not had a goal which might have been *exactly* as well achieved by shortening the lives of the first social class as by lengthening the lives of the fifth, or of course by reducing both still further to any situation whatever of equal lifetimes. It needs to be seen clearly that exactly such a benightedness or awfulness, one which has these possibilities within it, is exactly what is assigned to the Left by those who identify it with the principle of equality of results, or that principle as it can be understood. The traditions of the Left have not conceivably had a goal which in conceivable circumstances might have been perfectly achieved by producing equal ignorance, equally short lives, or an equal poverty, or an equal captivity and powerlessness, or a terrible equality of frustration with respect to our other fundamental desires. It cannot conceivably be that the concern or commitment of these traditions has been a relationship, a mere relativity. Anyone tempted to the silliness of saying otherwise can be cured by considering those societies which have actually made some progress towards the given ideal, and comparing them to what they were before.

The second essential proposition to be noted is that the Principle of Equality, whatever is to be said against it, is a *clear* and a *moral* principle. If it is open to objections, as any principle is, it is no mystery. There is no uncertainty or obscurity about its fundamental commitment. It is wholly different in this respect from the congeries of unsatisfactory things that falls under the heading the 'Principle of Desert'. As for its nature, it indubitably is a moral principle. We need not spend time on coming to a definition of the moral. Any conception of morality which failed to classify the Principle of Equality as a moral principle would itself be refuted by that consequence. It is a moral principle if only for the reason that it enjoins us to struggle to reduce distress, places that obligation on us. No injunction is more recognizably moral, or, as might be added, more distant from various factitious intrinsic goods we have noticed at several points in our reflections.

We now come to the conclusion to which all our reflections, from those on change and reform onwards, have tended. We are left with no conclusion but one.

There are saints among us, as it seems, but there are not many, and uncomfortable questions arise about them. For the rest, we are to a rather too noticeable extent self-interested. As was remarked in connection with human nature, when we were contemplating Conservative warnings about our lowness, we put first our own concerns and the concerns of those close to us. Our sympathies do not extend far. We put ourselves and these few others first with respect to satisfaction of the fundamental desires shared by all of us.

This universal fact has within it the fact of the self-interest of the Left. It has within it, to speak more sharply, the self-interest of those who propound and those who benefit by progress towards the ideal of the Left. The working class, as it was once called, votes with an eye to its own benefit, usually not a very clear eye. If it had more possessions, and others less, it would count as selfish. There is something else, however. What is also true is that it can justify itself. Its self-interest is in accord with a moral principle, the moral principle that may be thought to overcome all others. It has the justification of the Principle of Equality.

The universal fact of self-interest also has within it the self-interest, the selfishness, of Conservatives. The strength of truth, the impossibility of always following Burke's sordid injunction to be economical with it,[21] has led many Conservatives to concede the fact. Some, for whatever reason, do not long leave out of their reflections the relevant sentence of Adam Smith. 'It is not from the benevolence of the butcher, the brewer, or the baker, that we expect our dinner, but from their regard to their own interest.'[22] Russell Kirk is typical in admitting selfishness but adding a word of self-defence which allows for a certain complacency. 'Conservatism has its vice, and that vice is selfishness ... Radicalism, too, has its vice, and that vice is envy.'[23] Clinton Rossiter, although speaking at this moment as a kind of devil's advocate, does not much dissent from what he hears himself saying about Conservatism and a way of life in which private property is the indispensable element.

> Conservatism is selfish. The Conservative, hardly coincidentally, is well-served by this way of life. While claiming to defend an entire society, he really defends his own position in it. Conservatism is inherently an attitude of possession – whether possession of property, status, reputation, or power – and it fears change primarily because this means dispossession. All philosophies, it may be argued, are rationalizations of self-interest, but the interests of Conservatism are especially self-centred, for they are vested rather than pursued.[24]

All that is clear enough. The conclusion to which we come is not that Conservatives are selfish. It is that they are nothing else. Their selfishness is the rationale of their politics, and they have no other rationale. They stand without the support, the legitimation, of any recognizably moral principle. It is in this that they are distinguished fundamentally from those who are opposed to them.

This grim fact is the best and all that can be said in explanation of their various distinctions. That they are opposed to all change is false. The particular change to which they are opposed is change which is against their interests. It is against the interests of those who are identified, first, by their greater possession of private property. There is no other account of that change. So with the theory and ideology they are against, which is not, of course, all theory and ideology.

Their selfishness alone is what explains their various and more important commitments in connection with property and a market, commitments to such things as reward. It explains their resistance to what we have described too casually and abstractly as social freedom, decent lives for those who lack them. The resistance of Conservatives to decent lives for others has no other rationale but their selfishness. So too with their distinctions in the matters of government, society and equality. There is no other explanation than what it is precise to name as naked class interest. At a lighter moment in the course of our reflections, our subject was Macaulay, and the thought that his response to his Maker, on being asked to justify his politics, might have been that he always had an eye on the main chance. He had no other reply.

The grim fact of amorality is some large part of the explanation of Conservative style, or rather, of various styles and ways of proceeding. These include omission and inexplicitness, as in the case of the goal or end with respect to an incentive system. They include bombast, spirituality and plangency in place of definition. They include pretence of condescension, political metaphysics and a retreat from ordinary seriousness. They include very bad argument. It is in good part because he lacks what he would otherwise produce that Burke proceeds as he does. Conor Cruise O'Brien is too kind to say of the mighty farrago of the *Reflections on the Revolution in France* that it is the work of the master of the Whig manner, of the Gothic style, the pathetic, the ironic, the rolling period, the concise.[25] It is also the work of a partisan of a party with no principle. The grim fact must come to mind, too, with the lesser works of the New Right. But let us not think further on this lumpen-intelligentsia.

Let us also leave it to others to judge further of Conservatism, the politics and the life, which has, in the end, nothing to say for itself.

Afterword to
the Paperback Edition

This book is like Edmund Burke's *Reflections on the Revolution in France* in that it was written in a kind of passion, an anger that things have gone badly in a society. This strong feeling resulted in a book which in turn inflamed some of its many reviewers. Despite the book's passionate origin, and the protests to which it gave rise, I am now more persuaded of its truth. The affront that its conclusion gives, to my mind, is the particular affront that can attach only to truth. Certainly it is a wholly serious conclusion, and would almost certainly be drawn again if I began again. Indeed, I would somewhat strengthen it by enlarging on how natural it is. It accords with certain propositions advanced by moral philosophers about the use or function of morality in societies – there is no surprise whatever in critical and reflective morality being on a certain side in the long battle between Burke and his followers on the Right and their adversaries on the Left.

My renewed confidence in what is concluded about the rationale or fundamental principle of Conservatism is owed in large part to one fact. It is not the fact that many reviewers with something like my politics fell into agreement, and that others were inclined to it. It was a pleasure, but not one which gave new conviction, to have the imprimatur of Michael Foot. What produced new conviction was that no unhappy critic offered an alternative answer to the main question of what rationale, what commitment or set of commitments, lies under and informs the tradition of Conservatism.

Enoch Powell ruminated, wisely passing over in silence that part of his political past mentioned in the book; Anthony Quinton was passably witty and in a way improved on my answer to the main question; Ian Gilmour revealed to the world that among my little historical errors was the demotion of Rainborough from Colonel to Captain. He also said no one would pay attention to my book – said so, fortunately for me, in the course of writing at great length about it and so securing that many did. Conor Cruise O'Brien stood up for the character of Burke, who remains in need of friends in that particular regard.

None of these thinkers chose to unveil any alternative to what upset them. It was not that they failed to produce a good or an arguable alternative to the rationale assigned to Conservatism in this book, but that they produced none at all. These Right Honourable, ennobled and other mountains shuddered, laboured, and brought forth no mice at all.

Some implied that they had good reason to fail this challenge, the most fundamental challenge to what purports to be – and indeed in a clear sense must be – a great political tradition. For Enoch Powell, Conservatism is essentially a rhetorical appeal and hence is like the singing of a song. We are just to listen, and not to expect it to be a philosophy or to be logical. No song stands up to close examination, nor comes to anything definite. Ian Gilmour reports with approval the lines of a mentor of his, Michael Oakeshott, that Conservatives 'sail a boundless and bottomless sea' where 'there is neither harbour for shelter nor floor for anchorage, neither starting place nor appointed destination'. As you will gather, we had better not ask for further directions about where they are taking us. What we can best do, according to Bernard Crick, is not to look for anything clear, consistent, rational, principled or summative, but try to understand empathetically. For Bhikhu Parekh, Conservatism is just a mixed bundle of beliefs and feelings held together for a time by a vague vision. Roger Scruton is not outdone by any of this. He is sympathetic to the view that Conservatism is a kind of knowledge that cannot be contained in a single mind.

Putting aside that last depressing thought, I have some sympathy with one idea in all this, and indeed take it to be true. This idea is to the effect that the tradition of Conservatism has not often tried to sum itself up in an orderly and explicit way. We are given no help if someone appears at our shoulder and sings a little bit, or gestures at a vision, or keeps on intoning, 'Empathize with me, empathize with me.' Nor is it helpful if he utters numinous sentences about being lost at sea.

Does it follow that no one should try to bring Conservatism into succinct view? I cannot see that. To suppose so seems to be to fall into the mistake that an effective description of particularities must itself be particular rather than general, that a group of feelings cannot be seen to come to anything, that an analysis of the unclear must itself be unclear, that an account of the inchoate must itself be inchoate. If this were the history of ideas or the endeavour of the student of ideology then the worst suspicions of those labours on the part of some philosophers would be well confirmed. It is plain indeed, above all, that to eschew generalization about a subject is to rule out the possibility of useful knowledge of it and useful conclusions about it. Does anyone, whatever they may say, ever really attempt such a thing in their own thinking?

There is more to be said of the need for a clear summary of Conservatism. It is not just an object of study, a political tradition that does not go in for a certain kind of self-description, and so might be thought to raise an academic problem. That is not what is most important about it. It shares with other political traditions a certain character in that it tells us in some way or other what sort of society we ought to have, or ought to keep. Furthermore, and yet more important, it faces us not with a theoretical but a practical choice, a consequential choice in the real world. It proposes to affect lives and societies, and will do so or continue to do so if it has the support of enough of us.

Given this fact, we have an evident and not only intellectual need to get clear in general just what recommendation it is making to us. Obviously this is imperative, something about which there is some urgency. If we are considering whether to support the tradition of Conservatism we need to have a plain and effective summation of it. That a best summation exists is a certainty, and that it can be clear and short is as good as a certainty.

My perturbed reviewers sometimes offered a second and related kind of excuse for failing to produce their own summation of Conservatism. That excuse was that there was nothing to summarize. Ian Gilmour was to the fore here. It was sad enough that I was the archetypal rationalist of the nightmares of his mentor, but sadder still that I had offended against a certain dictum: 'It is just as well, when writing a book, to make sure, before you get very far, that the subject exists.' My book had no subject because no one can seriously believe that Ronald Reagan had the same politics as such decent Tories as Rab Butler, that the New Right had the same politics as the Old, or, to come closer to the bone, that Ian Gilmour had the same politics as Margaret Thatcher, who did not prolong his services in her government.

It was unfortunate for him that in writing that my use of 'Conservatism' picked out nothing, because of differences among Conservatives, he was forgetful of how he had begun his lengthy reflections. He had begun by some pronouncements on the history and the death of what he took to be a real subject, picked out by the word 'Socialism'. He clearly did not suppose that he had no subject because the tradition in question includes diversity, indeed diversity of which he gave some details. What he gave evidence of in his obituary was the truth, soon forgotten, that it is footling to suppose a thing does not exist or cannot be identified, well defined and discussed despite what will *always* be true: that it is made up of parts that are different.

If my critics did not hazard an alternative answer to my main question, and gave two bad excuses for not doing so, some of them also evidenced a further resistance to my posing and answering it as I did. It was that I was not overly scholarly. (It is true that the *Oxford Times* appeared to take a gratifyingly different view of the book in saying that 'it promises to become one of the textbooks of the Conservative faith', but this was a lone and puzzling voice.)

The complaint of unscholarliness has to do with the nature of philosophy, and in this case political philosophy. That is what my book is. It is different from a number of things, including good and bad history of ideas, let alone history of politics. My aim, one that is common among philosophers, was indeed to give a general and effective definition of a thing, appraise what is said for it, and finally judge it. This endeavour of construction commonly involves trying to arrive at what, according to one's lights, is the best account of something, since there is little point in examining anything else. The philosophical endeavour, obviously, is not in the end a scholarly or historical one, and is not sensibly looked at in that way. What is historical in it, what is reported of the opinions of others, may well be illustrative rather than the substance of the thing.

Early on in my researches, furthermore, a fact remarked on above became clear to me. It is that Conservatives give one little help in understanding their politics – as, indeed, they are all too ready to allow. They make a virtue of not trying. Thus I did not plough on as long as might have been useful in other such endeavours. Patten, Popper and Pym were not extensively consulted, and nor did I turn over every page of Burke.

I do not suppose that the philosophical way of proceeding is to the taste of everyone, or should be, despite the fact that it seems to me no arcane thing, but just intelligent inquiry of a clear-eyed, sceptical, persistent and systematic kind. The history of ideas and the study of ideology must certainly be allowed to flourish. It is hard to see, however, what other way than the philosophical there can be if one has the goal of effectively considering the proposal made to us by Conservatism, or any other political tradition.

Notes

Chapter 1: Change (pp. 1–16)

1. Anthony Quinton, *The Politics of Imperfection*
2. Peregrine Worsthorne's political column illuminates Conservatism more than quite a number of books on the subject
3. Quoted by Clinton Rossiter, *Conservatism in America*, p. 116
4. Edmund Burke, *Letter to a Noble Lord*, in L. I. Bredvold and R. G. Ross, eds., *The Philosophy of Edmund Burke*
5. Conor Cruise O'Brien, introduction to his edition of Burke's *Reflections on the Revolution in France*. The introduction, although sympathetic, is to my knowledge the best short account of Burke's thinking
6. Michael Oakeshott, 'On being Conservative', in his *Rationalism in Politics and Other Essays*, pp. 168–70
7. Edmund Burke, *Reflections on the Revolution in France*, pp. 194–5
8. Roger Scruton, *The Meaning of Conservatism*, p. 21
9. Noel O'Sullivan, *Conservatism*, p. 12

Chapter 2: Theory, Etc. (pp. 17–44)

1. Quoted by Robert Nisbet, *Conservatism: Dream and Reality*, p. 7
2. From the margin of Adams's copy of his *Discourses on Davila*, 1805. Excerpt in Russell Kirk, ed., *The Portable Conservative Reader*, p. 66
3. Kirk, op. cit., introduction, p. xiv
4. Quoted in Clinton Rossiter, *Conservatism in America*, p. 50

5. Speech, reprinted in Kirk, op. cit., p. 145
6. Kirk, op. cit., introduction, p. xviii
7. Michael Oakeshott, *Rationalism in Politics and Other Essays*, pp. 116 ff
8. Benjamin Disraeli, *A Vindication of the English Constitution*, extract in Kirk, op. cit., pp. 218 ff
9. Friedrich Hayek, *Economic Freedom and Representative Government*, p. 13
10. Edmund Burke, *Reflections on the Revolution in France*, p. 181
11. *The Private Papers of Henry Ryecroft*, 1903, excerpt in Kirk, op. cit., p. 378
12. Burke, op. cit., p. 119
13. Roger Scruton, *The Meaning of Conservatism*, p. 119
14. 'Conservatism', in Paul Edwards, ed., *The Encyclopaedia of Philosophy*, Vol. 2, p. 195
15. Burke, op. cit., p. 63
16. 'Conservatism', in Edwards, op. cit., p. 195
17. Anthony Quinton, *The Politics of Imperfection*, p. 11
18. Ibid., pp. 16–17
19. Burke, op. cit., p. 183; cf pp. 152–3
20. Scruton, op. cit., p. 33
21. Nisbet, op. cit., p. 19
22. G. A. Cohen, *Karl Marx's Theory of History: A Defence*
23. Nisbet, op. cit., p. vii
24. Noel O'Sullivan, *Conservatism*, pp. 7, 31
25. Quinton, op. cit., pp. 12–13
26. Ibid., p. 33
27. Ronald Dworkin, *Taking Rights Seriously*
28. Robert Nozick, *Anarchy, State, and Utopia*, p. 160

Chapter 3: Human Nature (pp. 45–81)

1. Christopher Berry, *Human Nature*, Chapters 1–3, esp. p. 36; cf Leslie Stevenson, *Seven Theories of Human Nature*, pp. 14–15
2. Edmund Burke, *Reflections on the Revolution in France*, p. 173
3. Thomas Carlyle, 'Shooting Niagara', *Works*, Vol. XXX, p. 40
4. Michael Oakeshott, *Rationalism in Politics and Other Essays*, pp. 174–5
5. G. A. Cohen, *Karl Marx's Theory of History: A Defence*, p. 103; but see also pp. 151–2
6. Berry, op. cit., pp. 6 ff
7. Cf John Finnis, *Natural Law and Natural Rights*
8. Burke, op. cit., p. 152
9. Clinton Rossiter, *Conservatism in America*, p. 23
10. Lincoln Allison, *Right Principles: A Conservative Philosophy of Politics*, p. 170
11. Ibid., p. 34
12. Burke, op. cit., pp. 187, 188
13. Anthony Quinton, *The Politics of Imperfection*, pp. 11–16
14. Christopher Berry, 'Conservatism and Human Nature', pp. 54, 55, 58, 63
15. Christopher Berry, *Human Nature*, pp. 68, 73, 79
16. Derek Parfit, *Reasons and Persons*, is a striking original work on the subject; Jonathan Glover's *I: The Philosophy and Psychology of Personal Identity* is the foremost general treatment
17. Christopher Berry, 'Conservatism and Human Nature', p. 62
18. Christopher Berry, *Human Nature*, p. 71
19. Ted Honderich, 'The Problem of Well-Being and the Principle of Equality'
20. Cf Allison, op. cit., p. 30
21. Jeremy Bentham, *Introduction to the Principles of Morals and Legislation*, p. 33
22. For something about reluctant wants, see my *A Theory of Determinism: The Mind, Neuroscience, and Life-Hopes*, p. 394
23. *The Letters of David Hume*, Vol. 1
24. William Godwin, *An Enquiry Concerning Political Justice*, p. 140
25. Quinton, op. cit.
26. Russell Kirk, *The Portable Conservative Reader*, pp. xxxv–xxxvi
27. Peregrine Worsthorne, 'Too Much Freedom', p. 149
28. Ted Honderich, *A Theory of Determinism: The Mind, Neuroscience, and Life-Hopes*
29. David Hume, *An Enquiry Concerning Human Understanding*, p. 82
30. Cohen, op. cit.
31. Robert Nozick, *Philosophical Explanations*; cf Honderich, *A Theory of Determinism: The Mind, Neuroscience, and Life-Hopes*, pp. 187–90
32. Immanuel Kant, *Philosophy of Law*, pp. 195–8
33. Ted Honderich, *Punishment: The Supposed Justifications*, Chapter 2

Chapter 4: Freedom (pp. 82–103)

1. The struggle is carried forward in 'On Liberty'. For an account, see my 'The Worth of J. S. Mill's "On Liberty",' *Political Studies*, 1974, and ' "On Liberty" and Morality-Dependent Harms', *Political Studies*, 1982
2. Roy Hattersley, *Choose Freedom: The Future for Democratic Socialism*
3. Edmund Burke, *Reflections on the Revolution in France*, p. 89
4. R. Levitas, 'Ideology and the New Right', and A. Belsey, 'The New Right, Social Order, and Civil Liberties', both in Levitas, ed., *The Ideology of the New Right*; Desmond S. King, *The New Right: Politics, Markets and Citizenship*
5. Friedrich Hayek, *The Constitution of Liberty* and like volumes
6. Keith Joseph and Jonathan Sumption, *Equality*, pp. 47 ff
7. Quoted in Robert Nisbet, *Conservatism: Dream and Reality*, p. 55
8. 'Property and Law', p. 442, as reprinted in Kirk, *The Portable Con-*

servative Reader. Paul Elmer More is far from being a lone voice in his affirmation of property. Many of his countrymen speak with him. His zeal was in a way exceeded by President James McCosh of Princeton, who announced property to be a *divine* right (Rossiter, *Conservatism in America,* p. 150)

9. Roger Scruton, *The Meaning of Conservatism,* p. 94

10. Lawrence Becker, *Property Rights: Philosophic Foundations,* and J.O. Grunebaum, *Private Ownership*

11. Murray Rothbard, *For a New Liberty: The Libertarian Manifesto*

12. *The Omega File,* reports of the Adam Smith Institute

13. A.M. Honore, 'Ownership', in A.G. Guest, ed., *Oxford Essays in Jurisprudence*

14. Edmund Burke, 'Thoughts and Details on Scarcity', quoted in Nisbet, op. cit., p. 36

15. Hugh Cecil, *Conservatism*

16. Quoted in Andrew Gamble, *The Conservative Nation,* p. 116

17. Rothbard, op. cit.

18. Robert Nozick, *Anarchy, State and Utopia*

19. Thomas Jefferson, First Inaugural Address, quoted by David Green, *The New Right: The Counter-Revolution in Political, Economic and Social Thought,* pp. 74–5

20. Adam Smith, *The Wealth of Nations,* Vol. 2, pp. 180–1; cf Milton Friedman, *Capitalism and Freedom,* p. 2, Chapter 2

21. Scruton, op. cit.

22. Burke, op. cit., p. 140

23. Green, op. cit., p. 1

24. Smith, op. cit., p. 400

25. Lincoln Allison, *Right Principles: A Conservative Philosophy of Politics,* p. 112

26. Hayek, op. cit., p. 29

27. Friedrich Hayek, *The Mirage of Social Justice,* p. 64

28. Cf David Smith, *The Rise and Fall of Monetarism*

29. Milton Friedman and Anna Schwarz, *A Monetary History of the United States*

30. Allison, op. cit., pp. 11–15

31. Scruton, op. cit., pp. 98, 15 ff

32. Alan Brown, *Modern Political Philosophy,* Chapter 4

33. Rossiter, op. cit., p. 38

34. 'Property and Law', in Kirk, op. cit., pp. 438–40

35. Friedman, op. cit., pp. 8, 7

36. Noel O'Sullivan, *Conservatism,* p. 27

37. Friedrich Hayek, *The Road to Serfdom*

38. Ludwig von Mises, *Socialism,* p. 511

39. Anthony Quinton, *The Politics of Imperfection,* p. 21

40. Quoted in O'Sullivan, op. cit., p. 149

41. Friedman, op. cit., p. 10

42. Ibid., p. 11

43. O'Sullivan, op. cit., pp. 142–3

44. Alan Ryan, *Property and Political Theory,* Chapter 1; Becker, op. cit., Chapter 4

45. Nozick, op. cit., Chapter 7, Section I. It is reprinted, by the way, in *Philosophy as It is,* edited by myself and Myles Burnyeat

46. Joseph and Sumption, op. cit., p. 58

47. On 10 November 1988, speaking to members of the Opposition in the House of Commons on the subject of the economy, the Prime Minister offered the reminder that 'everyone in this House has done very well out of it'.

48. Peter Thornton, *Decade of Decline: Civil Liberties in the Thatcher Years*

Chapter 5: Government (pp. 124–47)

1. Edmund Burke, *Reflections on the Revolution in France,* p. 94

2. Ibid., p. 99

3. Edmund Burke, *Appeal from the New to the Old Whigs,* excerpt in Kirk, *The Portable Conservative Reader,* p. 44

4. John Randolph, speech reprinted in Kirk, op. cit., pp. 131 ff

5. Benjamin Disraeli, *A Vindication of the English Constitution*

6. Thomas Macaulay, letter (1857) reprinted in Kirk, op. cit., p. 215

7. Robert Salisbury, 'Disintegration', *Quarterly Review,* 1883

8. Hugh Cecil, *Conservatism*

9. Noel O'Sullivan, *Conservatism*, Chapters 4, 5, p. 136

10. T. S. Eliot, *Selected Prose*, p. 222

11. Roger Scruton, *The Meaning of Conservatism*, pp. 16, 53

12. Clinton Rossiter, *Conservatism in America*, p. 61; see also p. 63

13. Robert Nisbet, *Conservatism: Dream and Reality*, p. 40

14. Lincoln Allison, *Right Principles: A Conservative Philosophy of Politics*, p. 168

15. Edmund Burke, *Reflections on the Revolution in France*, p. 150

16. Peregrine Worsthorne, 'Too Much Freedom', pp. 141–3, in Maurice Cowling, ed., *Conservative Essays*

17. Edmund Burke, *Appeal from the New to the Old Whigs*, excerpt in Kirk, op. cit.

18. Edmund Burke, *Reflections on the Revolution in France*, p. 139

19. Anthony Quinton traces them back to earlier conservatisms we are not considering, including that of the sixteenth-century theologian and philosopher Richard Hooker

20. David Hume, *Essays Moral, Political and Literary*, p. 33

21. Quoted by Nisbet, op. cit., p. 71

22. Rossiter, op. cit., p. 103

23. Allison, op. cit., pp. 163–4

24. Edmund Burke, *Reflections on the Revolution in France*, p. 86 (Everyman edn)

25. Henry Bolingbroke, *Dissertation on Parties*, Letter 10

26. Edmund Burke, *Reflections on the Revolution in France*, p. 105

27. Anthony Quinton, *The Politics of Imperfection*, p. 90

28. Friedrich Hayek, *Law, Legislation and Liberty*, Vol. I p. 95, Vol. III p. 119

29. Conor Cruise O'Brien, introduction to his edition of Burke's *Reflections*, pp. 56 ff

30. Edmund Burke, *Reflections on the Revolution in France*, p. 342

31. Quoted in Nisbet, op. cit., p. 44

32. Thomas Macaulay, letter (1857) reprinted in Kirk, op. cit., pp. 215–16

33. O'Sullivan, op. cit., pp. 108–12

34. Quoted ibid., p. 102

35. Edmund Burke, *Letter to a Member of the National Assembly*, excerpt in Kirk, op. cit., p. 148

36. Scruton, op. cit., pp. 111, 84

37. Stuart Hall, 'The Great Moving Right Show', in Hall and Martin Jacques, eds, *The Politics of Thatcherism*; Andrew Belsey, 'The New Right, Social Order and Civil Liberties', in R. Levitas, ed., *The Ideology of the New Right*; Desmond S. King, *The New Right: Politics, Markets and Citizenship*, pp. 120 ff

38. For example, Stanley G. Payne, *Fascism: Comparison and Definition*. I am not quite so keen on Noel O'Sullivan's *Fascism*, which might be thought to be other than plain political science

39. Levitas, op. cit., p. 8

40. Adolf Hitler, *Mein Kampf*, quoted in Rick Wilford, 'Fascism', p. 233, in Robert Eccleshall *et al.*, *Political Ideologies*

41. Novalis, otherwise known as Friedrich Leopold, Freiherr von Hardenberg, quoted in O'Sullivan, op. cit., p. 59

Chapter 6: Society (pp. 148–68)

1. Quoted by F. J. C. Hearnshaw, *Conservatism in England*, p. 241

2. Edmund Burke, *Reflections on the Revolution in France*, pp. 194–5

3. Ibid., p. 120

4. Ibid., p. 193

5. Hearnshaw, op. cit., pp. vi, 6

6. Ibid., p. 23

7. Clinton Rossiter, *Conservatism in America*, p. 27

8. Roger Scruton, *The Meaning of Conservatism*, p. 23

9. Lincoln Allison, *Right Principles: A Conservative Philosophy of Politics*, pp. 16–17

10. Anthony Quinton, *The Politics of Imperfection*, p. 16

11. For a brief account of 'the whole is greater than the sum of its parts', as it turns up in biology, where alas it does,

see Morton O. Beckner, 'Organismic Biology, in Paul Edwards, ed., *The Encyclopaedia of Philosophy*; for a typically acute and sensitive discussion of such an idea in moral philosophy, see Timothy Sprigge, *The Rational Foundations of Ethics*, pp. 36–43

12. Burke, op. cit., p. 194
13. Scruton, op. cit., pp. 21–2
14. Quoted by Irving Babbitt, 'Burke and the Moral Imagination', in Kirk, *The Portable Conservative Reader*, p. 455
15. Hearnshaw, op. cit., p. 28
16. Quoted by George F. Will, foreword to Rossiter, op. cit., p. x
17. Hearnshaw, op. cit., p. 23
18. For a good account of recent attitudes, see Gill Seidel, 'Culture, Nation and "Race" in the British and French New Right', in Levitas, ed., *The Ideology of the New Right*
19. Burke, op. cit., p. 138
20. Scruton, op. cit., p. 68
21. John Casey, quoted by Seidel, loc. cit., p. 113
22. Anthony Flew, quoted by Seidel, ibid., p. 119
23. Quoted by Paul Foot, *The Rise of Enoch Powell*, p. 71
24. J.E. Powell, *Freedom and Reality*, speeches, ed. John Wood, p. 214
25. Isaiah Berlin, *Against the Current: Essays in the History of Ideas*, pp. 286 ff
26. Eliot's anti-semitism is discussed in 'Eliot's Uglier Touches', by Christopher Ricks, *The Times Literary Supplement*, 4–10 November 1988
27. Burke, op. cit., p. 173; Dr O'Brien has another word to say in exculpation of Burke
28. Quoted by O'Sullivan, *Conservatism*, p. 98
29. George Santayana, *Soliloquies in England and Later Soliloquies*, reprinted in Kirk, op. cit., pp. 476–7
30. Robert Nisbet, *Conservatism: Dream and Reality*, p. 45
31. John Stuart Mill, *On Liberty*
32. Burke, op. cit., p. 372

33. Quoted by Miriam David, 'Moral and Maternal: The Family in the Right', in Levitas, op. cit., p. 158

Chapter 7: Equality (pp. 169–207)

1. John Adams, letter reprinted in Kirk, ed., *The Portable Conservative Reader*, pp. 69–70
2. Edmund Burke, *Reflections on the Revolution in France*, p. 124
3. Ibid., p. 169
4. Peregrine Worsthorne, 'How Egalitarianism Breeds Robbery and Yobbery', *Sunday Telegraph*, 19 June 1988
5. David Cooper, *Illusions of Equality*, pp. ix, 2
6. William Letwin, *Against Equality*, pp. 69–70, 3
7. Keith Joseph and Jonathan Sumption, *Equality*, pp. 72–5 *et passim*
8. Duke of Edinburgh, *Men, Machines and Sacred Cows*, speeches; this book brings to mind another, much to be recommended: Edgar Wilson, *The Myth of British Monarchy*
9. Adams, loc. cit., p. 69
10. James Fenimore Cooper, 'On Equality', partly reprinted in Kirk, op. cit., p. 187
11. Anthony Flew, *The Politics of Procrustes*, pp. 32–3
12. Letwin, op. cit., p. 13
13. Joseph and Sumption, op. cit., p. 66
14. Flew, op. cit., p. 32. The best-known modern work on egalitarianism, by the way, R. S. Tawney's *Equality* (1931), makes clear that it is not committed to factual equality
15. Kirk, op. cit., p. xvii
16. Burke, op. cit., p. 124
17. Quoted in C. H. Firth, ed., *The Clarke Papers*, Vol. 1, p. 301
18. Flew, op. cit., pp. 67 ff; David Cooper, op. cit., pp. 20 ff
19. Joseph and Sumption, op. cit., p. 33
20. David Cooper, op. cit., pp. 67 ff

21. Lincoln Allison, *Right Principles: A Conservative Philosophy of Politics*, pp. 78 ff

22. Letwin, op. cit., pp. 34 ff

23. I do attend to the argument in my *Violence for Equality: Inquiries in Political Philosophy*, pp. 117 ff

24. John Rawls, *A Theory of Justice*, p. 61. I have since learned, alas, after my book was finished, that Rawls has since made good the omission, in 'The Basic Liberties and Their Priority', the 1981 Tanner Lectures, included in S. M. McMurrin, ed., *Liberty, Equality and Law*

25. Joseph and Sumption, op. cit., pp. 20, 5–6, 63

26. Milton Friedman, *Free to Choose*, p. 166

27. Letwin, op. cit., p. 3

28. Tawney, op. cit., pp. 48–9, 45–7, 57

29 George Saintsbury, *A Scrap Book*, excerpt in Kirk, op. cit., p. 382

30. Joseph and Sumption, op. cit., pp. 27–8

31. Burke, op. cit., p. 204

32. Paul Elmer More, 'Property and Law', reprinted in Kirk, op. cit., p. 447; Flew, op. cit., p. 59; Friedman, op. cit., pp. 173 ff

33. Joseph and Sumption, op. cit., pp. 17–18

34. Ibid., p. 20

35. Quoted by Tawney, op. cit., p. 34

36. Burke, op. cit., p. 138

37. Quoted by Robert Eccleshall, *Political Ideologies*, p. 90

38. Robert Salisbury, 'Disintegration', *Quarterly Review*, 1883, quoted by Noel O'Sullivan, *Conservatism*, p. 108

39. Robert Nozick, *Anarchy, State and Utopia*, pp. 160–4

40. Joseph and Sumption, op. cit., p. 52

41. Ibid., pp. 21, 22

42. Quoted by Eccleshall, op. cit., p. 91

43. Friedrich Hayek, *The Constitution of Liberty*, p. 44

44. Letwin, op. cit., pp. 29–34

45. Friedman, op. cit., p. 182

46. Ibid., pp. 177–8

47. Anthony Flew, *Equality in Liberty and Justice*, pp. 188–9

48. Roy Hattersley, in *Choose Freedom*, pp. 58 ff, is rightly firm about the point

49. John Baker, *Arguing for Equality*, p. 94

50. Anthony Flew, *The Politics of Procrustes*, p. 83

51. David Cooper, op. cit., p. 24

52. Friedman, op. cit., p. 177

53. Anthony Flew, *The Politics of Procrustes*, p. 81

54. John Lucas, *On Justice*, pp. 194, 18, 170

55. David Cooper, op. cit., pp. 5, 6, 28

56. Joseph and Sumption, op. cit., p. 83

57. Anthony Flew, *Equality in Liberty and Justice*, p. 185

58. Letwin, op. cit., p. 27

Chapter 8: Conclusion (pp. 208–39)

1. Robert Nozick, *Anarchy, State and Utopia*, p. 160

2. Alan Ryan, *Property and Political Theory*, p. 33; Lawrence Becker, *Property Rights: Philosophic Foundations*

3. Quoted by Clinton Rossiter, *Conservatism in America*, p. 121

4. Edmund Burke, *Reflections on the Revolution in France*, p. 138

5. Ibid., p. 196

6. This line is quoted from one of Mrs Gaskell's novels by Keith Joseph and Jonathan Sumption in *Equality*, p. 93; it expresses, we are told, the conventional wisdom of the nineteenth century, but is put aside as untrue and repellent by our authors

7. Quoted by Robert Eccleshall, *Political Ideologies*, p. 91

8. Anthony Quinton, *The Politics of Imperfection*, p. 90

9. Anthony Flew, *The Politics of Procrustes*, p. 81

10. John Lucas, *On Justice*, pp. 197, 200

11. George Sher, *Desert*

12. Joseph and Sumption, op. cit., p. 73

13. My own view of them is given in *Punishment: The Supposed Justifications*, and further developed in Chapter 10 of *A*

Theory of Determinism: The Mind, Neuroscience, and Life-Hopes

14. George Sher, op. cit.

15. See my own *A Theory of Determinism: The Mind, Neuroscience, and Life-Hopes*

16. I wish these were the conclusions drawn after some careless thought on the subject by me at the end of ibid; see p. 612 for the worst conclusion

17. Roy Hattersley, in his *Choose Freedom*, has the distinction among politicians of making the point clearly, pp. xvii, 21–2

18. Roy Hattersley of the Labour Party in Britain offers a version of the principle most succinctly when he writes: 'Liberty is our aim. Equality is the way in which it can truly be achieved' (op. cit., p. 23). His colleague, Bryan Gould, writes similarly: '... the diffusion and equalization of power – the true basis of socialism – is ... the only way to achieve a truly free society in which each individual enjoys the maximum degree of freedom commensurate with a similar degree of freedom for all others' (*Socialism and Freedom*, p. 106)

19. 'The Problem of Well-Being and the Principle of Equality', *Mind*, 1981. The essay is also Chapter 2 of the revised 1989 edition of my *Violence for Equality: Inquiries in Political Philosophy*. David Cooper is firm that it is an illusion that the Principle of Equality has anything much to do with egalitarianism, since the latter is necessarily just a matter of mere relativities. See his *Illusions of Equality*, pp. 4–5. Anthony Flew discusses shortcomings of the principle, as well as some of my own, in the final pages of his *Equality in Liberty and Justice*

20. For a summary of the truth, see my *Violence for Equality: Inquiries in Political Philosophy*, rev. ed., pp. 2 ff; for very recent statistics, see Peter Goldblatt, 'Mortality by Social Class, 1971–85', *Population Trends* 56, Summer, 1989

21. Edmund Burke, *Letters on a Regicide Peace*, 1796; see *Works*, V, p. 230

22. Adam Smith, *The Wealth of Nations*, Vol. 1, p. 13

23. Russell Kirk, *The Portable Conservative Reader*, p. xxiii

24. Rossiter, op. cit., pp. 59–60

25. Introduction to his edition of Edmund Burke, *Reflections on the Revolution in France*, pp. 42 ff

Bibliography

ALLISON, L., 1984: *Right Principles* (Oxford: Blackwell)

AYER, A.J., 1988: 'The Onslaught of Burke', in *Thomas Paine* (London: Secker and Warburg)

AYLING, S., 1988: *Edmund Burke* (London: John Murray)

BAKER, J., 1987: *Arguing for Equality* (London: Verso)

BARRY, N. P., 1987: *The New Right* (Beckenham: Croom Helm)

BECKER, L. C., 1977: *Property Rights: Philosophic Foundations* (London: Routledge and Kegan Paul)

BENTHAM, J., 1962 (1838): *Introduction to the Principles of Morals and Legislation*, in Mary Warnock, ed.: *Utilitarianism* (London: Fontana)

BERLIN, I., 1988: *Against the Current: Essays in the History of Ideas* (Oxford: Clarendon)

BERRY, C., 1983: 'Conservatism and Human Nature', in I. Forbes and S. Smith, eds: *Politics and Human Nature* (London: Frances Pinter)

BERRY, C., 1986: *Human Nature* (London: Macmillan)

BOLINGBROKE, H., 1754: *Dissertation on Parties*, in *Works*, ed. D. Mallet (London)

BROWN, Alan, 1986: *Modern Political Philosophy* (Harmondsworth: Penguin)

BROWN, Gordon, 1989: *Where There is Greed . . .* (Edinburgh: Mainstream)

BURKE, E. 1960 (1756–1796): *The Philosophy of Edmund Burke*, ed. L. I. Bredvold and R. G. Ross (Ann Arbor: University of Michigan Press)

BURKE, E., 1968 (1790): *Reflections on the Revolution in France*, ed. Conor Cruise O'Brien (Harmondsworth: Penguin)

BURKE, E., 1975 (1756–1796): *Edmund Burke on Government, Politics and Society*, ed. B. W. Hill (London: Fontana)

CARLYLE, T., 1899: *Works* (London: Chapman and Hall)

CASEY, J., 1982: 'One Nation: The Politics of Race', *Salisbury Review*

CECIL, H., 1912: *Conservatism* (London: William and Norgate)

COHEN, G. A., 1978: *Karl Marx's Theory of History: A Defence* (Oxford University Press)

COOPER, D., 1980: *Illusions of Equality* (London: Routledge and Kegan Paul)

COWLING, M., 1978, ed.: *Conservative Essays* (London: Cassell)

DISRAELI, B., 1913 (1835): *A Vindication of the English Constitution*, in *Of Whigs and Whiggism*, ed. W. Hutcheon (London: Murray)

DIXON, K., 1986: *Freedom and Equality* (London: Routledge and Kegan Paul)

DWORKIN, R., 1977: *Taking Rights Seriously* (London: Duckworth)

ECCLESHALL. R., 1984: 'Conservatism', in Eccleshall *et al.*: *Politics and Ideologies*

ECCLESHALL, R., GEOGHAGEN, V., JAY, R., WILFORD, R. V., eds, 1984: *Political Ideologies* (London: Hutchinson)

ELIOT, T.S., 1939: *The Idea of a Christian Society* (London: Faber)

ELIOT, T.S., 1953: *Selected Prose*, ed. J. Hayward (Harmondsworth: Penguin)

FEAVER, G., and ROSEN, R., 1987, eds: *Lives, Liberties and the Public Good* (London: Macmillan)

FINNIS. J., 1980: *Natural Law and Natural Rights* (Oxford: Clarendon)

FIRTH, C.H., 1891: *The Clarke Papers* (London: Clarendon)

FLEW, A., 1981: *The Politics of Procrustes* (London: Temple Smith)

FLEW, A., 1984: 'The Race Relations Industry', *Salisbury Review*

FLEW, A., 1989: *Equality in Liberty and Justice* (London and New York: Routledge)

FOOT, P., 1969: *The Rise of Enoch Powell* (Harmondsworth: Penguin)

FRIEDMAN, M., 1962: *Capitalism and Freedom* (University of Chicago Press)

FRIEDMAN, M., and FRIEDMAN, R., 1980: *Free to Choose* (Harmondsworth: Penguin)

GAMBLE, A., 1974: *The Conservative Nation* (London: Routledge and Kegan Paul)

GLOVER, J., 1989: *I: The Philosophy and Psychology of Personal Identity* (London: Allen Lane)

GODWIN, W., 1976, (1798): *An Inquiry Concerning Political Justice* (Harmondsworth: Penguin)

GOLDBLATT, P., 1989: 'Mortality by Social Class, 1971–85', *Population Trends* 56, Summer 1989 (London: HMSO)

GOULD, B., 1985: *Socialism and Freedom* (London: Macmillan)

GREEN, D., 1987: *The New Right: The Counter Revolution in Political, Economic and Social Thought* (Brighton: Wheatsheaf)

HALL, S., and JACQUES, M., 1983, eds: *The Politics of Thatcherism* (London: Lawrence and Wishart)

HATTERSLEY, R., 1987: *Choose Freedom: The Future for Democratic Socialism* (Harmondsworth: Penguin)

HAYEK, F., 1960: *The Constitution of Liberty* (London: Routledge and Kegan Paul)

HAYEK, L., 1963: *Economic Freedom and Representative Government* (London: Institute of Economic Affairs)

HAYEK, F. 1976: *The Road to Serfdom* (London: Routledge and Kegan Paul)

HAYEK, F. 1978: *New Studies in Philosophy, Politics, Economics and the History of Ideas* (London: Routledge and Kegan Paul)

HAYEK, F., 1979: *Law, Legislation and Liberty:* Vol. 1 *Rules and Order*, Vol. 2 *The Mirage of Social Justice*, Vol. 3 *The Political Order of a Free People* (London: Routledge and Kegan Paul)

HEARNSHAW, F.J.C., 1967 (1933): *Conservatism in England* (New York: Howard Fertig)

HONDERICH, T., 1981: 'The Problem of Well-Being and the Principle of Equality', *Mind*; reprinted as Chapter 2 of Honderich, 1989

HONDERICH, T., 1984, 1990: *Punishment: The Supposed Justifications*, rev. ed. (Harmondsworth: Penguin; Oxford: Polity)

HONDERICH, T., 1989: *Violence for Equality: Inquiries in Political Philosophy*, rev. ed. (London: Routledge)

HONDERICH, T., 1988: *A Theory of Determinism: The Mind, Neuroscience and Life-Hopes* (Oxford University Press). Also published in two paperback volumes as *Brain and Mind* and *The Consequences of Determinism*

HONORE, A.M., 1961: 'Ownership', in A.G. Guest, ed.: *Oxford Essays in Jurisprudence* (Oxford: Clarendon)

HUME, D., 1932: *The Letters of David Hume* (Oxford: Clarendon)

HUME, D., 1963, (1748): *An Enquiry Concerning Human Understanding* (Oxford: Clarendon)

HUME, D., 1969: *Essays Moral, Political and Literary* (Oxford University Press)

JOSEPH, K. and SUMPTION, J., 1979: *Equality* (London: John Murray)

KANT, I., 1887: *Philosophy of Law*, trans. W. Hastie (Edinburgh: Clark)

KING, D. S., 1987: *The New Right: Politics, Markets and Citizenship* (London: Macmillan)

KIRK, R., 1953: *The Conservative Mind* (London: Faber)

KIRK, R., 1982: *The Portable Conservative Reader* (New York: Viking Penguin)

KRISTOL, I., 1983: *Reflections of a Neo-Conservative* (New York: Basic Books)

LETWIN, W., 1983: *Against Equality: Readings on Economics and Social Policy* (London: Macmillan and the Foundation for Education in Economics)

LEVITAS, R., 1985, ed.: *The Ideology of the New Right* (Oxford: Polity Press)

LUCAS, J., 1965: 'Against Equality', *Philosophy*

LUCAS, J., 1977: 'Against Equality Again', *Philosophy*

LUCAS, J., 1980: *On Justice* (Oxford: Clarendon)

McMURRIN, S. M., 1987, ed.: *Liberty, Equality and Law* (Cambridge University Press)

MILL, J. S., 1859; *On Liberty* (many editions)

MINOGUE, K., 1967: 'Conservatism', in P. Edwards, ed.: *The Encyclopaedia of Philosophy* (New York: Macmillan)

MORE, P. E., 1915: 'Property and Law', in his *Aristocracy and Justice* (Boston: Clarke)

NISBET, R., 1986: *Conservatism: Dream and Reality* (Milton Keynes: Open University Press)

NORMAN, R., 1987: *Free and Equal* (Oxford University Press)

NOZICK, R., 1974: *Anarchy, State and Utopia* (Oxford: Blackwell)

NOZICK, R., 1981: *Philosophical Explanations* (Oxford: Clarendon)

OAKESHOTT, M., 1962: *Rationalism in Politics and Other Essays* (London: Macmillan)

O'BRIEN, C. C., 1968: Introduction to his edition of Burke, *Reflections on the Revolution in France* (Harmondsworth: Penguin)

O'SULLIVAN, N., 1976: *Conservatism* (London: Dent)

O'SULLIVAN, N., 1983: *Fascism* (London: Dent)

PARFIT, D., 1984: *Reasons and Persons* (Oxford: Clarendon)

PAUL, E. F., MILLER, F. D. and PAUL, J., 1985, eds: *Ethics and Economics* (Oxford: Blackwell)

PAYNE, S. G., 1980: *Fascism: Comparison and Definition* (Madison: University of Wisconsin Press)

POWELL, J. E., 1969: *Freedom and Reality*, ed. J. Wood (London: Batsford)

POWELL, J. E., 1982: 'Our Loss of Sovereignty', *Salisbury Review*

QUINTON, A., 1978: *The Politics of Imperfection: The Religious and Secular Traditions of Conservative Thought in England from Hooker to Oakeshott* (London: Faber)

RENTOUL, J., 1987: *The Rich Get Richer: The Growth of Inequality in Britain in the 1980s* (London: Unwin)

ROSSITER, C., 1982: *Conservatism in America*, rev. ed. (New York: Knopf)

ROTHBARD, M., 1978: *For a New Liberty: The Libertarian Manifesto* (Collier)

ROTHBARD, M., 1982: *The Ethics of Liberty* (Humanities Press)

RYAN, A., 1984: *Property and Political Theory* (Oxford: Blackwell)

SCRUTON, R., 1980: *The Meaning of Conservatism* (Harmondsworth: Penguin)

SEIDEL, G., 1986: 'Culture, Nation and "Race" in the British and French New Right', in Levitas, 1986

SHER, G., 1987: *Desert* (Princeton University Press)

SMITH, A., 1977, (1776): *The Wealth of Nations* (London: Dent, Everyman edition)

SMITH, D., 1987: *The Rise and Fall of Monetarism* (Harmondsworth: Penguin)

SPRIGGE, T., 1988: *The Rational Foundations of Ethics* (London: Routledge)

STEVENSON, L., 1974: *Seven Theories of Human Nature* (Oxford University Press)

TAWNEY, R.H., 1964 (1931): *Equality* (London: Allen and Unwin)

THORNTON, P., 1989: *Decade of Decline: Civil Liberties in the Thatcher Years* (London: National Council for Civil Liberties)

TOWNSEND, P. 1984: *Why are the Many Poor?* (London: Fabian Society)

TOWNSEND, Peter, DAVIDSON, Nick, WHITEHEAD, Margaret, 1988: *Inequalities in Health* (Harmondsworth: Penguin)

TRIGG, R., 1988: *Ideas of Human Nature* (Oxford: Blackwell)

VON MISES, L., 1936: *Socialism* (London: Cape)

WILFORD, R., 1984: 'Fascism', in Eccleshall *et al.*: *Political Ideologies*

WILSON, E., 1989: *The Myth of British Monarchy* (London: Journeyman/Republic)

WORSTHORNE, P., 1978: 'Too Much Freedom', in Cowling, ed.: *Conservative Essays*

Index

FOR THE BEST IN PAPERBACKS, LOOK FOR THE

In every corner of the world, on every subject under the sun, Penguin represents quality and variety – the very best in publishing today.

For complete information about books available from Penguin – including Puffins, Penguin Classics and Arkana – and how to order them, write to us at the appropriate address below. Please note that for copyright reasons the selection of books varies from country to country.

In the United Kingdom: Please write to *Dept E.P., Penguin Books Ltd, Harmondsworth, Middlesex, UB7 0DA.*

If you have any difficulty in obtaining a title, please send your order with the correct money, plus ten per cent for postage and packaging, to *PO Box No 11, West Drayton, Middlesex*

In the United States: Please write to *Dept BA, Penguin, 299 Murray Hill Parkway, East Rutherford, New Jersey 07073*

In Canada: Please write to *Penguin Books Canada Ltd, 2801 John Street, Markham, Ontario L3R 1B4*

In Australia: Please write to the *Marketing Department, Penguin Books Australia Ltd, P.O. Box 257, Ringwood, Victoria 3134*

In New Zealand: Please write to the *Marketing Department, Penguin Books (NZ) Ltd, Private Bag, Takapuna, Auckland 9*

In India: Please write to *Penguin Overseas Ltd, 706 Eros Apartments, 56 Nehru Place, New Delhi, 110019*

In the Netherlands: Please write to *Penguin Books Netherlands B.V., Postbus 195, NL–1380AD Weesp*

In West Germany: Please write to *Penguin Books Ltd, Friedrichstrasse 10–12, D–6000 Frankfurt/Main 1*

In Spain: Please write to *Alhambra Longman S.A., Fernandez de la Hoz 9, E–28010 Madrid*

In Italy: Please write to *Penguin Italia s.r.l., Via Como 4, I-20096 Pioltello (Milano)*

In France: Please write to *Penguin Books Ltd, 39 Rue de Montmorency, F-75003 Paris*

In Japan: Please write to *Longman Penguin Japan Co Ltd, Yamaguchi Building, 2-12-9 Kanda Jimbocho, Chiyoda-Ku, Tokyo 101*